Academic Transformation

THE ROAD TO COLLEGE SUCCESS

SECOND EDITION

De Sellers, Ph.D.
Cerridwen, Inc.

Carol W. Dochen, Ph.D.
Texas State University-San Marcos

Russ Hodges, Ed.D
Texas State University-San Marcos

Boston   Columbus   Indianapolis   New York   San Francisco   Upper Saddle River   Amsterdam
Cape Town   Dubai   London   Madrid   Milan   Munich   Paris   Montreal   Toronto   Delhi
Mexico City   Sao Paulo   Sydney   Hong Kong   Seoul   Singapore   Taipei   Tokyo

We dedicate this book to our past, present, and future students.

Editor in Chief: Paul A. Smith
Executive Editor: Sande Johnson
Editorial Assistant: Clara Ciminelli
Vice President Marketing and Sales Strategies:
  Emily Williams Knight
Vice President, Director of Marketing: Quinn Perkson
Marketing Coordinator: Kate Romano
Executive Marketing Manager: Amy Judd
Marketing Assistant: Robin Holtsberry
Senior Managing Editor: Central Publishing

Operations Specialist: Laura Messerly
Senior Art Director: Jayne Conte
Cover Designer: Bruce Kenselaar
Photo Researcher: Annie Pickert
Cover Art: Shutterstock
Full-Service Project Management: Sudip Sinha/Aptara®, Inc.
Composition: Aptara®, Inc.
Printer/Binder: R. R. Donnelley/Harrisonburg
Cover Printer: R. R. Donnelley/Harrisonburg
Text Font: Times

Credits and acknowledgments borrowed from other sources and reproduced, with permission, in this textbook appear on appropriate page within text.

Photo Credits: ALEXANDER KALINA/Shutterstock, pp. 87, 109, 133; Andresr/Shutterstock, pp. 89, 111; COMSTOCK/Thinkstock, p. 188; Doug Menuez/Getty Images - Photodisc-Royalty Free, p. 235; Elnur/Shutterstock, pp. 165, 183, 207; Jupiter Images/Getty Images/Jupiter Unlimited, p. 318; Leva Geneviciene/Shutterstock, p. 136; Lykovata/Shutterstock, pp. 233, 255, 281, 313; Michael Jung/Shutterstock, p. 175; Monkey Business Images/Shutterstock, pp. 46, 69, 284; Supri Suharjoto/Shutterstock, p. 29; Thinkstock, p. 210; Yuri Arcurs/Shutterstock, pp. 1, 21, 37, 61.

Library of Congress Cataloging-in-Publication Data
Sellers, De.
  Academic transformation : the road to college success / De Sellers, Carol W. Dochen, Russ Hodges.—2nd ed.
    p. cm.
  ISBN-13: 978-0-13-700756-1
  ISBN-10: 0-13-700756-6
  1. Study skills.   2. Learning, Psychology of.   3. Academic achievement.   4. College student orientation.
I. Dochen, Carol W.   II. Hodges, Russ, 1958—   III. Title.
  LB2395.S45 2011
  378.1'70281—dc22

                                                                    2010000648

10 9 8 7 6 5 4 3 2 1

www.pearsonhighered.com

ISBN 10:   0-13-700756-6
ISBN 13: 978-0-13-700756-1

About the Authors

Dr. De Sellers began one of the earliest cognitive-based learning strategies courses for college students in the United States in 1973 at Texas State University–San Marcos, incorporating both the emerging theory and the research-based practice from subdisciplines in psychology and educational psychology into the course. She continued to teach the course for more than 25 years before retiring. Some of her administrative posts included Dean of the College of General Studies, Director of the Student Learning Assistance Center, and Director of the International Office. She holds both an M.A. and a Ph.D. from the University of Texas at Austin, where she focused her studies on adult learners. De is now the president of Cerridwen, Inc., a consulting company for educational and psychological services.

Dr. Carol W. Dochen is currently the Director of the Student Learning Assistance Center at Texas State University–San Marcos. She also teaches undergraduate courses in University College and occasionally teaches in the College of Education. Carol earned her Ph.D. in Higher Education Administration, with a minor in Educational Psychology, from the University of Texas at Austin. She is actively involved in state and national developmental education organizations and was a founding member of the annual statewide College Academic Support Programs conference and the Texas Association for Developmental Education (TADE). Carol is a frequent presenter at state and national conferences and received a College Academic Support Programs award for Outstanding Conference Institute. She has published in a variety of journals and books; has obtained numerous grants; and has established model Supplemental Instruction (SI), Online Tutoring, and other learning assistance programs at Texas State.

Dr. Russ Hodges has worked at Texas State University–San Marcos since 1986 and coordinates the university's undergraduate learning frameworks course titled Effective Learning. Russ also teaches master's- and doctoral-level courses in the College of Education. Russ currently serves as chair of the Council of Learning Assistance and Developmental Education Associations (CLADEA) and is a past president of the College Reading and Learning Association (CRLA), serving from 2004 to 2005. Russ has received the Outstanding Article Award from the *Journal of Developmental Education* in 2001, the Robert Griffin Award for Long and Outstanding Service from CRLA in 2007, the College Academic Support Programs (CASP) Lifetime Achievement Award in 2008, and was inducted as a CLADEA Fellow for his lifetime contributions to the fields of Learning Assistance and Developmental Education in 2009.

Contents

2   Thinking and Intellectual Performance   37
I think, ergo I learn.

3   Learning in Class   61
But I slept through class in high school.

Learning Outside Class 87

Outside of class?!? The brochure didn't say anything about this.

5 Academic Learning and Neural Development 109

My, what big dendrites you have.

6 Preparing for Performance 133

Lights, cameras, action!

Establishing Direction in Your Life   165

The promised land.

Self-Regulation, Will, and Motivation   183

I know I can, I know I can.

9 Strengthening Academic Self-Regulation   207
Pumping iron (will).

Making Behaviors Work for You   233
Walking the academic tightrope.

Patterns in Human Development   255
All these people are like me?

12   Exploring the Diversity of Individuality   281

I've just gotta be me.

13 Appropriate Stress Reduction Techniques   313
AAUUUGH *%^$#&!@ (I feel much better now).

Preface

More than three decades ago, I walked to the other side of the desk and began teaching. The classroom had always been my arena of competition, and I was routinely successful as a student. If I ever gave any thought to other students who were not as successful as I, I just assumed they were lazy. It was not until I began to teach that I noticed many of my students tried to learn but failed nonetheless.

Suddenly, teaching was not as easy as I had assumed it would be. It was not simply a matter of presenting content. Each day during that first year of teaching brought questions. Was I teaching if they did not learn? Why was learning difficult for some students? Why was it so easy for me? The questions continued to pour in. Clearly, many of my students were intelligent, and I could witness their effort, but why did they often struggle to learn? What was the cause? It would have been simple to retreat to the ivory tower and proclaim that their high school preparation was poor, that they just didn't try hard enough, that not everyone could benefit from a higher education.

Instead, I started to ask real questions. How do we learn academically? Could anyone learn more effectively? The journey that started so long ago led me back to graduate school, then on to decades of teaching, and now to this text. Along the way, I have been blessed with dynamic and innovative colleagues, challenging and adventurous students, honest teachers, and administrators who knew when to turn a blind eye to daringly experimental programs.

My seemingly simple questions came to have complicated answers. My colleagues and I searched in numerous fields, unearthing both theoretical and research answers. Over the decades, we have been part of this new field of developmental education. Developmental education has emerged in response to the needs of thousands of American students who want to be more successful academically and to the desires of institutions that want these students to succeed.

This text is the amalgamation of our experiences. These are the concepts and practices based in theory and research that help our students reach their academic goals. These concepts and practices are rooted in the ideal of an autonomous student, a person fully equipped to meet the learning challenges in academics as well as the work world.

De Sellers

ABOUT THIS EDITION

In this revised text, we focus primarily on one aspect of learning—collegiate learning. As teachers with decades of collective experience under our belts, we have come to understand that competency as a college student can be learned. Academic success courses that foster development in college learners have a long history in higher education. They have many names, emerge from differing academic disciplines, and help diverse students. They foster students' abilities to monitor and regulate their own learning through the development of a perspective about themselves as learners. Theories from cognitive and behavioral psychology are deeply rooted in the course curriculum. This text flows from the traditions of this field, although we incorporate theories and strategies from other disciplines, such as personality theory, business, and philosophy.

We also use stories representative of the many students we have worked with over the years. Their stories explain and illustrate critical theories and strategies that can help students achieve academic success. The exercises scattered within each chapter and the journal questions at the end of each chapter give students specific opportunities to adapt the concepts to their own lives.

In preparation for revising this text, we spent the past couple of years soliciting feedback from colleagues across the nation who were using our text in their classes. Their enthusiasm and encouraging comments about what worked, and candid criticism for what needed to be changed, led us to reflect deeply about the content to include, but more importantly, to resequence the content in a way that was more intuitive for students to learn and teachers to teach. Thus, the second edition is a true collaboration that we are excited to share with our colleagues.

NEW TO THIS EDITION

Students and teachers will benefit from a variety of new content and features in this edition, including:

- An entirely new "pre-chapter" titled "Packing the Essentials," which consists of a brief introduction, three proven organizational tools (i.e., Syllabi Matrix, Academic Calendar, and Comprehensive Notebook), strategies for managing time, working in virtual learning environments, preparing for and taking college tests, and a final section on commitment.

- New and revised (shorter) case studies that allow students to analyze real issues facing today's diverse college population.

- Case study questions embedded within each chapter to promote class discussion and analysis of each case study.

- Material on learning, knowing, and thinking with types of knowledge (i.e., declarative, procedural, metacognitive) and levels of intellectual performance (using the recently revised Bloom's Taxonomy for the cognitive domain) in Chapter 2, all of which originally appeared in different and later chapters.

- New content on guided notes and virtual learning environments (Chapter 3) and on text-reading strategies and learning from academic networking (Chapter 4).

- An expanded and updated section on brain learning theory research with all new images of neurological structures and material on the new concept of "continuous partial attention" (Chapter 5).

- A redesigned concluding chapter for the academic learning section that synthesizes material on different approaches to learning (i.e., surface, deep, achievement), academic performance, and simple and advanced study techniques (Chapter 6). These topics were scattered throughout later chapters in the original text, but our colleagues and reviewers strongly encouraged us to cover them earlier and together in the revised edition.

- An integrated and comprehensive coverage of the impact of self-regulation on student success by weaving this topic throughout four chapters (7–10). New and revised topics include setting and attaining achievable goals; academic self-regulation, will, and motivation; our own stage model of self-regulatory ability; strategies for increasing and maintaining academic motivation, improving time management, reducing procrastination and balancing our lives; and using self-change as a holistic approach to changing behaviors.

- Chickering's Vector theory, at the request of our colleagues and reviewers, in the chapter (11) on "Patterns in Human Development."

- An Appendix titled "Overcoming Specific Academic Anxieties" that contains updated research, strategies, and websites for coping with and reducing anxieties involving public speaking, taking tests, mathematics, and writing.

ACKNOWLEDGMENTS

We have relied on many colleagues, friends, and family members to help us through the lengthy, complicated process of revising and producing this second edition, and to them we owe our utmost appreciation and gratitude:

- Patricia Foster, currently a faculty member at Stephen F. Austin State University and our summer teaching colleague at Texas State, for spending several days with us, dissecting the first edition, page by page, rearranging topics, and brainstorming new ideas to make this textbook more user-friendly to students and faculty members.

- Dr. Joel McGee and the Student Learning Center faculty members at Texas A&M University for providing valuable feedback about what textbook material to keep, what to delete, and how the topics and chapters could be rearranged more effectively.

- John McVey, our long-time friend, for his creativity with the table of contents (both editions!) and his willingness to provide the essential brainpower, typing, and editing skills when De became incapacitated with a broken arm three-quarters of the way through the textbook revision.

- Jency James, editor extraordinaire and dear friend, for turning our manuscript into a true polished work of art! Her exceptional editing, along with thoughtful questions and content contributions, has improved the quality of this edition tremendously.

- Raechel Friedman, the invaluable and resourceful student assistant who was completely undaunted by any task delegated—from editing content from a student's point of view, to researching and recommending new material, to combing through each chapter countless times for numerous reasons to make sure we met production deadlines.

- Randy Dale, doctoral research assistant, for locating valuable resources and providing research support throughout this project.

- Lisa Whittaker and Russell Miller, Student Learning Assistance Center (SLAC) tech support staff at Texas State, for supporting and safe-guarding this textbook revision (electronically and physically) from the very first day until the final copy was completed and sent.

- Lindley Workman Alyea, Kathi Ritch, James Mathews, René LeBlanc, Holly Floyd, and Cynthia Sullivan, the Student Learning Assistance Center staff at Texas State, for keeping the learning center running smoothly while their director was preoccupied with co-writing, editing, and managing the revision of this book.

- Dr. Ron Brown, Dean of University College at Texas State, for understanding and supporting the need to maintain a regular off-campus writing schedule until project completion as well as encouraging professional development through scholarly research and writing.

- Our reviewers, who offered constructive suggestions: Lewis Gray, Middle Tennessee State University; Stephanie Marsh, United States Military Academy Preparatory School; Tobin Quereau, Austin Community College; Sherry Shutin, Pennsylvania Highlands Community College; and Shirley Yu, University of Houston.

- Our respective family members and significant others, for their unwavering support, patience, and for cheering us on, once again!

De Sellers
Carol Dochen
Russ Hodges

Succeed in college and beyond!
Connect, practice, and personalize with MyStudentSuccessLab.

www.mystudentsuccesslab.com

MyStudentSuccessLab is an online solution designed to help students acquire the skills they need to succeed. They will have access to peer-led video presentations and develop core skills through interactive exercises and projects that provide academic, life, and career skills that will transfer to ANY course.

It can accompany any Student Success text, or be sold as a stand-alone course offering. Often students try to learn material without applying the information. To become a successful learner, they must consistently apply techniques to their daily activities.

MyStudentSuccessLab provides students with opportunities to become successful learners:

Connect:
• Engage with real students through video interviews on key issues.

Practice:
• Three skill-building exercises per topic provide interactive experience and practice.

Personalize:
• Apply what is learned to your life.
• Create a personal project that will be graded and can be posted to your portfolio.
• Journal online and set short- and long-term goals.

JAMES
freshman

MyStudentSuccessLab provides tools and support for students and instructors:

Student Tools/Support – Supplies these tools in addition to the video, exercises, and projects:
　Resources – Use of Plagiarism Guide, Dictionary, Calculators, and a Multimedia index of Interactive case studies and activities.
　Assessments - Includes Career Assessment tool, Learning Styles, and Personality Styles.

Instructor Tools/Support – Saves class prep time and supports implementation while engaging students:
　Sample syllabus – Ensures easy course implementation.
　Instructor's guide – Describes each activity, the skills each addresses, an estimated student time on task for each exercise, and a grading rubric for the final Apply activity.
　Additional Assignments – Suggests extra activities to use with each topic:
　• General activity related to an important objective for each topic.
　• Internet Assignment (e.g. Google "You Tube" video on topic) to find a video on key strategies and write a critique and present it to the class.
　• Resources usage – ie. Read and take online notes on the main points of the Understanding Plagiarism guide.

MyStudentSuccessLab is easy to use and assign. Visit **www.mystudentsuccesslab.com** for additional information.
Technical support at http://247pearsoned.custhelp.com.

CUSTOMIZE THIS BOOK WITH

PEARSON LEARNING SOLUTIONS

FOR STUDENT SUCCESS AND CAREER DEVELOPMENT

The Pearson Custom Library Catalog

With Pearson Custom Library, you can create a custom book by selecting content from our course-specific collections. The collections consist of chapters from Pearson titles like this one, and carefully selected, copyright cleared, third-party content, and pedagogy. The finished product is a print-on-demand custom book that students can purchase in the same way they purchase other course materials.

Custom Media

Pearson Learning Solutions works with you to create a customized technology solution specific to your course requirements and needs. We specialize in a number of best practices including custom websites and portals, animation and simulations, and content conversions and customizations.

Custom Publications

We can develop your original material and create a textbook that meets your course goals. Pearson Learning Solutions works with you on your original manuscript to help refine and strengthen it, ensuring that it meets and exceeds market standards. Pearson Learning Solutions will work with you to select already published content and sequence it to follow your course goals.

Online Education

Pearson Learning Solutions offers customizable online course content for your distance learning classes, hybrid courses, or to enhance the learning experience of your traditional in-classroom students. Courses include a fully developed syllabus, media-rich lecture presentations, audio lectures, a wide variety of assessments, discussion board questions, and a strong instructor resource package.

In the end, the finished product reflects your insight into what your students need to succeed, and puts it into practice. Visit us on the web to learn more at www.pearsoncustom.com/studentsuccess 800-777-6872

Packing the Essentials

Toothbrush? Check! Backpack? Check! Commitment? Check!

CHAPTER HIGHLIGHTS

- Introduction
- Course Syllabus
- Time Management
- Comprehensive Notebook
- Virtual Learning Environment
- Test Preparation Strategies
- Test-Taking Strategies
- Analysis of Performance
- Commitment

INTRODUCTION

The start of the new semester is a hopeful time. The move from high school to college can be both exciting and anxiety provoking. As freshmen enter into this new phase in their lives, they face an academically challenging educational environment because of the dramatic shift in expectations between high school teachers and college professors. For those students new to the collegiate environment, the material in this section is crucial as the information and strategies will help you start the academic transformation process with confidence. Those who are experienced college students wanting to improve their academic performance should read this material carefully and determine which strategies will help you in becoming an even better student.

We have purposely designed this section of the textbook to share several strategies and tools that our most successful students use to organize their academic lives at the beginning of each semester. These include how to effectively use course syllabi, time planners, and virtual learning environments to create comprehensive notebooks for each course.

You will have many tests this term. Because we cannot predict how quickly those tests will come, we have put extensive material on test preparation and test-taking strategies in this introductory material. Please use this information before you study for your first test. The chapter ends with a reflective view of your commitment to this enterprise—becoming a successful student.

COURSE SYLLABUS

The dominant organizational tool of a college course—the academic syllabus—is an essential survival tool. It used to be just a simple list of topics for the course, but now it can include

- course title and number,
- instructor's name and contact information,
- office hours,
- instructor's philosophy of teaching,
- purpose of the course,
- course goals or objectives,
- textbooks, required materials, and learning resources,
- Web-based course components,
- required learning activities,
- course calendar or outline with exam and assignment due dates,
- grading criteria,
- attendance policy, and
- disability statement.

Once professors have given you this information, they expect you to keep it and refer to it often. Professors may not mention key dates listed on the syllabus until immediately before an assignment is due or a test is to be given. However, they should give you, in writing, all the departmental and school policies, as well as their own policies about attendance and grading. It is really a contract; it tells you the professor's expectations of your work and how you will earn your grade. Many professors never pass out a syllabus. They just put it on the course website and expect you to print a copy.

The collegiate environment prepares you for professional life by the complexity of the academic demands of numerous courses. You are responsible for determining the priorities and managing the conflicting demands of exams, papers, and projects. Completing the following Syllabi Matrix is the first strategy you can use to gain an overview of your academic demands this term.

FIGURE E.1 Syllabi Matrix

Course Title & Number	Course Title & Number	Course Title & Number	Course Title & Number	Course Title & Number	Course Title & Number
Instructor	Instructor	Instructor	Instructor	Instructor	Instructor
Contact Info.	Contact Info.	Contact Info.	Contact Info.	Contact Info.	Contact Info.
Office Hours	Office Hours	Office Hours	Office Hours	Office Hours	Office Hours
Absence Policy	Absence Policy	Absence Policy	Absence Policy	Absence Policy	Absence Policy
Assignment Due Dates	Assignment Due Dates	Assignment Due Dates	Assignment Due Dates	Assignment Due Dates	Assignment Due Dates
Test Dates	Test Dates	Test Dates	Test Dates	Test Dates	Test Dates
Final Exam Date & Time	Final Exam Date & Time	Final Exam Date & Time	Final Exam Date & Time	Final Exam Date & Time	Final Exam Date & Time

TIME MANAGEMENT

Planning and managing time are the primary challenges for college students. It seems, at first glance, that you have much more free time in college than in high school. However, this is deceptive because you will have much more material than you did in high school to read, study, write outside of class. Unlike high school, where your academic time is planned, in college *you* are the planner. We strongly recommend that you create a system that will incorporate all your obligations—academic, work, social, and personal—in one place. This second strategy is a good stress buster as it can prevent nasty surprises down the road.

Here are some suggestions for using your planner:

- Enter important academic due dates (and place a reminder several days ahead).

- List your committed times (classes, work, meals, commuting, and so on).

- Identify your best times to study. Do you read better during the early evening hours? Are you a better writer during the early morning hours? Complete your academic tasks when you are most alert and able to concentrate.

- Realistically determine how much study time you need. Some students use the rule of two hours of study time for every hour of class time. We do not believe there is any one formula that ensures success. You must decide how much time you need to stay engaged in learning. If you are a beginning college student, we recommend you add 50 percent to your estimate. Remember that studying is a behavior—you will be thinking, reading, writing, creating, practicing, and teaching. Be as specific as you can on your planner about the behavior you intend to complete.

- Mark the hours you are at work, including drive time.

- List social or family plans, including dates, parties, and meetings.

- If you have regularly scheduled exercise and/or mediation time, enter it on the planner.

- Plan for some downtime; such personal time is necessary for rest and refreshment.

- Make sure you have some time each day that is not allocated. This time is what you will need to handle the unexpected crises of work, children, car repairs, and so forth.

- Keep your planner with you. It will help keep you on track.

- If you already have a calendar program on your computer, use it. If not, try one of the online calendar tools such as Google™ calendar as these tools are available to you anywhere you have Internet access.

FIGURE E.2 Weekly Planner

	Sunday	Monday	Tuesday	Wednesday	Thursday	Friday	Saturday
6:00							
7:00							
8:00							
9:00							
10:00							
11:00							
12:00							
1:00							
2:00							
3:00							
4:00							
5:00							
6:00							
7:00							
8:00							
9:00							
10:00							
11:00							
12:00							
1:00							
2:00							
3:00							
4:00							
5:00							

COMPREHENSIVE NOTEBOOK

The third strategy employed by several of our successful students is to create a comprehensive notebook—a notebook that holds *everything* you need for one class and its lab if there is one. You can use either loose-leaf notebooks or spiral notebooks for each course. Put the syllabus, class notes, handouts, printouts from the course website, assignments, and test review questions in this one place. In either case, put a zippered bag in your backpack with a stapler, pens, highlighters, blue books, answer sheets, and so on.

If you use spiral notebooks, just staple handouts next to the lecture notes. Put the syllabus in the front pocket. The same principle applies to loose-leaf notebooks. Different color notebooks, as well as other color-coding tools, will help keep you organized and less stressed.

Setting up your notebooks can almost be fun; it is the first of the semester and good intentions usually rule. It is the maintenance of your system that has the power to improve your academic performance. You are less likely to make costly mistakes, and your study efforts will be more efficient.

For learning to occur, information must be organized and meaningful. As you attempt to master college-level material, you may find that your individual preferences for learning do not always match your instructor's style of teaching. Your individual preference for learning is your own natural ability to organize and make meaning of the material. You may learn best by seeing information and can easily recall printed information in the form of words, phrases, or sentences. Or you might be more inclined to recall information presented in pictures, charts, or diagrams. Perhaps you learn best by listening, whereby information that you hear becomes easily remembered. Maybe you learn best by doing, as you create and manipulate objects. For many of us, using a combination of these techniques is extremely helpful.

Constructing an organized, comprehensive notebook will enhance your ability to learn college material on your terms. The notebook is more than simply a place to record notes; you can integrate note-taking, visual aids, test preparation, and reviewing systems into the notebook. It is also a place to reflect on the course content through journaling and guided questions. Think of the possibilities as you adopt ways to organize, associate, expand, apply, analyze, visualize, synthesize, and evaluate course content. Creating maps, networks, hierarchies, comparison charts, time lines, sample test questions, and many other learning techniques will become second nature to you. As we introduce you to new learning strategies, we want you to experiment and explore new ways of learning that enhance your individual preferences through the integrative notebook.

Your notebook should allow for flexibility so you can find, add, and move materials easily. To do this, organization is paramount. If you decide to use a loose-leaf notebook, we suggest that you begin by dividing it (using labeled dividers) into sections.

Exercise E.1

Comprehensive Notebook

Set up a comprehensive notebook for one or more of your courses. You will need to purchase one or more loose-leaf notebooks, loose-leaf paper, and section dividers. Divide the notebook(s) into the following categories and begin to place items in the notebook(s).

- Course syllabus

- Semester course calendar or outline

- Lecture notes

- Handouts

- Textbook notes

- Supplemental resources from the library or the Internet

- Assignments and/or exercises

- Review materials

- Test preparations and/or sample test questions

This exercise will assist you in organizing class material and facilitate your ability to review.

One important rule: **NEVER LEND YOUR NOTEBOOK**. If someone asks to borrow or copy your notes, walk with them to a copy machine and let them copy.

One final organizational tip, no matter how the rest of your room looks: make sure your desk is neat. It is only for study. Set it up so that you have room for your laptop, printer, and all your supplies. Buy a good study light too. Any bulletin boards above or next to your desk are just for academics, such as reminders about assignments and study sessions. Keep pictures and other distractions around your work area to a minimum.

VIRTUAL LEARNING ENVIRONMENTS

Most colleges and universities have installed virtual learning environments and require professors to use them. In common language, these are Internet-based academic course management systems. Almost certainly, you will need easy and rapid access to a computer and the Internet on a *daily* basis to check postings for up-to-date information and to find all of the detailed information you need to record on your Syllabi Matrix and Academic Planner. Besides providing the syllabus, administrative information (including how to get help), additional learning resources, online self-assessment and testing, threaded discussions and chat rooms, professors will often communicate with your class directly through electronic postings. Typical postings include announcements about upcoming guest speakers, field trip reminders, and last minute class cancellations; extra credit assignments or opportunities; and your grades on quizzes, papers, projects, and major exams.

As soon as you are registered and the semester has begun, you will have access to the virtual learning environment for your courses. Make sure you know how to access and use the specific system your institution has selected, and call or go by the student computer help desk when you have questions or problems.

TEST PREPARATION STRATEGIES

How do I choose and organize the content material for a test?

Start early enough to really do the job. Three to four days before a test, write a list of all the content to be covered and the expected level of learning you will need to perform it. Do you have all the lecture notes? If not, get copies of any lectures you missed. Get all the handouts or material from the instructor's website. The most important question to ask is "Have I done the initial learning of this material—read the required materials, gone to class, used other required sources?" If the answer is no, then get started!

The initial learning of any material takes time, especially if it is procedural knowledge, and such learning is most efficient when anxiety is low. However, relearning material that is already familiar but not readily retrievable is usually much faster, and even moderate anxiety does not interfere. The marker for many experienced students is 24 hours before the test. By that marker, most students feel some anxiety, but if what they have to do is simply relearn the material and practice storing/retrieving to prepare for the test, then they can usually do that efficiently.

How do I select the most important items to study?

List all the content for the test, then look for all the clues about what will actually be on the test. What has the instructor or the teaching assistant emphasized? What will be the structure of the test—objective, short answer, essay? What is on any handouts or the instructor's website? Does the study manual or CD of your text have practice questions? What does the instructor say on the last day before the test? What is the focus of the review session (be sure to go!)? Talk to students who have had this course and instructor before. If you have exams from earlier in the term, use them to get an idea of what type of items your instructor tends to choose.

There is so much information! How can I do this?

Hold on now—don't let the amount of information intimidate you! You have to get in front of it and organize it. Organizing helps us chunk the material so that we can remember it. Because you have to do this in as many as four or five courses, organization is your best weapon.

Exercise E.2

Using a Test Prep

The purpose of this exercise is to help you differentiate between preparing to study and actually studying for an upcoming test as well as to create an organized study plan. Completing this exercise will give you an opportunity to apply many of the techniques discussed previously while you prepare for your test.

1. Select material that you are currently preparing to study for a major test.

2. Test date: _____

3. Complete the following chart:

Specific material test will cover	Uncompleted Tasks		Completed Tasks	
	Test material	Time needed to complete	Test material	Time needed to review
Textbook chapters:				
Outside readings:				
Class notes:				
Other resources:				

4. Next to each of the following types of questions write the number of them that will be on the test:

_____ True/False	_____ Fill-in-the-blank
_____ Multiple choice	_____ Short answer
_____ Matching	_____ Essay

5. What is the time limit for completing the test? _____

6. Identify and list all major topics covered on the test:

       _____

       _____

       _____

       _____

       _____

       _____

7. Select one or more of the following simple techniques to practice memory and retrieval of the test material (see Chapter 6):

    a. Create 10–20 note cards using at least three of the following note card formats:

Vocabulary	Example
Identification	Concept
Formula	Practice problem
Simple diagram	Comparison/contrast

    b. Make time lines and/or stories to associate dates, names, events, and so on.

    c. Create mnemonics using at least two of the following types:

Jingles	Key words
Rhymes	Created words
Acronyms	Created sentences

8. Select one or more of the following activities to help you learn the test material at a deeper level (see Chapter 6):

    a. Summarization—Create a one- to two-page summary sheet of information from the lecture or readings.

    b. Visual or graphic organizers—Create two organizers using more than one of the following formats:

Matrix	Spider concept map
Hierarchy	Network
Bubble concept map	

9. Predicted test questions—Create questions and answers based on the type of test you expect:

   10–15 Multiple choice and True/False

   Matching and fill-in-the-blank if appropriate

   5–7 Short answer

   3–5 Essay

What do I do when I have two tests in one day?

If these are declarative knowledge courses, then use color coding and different learning techniques so you can keep the content distinctly different in your mind. Study the material for the second test first; then study the material for the first test before you go to sleep. The next morning, review the material for the first test and take it. Then review the material for the second test and take it.

If one test is declarative knowledge and the other procedural knowledge, practice the procedural knowledge first until you reach mastery level. Then study for the declarative knowledge course. The night before the tests, practice the procedures again. End your study that night with the material for the first test.

If both tests are procedural, start very early to master the procedures you will need to perform on the test. The night before the test, practice for one test, then take a 30-minute break, and then practice for the second test.

How do I stay awake when I study?

Use active study techniques—with friends in a study group, reciting aloud, spacing study with some quick exercise breaks or some fast household chores. Stand up and walk around as you rehearse. Music may help some of you, but for others it is a distraction. Study in the library or another place without the distractions of telephones, family, friends, and so forth. During finals, you might put the television away in the closet. Study before your family or roommates wake up or after they go to bed. Get some sleep each night (all-nighters tend to destroy test performance). Use snacks, healthy if possible. Fresh air, opening a window or walking outside, can help.

Do I need to study differently for objective, short-answer, and essay tests?

Absolutely. Objective tests require much more specific recognition and recall, so using various types of note cards and graphic organizers can help.

Collegiate-level multiple-choice questions usually require you to select the best answer (many of the alternatives may be correct) or they may require you to function at the application level, such as mathematics, economics, and accounting. Try to think like your teacher—what kind of questions would you write for this test?

Short-answer tests often require that you demonstrate that you understand a concept or an important fact. Sheer memory is not enough; you have to be able to explain the material. Practice by explaining concepts, identifications, or definitions to yourself, your dog, anyone who will listen.

Essay tests require a very different type of preparation. To prepare well, you will need to study at the analysis level. Once you have learned the major concepts, write practice questions comparing/contrasting two or more of the concepts *or* tracing the development of an idea or historical event *or* analyzing the cause/effect relationships between several topics *or* considering the significance of certain occurrences. After you create some study questions, practice writing a thesis statement and a list of major points that you would want to make in your answer. Thinking about the material at this level of analysis is a powerful preparation strategy for essay tests.

TEST-TAKING STRATEGIES

In this section we provide some of our favorite test-taking strategies.

I need some help on taking a test. What do you suggest?

Learning how to play the game and becoming an effective collegiate test taker are major goals of your first year in school. The first rule is simple: Nothing helps more than really knowing the material. If you learn the content and practice it at the appropriate level of learning, then the rest is just technique and common sense.

Here are some strategies for making the most of your test-taking experience:

BEFORE THE TEST

- Make sure you have all the supplies you need, as well as a watch.

- Arrive 5–10 minutes early.

- Do not hang out with other students who tend to catastrophize or psych each other out about what might be on the test.

- Sit away from your friends if they make you nervous or tend to finish earlier than you.

- Use positive self-talk and breathe deeply to relax.

AT THE BEGINNING OF THE TEST

- Write down formulas, theorems, or processes you will need.

- Look over the entire test, noting how much each part of the test is worth. Mentally decide which parts you want to answer first and how much time you will allocate to each section. (You might want to start with the section that seems easiest to you.)

- Read and underline key words in the test directions. Be sure to note if the directions say to answer only some but not all of the questions (common on essay tests).

DURING THE TEST

- If you begin to feel nervous or blank out on a question, stop, take a deep breath, and say to yourself, *I prepared for this test, and I can answer these questions. I will move on and come back to this question later.* Take another deep breath and read the next question, paying close attention to monitor your self-talk as you progress through the test.

OBJECTIVE QUESTIONS (MULTIPLE CHOICE, TRUE/FALSE, MATCHING)

- Read every question carefully. On multiple-choice questions, try to answer the question before you look at the options. If that does not work, read each option and cross out those that are incorrect, ones that are too similar to distinguish between (unless there is an option such as "a and c" or "all of the above"), and those that are grammatically incorrect. Also examine options that are complete opposites of all the others; they are often correct.

- When you are confused by a multiple-choice question, read the stem and each option as a true/false question. This allows you to focus on each piece of information separately before trying to look at the question and options as a whole.

- Attempt to answer each question, but mark any that you are unsure of so you can return to them before the end of the test. Often you will find clues to the answer later on in the test.

- On true/false questions, look for absolute terms such as *all, always, never, none.* Such words are rarely found in correct answers, except in science courses such as physics and chemistry. Questions containing words such as *usually, frequently, rarely,* and *seldom,* especially in social science courses, allow for exceptions and are more likely to be true.

- If you can think of an exception to any part of a true/false question, then it is false. Be careful not to make assumptions or read anything that is not explicitly stated into a question.

- Beware of negatives because they change the meaning of the sentence. Circle the negative (*no, not, cannot, dis-, il-, im-, non-, un-*) and get the meaning of the statement without the negative. Then reread the statement with the negative. Remember that two negatives in one sentence cancel each other out.

- Determine the relationship between columns on matching questions and then start with the column with the longest list of items.

SUBJECTIVE QUESTIONS (IDENTIFICATION, SHORT ANSWER, ESSAY)

- Remember that identification questions require these specific elements: when, what or who, where, and significance (importance or impact).

- On a short-answer question, define or describe the term or concept, cite a source, and give an example.

- Because many essay questions are quite long and involve several imbedded questions, be sure to read the entire question and briefly outline your answer to each part.

- Determine whether the essay questions are really statements, not questions. If this is the case, turn the statement into a question, identify limiting or directional words (these include *analyze, compare, contrast, define, describe, diagram, discuss, enumerate, evaluate, explain, identify, illustrate, interpret, justify, list, outline, prove, state, summarize, support*), outline your answer, answer the question in the first paragraph, give examples and details in the body, and provide a *big-picture* conclusion.

AT THE END OF THE TEST

- Take the last 10 minutes of the test time to review your work.

- For any unanswered multiple-choice questions, look at the items you are still considering. Reread the question and choose the one that sounds as if it completes the stem the best (at least you have a 25 percent chance or better of getting it right).

- For any unanswered true/false questions, if the items contain unfamiliar terminology or facts, mark the statement false. If you are still unsure, pick true because it is harder to write a false statement that is not too obvious.

- Do not change answers unless you have remembered something or learned something from the test that contradicts the option you selected previously.

- Reread any essay questions and answers and correct any grammatical or logical errors. Check to see that you have included all the relevant information. If you run out of time, outline the rest of your response.

ANALYSIS OF PERFORMANCE

The purpose of a test is to see how much you know, not merely to achieve a grade. Making mistakes, or even failing a test, is human. Rather than ignoring mistakes, examine them and learn from them as you learn from mistakes on the job and in your relationships. Working through your mistakes will help you avoid repeating them again on another test—or outside school life. (Carter, Bishop, & Kravits, 2002, p. 338)

When a test is returned to you, examine it carefully to see where your strengths were (and celebrate your successes!). Then look at your errors—were they careless or content errors? Content errors occur when we misunderstand a concept or do not remember factual information. Perhaps you never learned the concept or information in the first place. When you receive a graded paper or project, read the comments carefully. If the comments are few or confusing, make an appointment with your instructor to discuss how you can improve your work.

Exercise E.3

Analysis of Preparation and Performance

You can learn to enhance your performance by analyzing and reflecting on the results of a recent test, paper, or project. This exercise is designed to assist you with that process.

PREDICTIONS

1. How difficult did you think this test, paper, or project was going to be?

2. What grade did you think you would receive before and after? Explain any difference.

PREPARATION

3. How much time did you spend?

4. What methods did you use?

5. How well did you learn?

PERFORMANCE

6. How well did you follow directions?

7. How well did you read the questions or assignment?

8. How well did you manage your time?

9. What effect did stress (positive or negative, anger or anxiety or excitement) have on your performance?

EVALUATION

10. Were you surprised about your grade? Why or why not?

11. Why do you think you made that grade?

12. Do you wish to challenge any answer or grade? Do so respectfully in class, if appropriate, or schedule an appointment.

NEXT TIME

13. How will you prepare differently for your next performance?

COMMITMENT

Students who have a strong commitment to a college education and the acquisition of a degree are more likely to graduate than those students who do not (Astin, 1993; Tinto, 1987). When we really want something, we will try long and hard to make it happen. That effort is **commitment,** a powerful word that reflects *a promise we make to an idea, a group, another person, or ourselves.* The strength of our commitment rests on our determination to fulfill that promise. One of the most important tasks of childhood and adolescence is learning how to choose commitments and honor them. Most of us have had the experience of joining a group or activity and then wanting to quit halfway through. Do we quit? Or do we honor the promise we made to the other participants of the group? Usually, we begin to learn quickly that we need to choose carefully, even when what we are choosing is a friend or a romantic relationship. A hard life lesson is the realization that life does not just happen to us—we choose it. Choosing our commitments carefully and honoring them is a characteristic of successful students. Honoring our commitments supports good self-esteem and self-discipline.

Life without serious commitments can be a life filled with a sense of purposelessness. What makes the difference is whether we are thoughtfully searching for those commitments that form the foundation of a good life or whether we are simply wandering from one casual interest to another. Such a search permeates every facet of life as we look to those ideas, groups, and individuals to which we commit our beliefs and our actions. Although this discussion focuses on the academic commitments we have, it is noteworthy that college life (at whatever age) is usually a time of exploration of all categories of commitments—intellectual, spiritual, social, personal, occupational, physical. We may retain some of our commitments from earlier times, but even these are shaped by the crucible of college.

Personal and Institutional Commitments

There are two types of academic commitments: *personal* and *institutional* (Tinto, 1987). It is normal for you to desire a sense of belonging and loyalty to the institution where you study. You may be attending the same college as your parents or older siblings and your loyalty started years before you enroll. It is helpful to attend orientation programs and learn the history of the campus. In any case, expect the old ties to your former school to lessen as you become more invested in your new community. A strong commitment to the institution can help you persist and succeed in college.

In general, research on the retention of college students over the past 25 years indicates that both types of academic commitment increase the likelihood of academic success and graduation (Dochen, 1993). The institutional commitment seems to play a greater role in the initial years of college, whereas the personal commitment becomes much more important as students move deeply into their majors and begin to set specific career goals. Most institutions make serious efforts to attract and acclimate new students to the campus and its traditions. Commitment often begins with a student's initial choice of the college if that choice has been carefully made.

Strategies for Assessing Our Commitments

Reflecting and *journaling* are the two most powerful tools that can help you understand your own level of commitment. What are your thoughts and feelings about the institution you attend? Are you proud to be a student there? Is it important that your degree come from this institution? Do you feel a sense of belonging—in other words, is this institution a *good fit* for you? Are you comfortable in your dealings with the faculty, the staff, and other students? Have you relinquished your bonds to your former school and transferred your loyalties to this one? These and other reflective questions can help you evaluate your sense of commitment to your institution.

Another set of reflective questions will focus your attention on your commitment to *personal academic goals.* How important is it to you to have a college degree and the resulting professional career? Have you made a clear choice of a major? What are your academic ambitions, including grade point average (GPA) and honor societies? Have you investigated graduate or professional programs? Have you completed internships or volunteered or worked part-time in the field?

Of course, commitments occur in other areas of our lives: spiritual, physical, social, family. Early in their college years, students often seriously commit their time and talent to social or family relationships, to religious ideals or organizations, to athletics, to work. At times such commitments

Keeping a Commitment

- State your commitment by putting it in writing.
- Reflect on the importance of keeping your commitment. Answer the question: "Why is this commitment important to me?" Write about your thoughts and feelings as they relate to the commitment.
- Monitor and assess your progress.
- Reward yourself for progress.
- Evaluate your success.

enhance our academic commitments, but it is easy to get unbalanced and allow other commitments to devour all of our time and attention. The balance of commitments is especially difficult for freshmen. The college years are a time during which we should learn how to develop, deepen, and balance our commitments. The first step is self-awareness, and that is achieved by persistent reflection, both in conversation with people we trust and in journal writing. Taking an inventory of what we really value, not what others tell us we should value, is sometimes painful. The key is to look at our behaviors. What do we do? Not what do we say we should do, but *what do we do?* How do we spend our time, our money? Do we say that academic achievement is important to us and then cut class several times a week? Do we say that we are committed to our friends and then gossip about them? Do we say that we value physical health and then avoid exercise and eat junk food? Do we say that we do not have serious problems and then get drunk three times a week or make ourselves vomit once or twice a day because we believe we ate too much?

A *realistic inventory* pushes us to consider what we really value and what we want as our life commitments. Any list of commitments should include the behaviors that would demonstrate our willingness to choose each commitment. The list should also reveal priorities: Which commitments are most important? Least important? One method is to deliberately create an intention statement. Many of the chapters in this book illuminate the techniques necessary to turn intention statements into specific goal statements into specific behaviors.

Exercise E.4

Are You Committed?

How strongly are you committed to college? Answering the following questions will help you clarify and reflect on your current experiences and commitment to college.

1. Your thoughts and feelings about the institution you attend:

   a. Are you proud to be a student there?

   b. Is it important that your degree come from this institution?

   c. Do you feel a sense of belonging—in other words, is this institution a *good fit* for you?

   d. Have you relinquished your bonds to your former school and transferred your loyalties to this one?

   e. Are you comfortable in your dealings with the faculty, the staff, and other students?

2. Your goals for attending college:

   a. What is your main goal for attending college?

   b. Have you made a clear choice of a major or selected a program of study?

   c. Is it important for you to have a college degree or to get certified in a particular program?

   d. Will attending college result in a better job or change in career?

   e. Have you investigated graduate or professional programs?

   f. Have you completed any internships or volunteered or worked part-time in a field related to your academic goal?

   g. What are your academic ambitions, including GPA and honor societies?

3. Support from family members:

   a. Does your family support your desire to attend college?

   b. If you live at home, do family members make it possible for you to study?

   c. Do family members help you financially?

The Last Word

WE WISH YOU THE BEST POSSIBLE SEMESTER as you become the successful student you wish to be. This text and your faculty are your guides for this adventure.

—*De Sellers*
Carol Dochen
Russ Hodges

The Road to Autonomous Learning

I don't know where I'm going, but I'm making good time.

CHAPTER HIGHLIGHTS

- Introduction
- A Quality World
- Academic Transformation
- Becoming an Autonomous Learner

As twenty-first century citizens, we are experiencing an increasingly complex and challenging world. Each year millions of us choose higher education as a way to prepare ourselves for this ever-changing world. Yet many of us have conflicted emotions about our studies.

"Is it all about grades? I have to do well because my family has such high aspirations for me; a degree is my ticket to a good life."

"I try so hard, but then I blow it on the test."

"I do really well in a class if the teacher is interesting."

"How can I juggle all my family responsibilities and all these assignments?"

"I know my future is on the line, but I just can't get motivated."

This book is a guide to show you how to become the collegiate student you wish to become—how to academically transform yourself. If you are not quite the student you wish to be (or not nearly the student you wish to become), then open your mind and your heart to the messages herein. We are learners, too, both as students and as teachers, and we have walked these roads before. Come with us and we will show you what college learning is all about and how you can master it.

Exercise 1.1

SELF-ASSESSMENT: My Willingness to Become a Successful Student

The first step in becoming a successful student is to assess your openness to the changes college demands. With 5 being "Almost Always" and 1 being "Almost Never," assess your readiness for changes you expect this semester. Rate each of the following statements honestly by circling the appropriate number.

	Almost Always		Sometimes		Almost Never
1. I am confident about my abilities to succeed in college.	5	4	3	2	1
2. I am open to change some of my academic behaviors and study habits.	5	4	3	2	1
3. I get personal satisfaction from completing goals.	5	4	3	2	1
4. I routinely initiate studying when assignments are made.	5	4	3	2	1
5. I engage in difficult academic tasks without giving up too easily.	5	4	3	2	1
6. I enjoy learning something new.	5	4	3	2	1
7. My grades are a good indicator of my abilities.	5	4	3	2	1
8. I try to think openly about issues even if they conflict with my ideas.	5	4	3	2	1
9. I use different learning strategies for different subjects.	5	4	3	2	1
10. I am hopeful about my success in college.	5	4	3	2	1

Add up the numbers you circled. Your total score will be between 10 and 50. The higher your score, the more likely you are to be open to necessary changes. For a score below 30, write or reflect on the items for which you have concerns and consider talking with a trusted friend, a family member, a teacher, a counselor, or an advisor.

INTRODUCTION

What a joy to be human! We have harnessed the physical world; we can reflect on our feelings. We can understand important aspects of this world, including ourselves. We can change what we do and how we feel. We can achieve what we wish. The opposites are also true. Our humanness can be a burden. We can be ignorant of the world and ourselves. We can stay stuck in old ways of being and feeling. We can fail ourselves and fail others.

What makes the difference between these two possibilities? It is our basic nature to survive and to invent and to achieve and to change. It is the nature of humans to learn, but fear and laziness get in the way. Although learning is a basic skill, it must also be developed.

At the heart of the learning process is a mystery. Scientists are just beginning to know how our brains work. For tens of thousands of years, this extraordinary ability has been hidden from us. Now technology is opening a vision of mental functioning. Each day we are discovering more about how humans learn and change. We know we have learned something when we experience a change in our thoughts, feelings, or actions. Those changes are evidence that we have learned from experiencing new information or circumstances (Lefrançois, 2000). Thus, learning happens continually as we interact with all that is our environment.

One fact about being human is not a mystery—we can direct our thoughts and feelings and choose our actions. In other words, we have free will. We exercise that will within a societal framework of laws and cultural expectations. You may not feel very free at all, but in a real sense, you are. As authors and teachers, we believe your abilities to choose goals and behaviors are foundational to becoming a successful student. Certainly as a college student you have made the choice to pursue a program or profession. In every class you are free to learn or not. You choose what receives your attention and effort. You choose what you value.

As teachers, we help students set priorities in their lives. Your first priority is to determine the life you want to have and the person you want to be.

A QUALITY WORLD

Humans are the only creatures who can imagine perfection but not attain it. Bookstores and magazine racks illustrate our yearning for perfection and for the control to attain it, but we are inherently imperfect. Are we ever smart enough, beautiful enough, good enough, fast enough, lovable enough, successful enough? The no-man's-land we all live in is in between our concept of perfection and our own state of imperfection. Although "trying to be perfect is the most tragic human mistake" (Kurtz & Ketcham, 1992, p. 5), we are loathe to relinquish our ambitions and slide into inaction. Finding the balance between the ideal and the real is the focus of the remainder of this chapter.

As humans, we dream of the lives we want—relationships, accomplishments, values, and possessions. That vision is one we begin to create from birth. William Glasser (1998), a noted American psychiatrist and developer of two important concepts—reality therapy and choice theory, calls it our **quality world,** and each is unique to the individual. Each of us has mental pictures of "(1) the *people* we most want to be with, (2) the *things* we most want to own or experience, and (3) the *ideas* or systems of *belief* that govern much of our behavior" (p. 45). It holds our deepest values and feelings. It holds our hopes for the way we would like to live. Our quality world holds the best ways to satisfy one or more of our basic psychological needs—love/belonging, power, freedom, fun. It is the place where we would feel completely loved and protected. These are the concepts about which we care passionately. We look upon each new experience—person, thing, or idea—from the perspective of whether it contributes or detracts from our quality world. Does it move us closer to that world, or farther away?

Even though we move back and forth between the everyday external world and our quality world numerous times each day, it is rare when we conceptualize, or imagine, our quality world as a *world,* a place that holds the summation of our hopes and beliefs. Every time we think about the perfect mate, the grades we want, the job we desire, or any one of the dozens of attractive images that come to mind during the day, we are thinking about our quality world. When we experience hope about a relationship, excitement about an idea, or longing for a possession, we are shaping and reshaping our quality world.

Are our quality worlds healthy and good? Not always. An addict yearns for the next rush; the power hungry fantasize about exerting their control over others; the selfish long for love without having to love in return; the lazy look for accomplishment without effort; the greedy want more than their share; the cruel enjoy the pain of others. As we mature, self-reflection can help us ascertain how healthy and ethical our quality worlds are. However, self-reflection in isolation rarely works. We desperately need feedback from the people and systems we respect. We have to use that feedback, not simply accept it unconditionally. Our parents cannot design our quality world; neither can our teachers, preachers, politicians, or peers. It is our job, our responsibility, to build our quality world; it is, according to Glasser (1998), the core of our life, no one else's.

Ironically, no one specifically tells us that we must build our own quality world; in fact, far too many people try to build it for us. College can be a brutal experience if our quality world is not congruent with, or does not match, the reality of that life.

Elements of Our Quality World
Our deepest values and feelings. Hope for the way we would like to live.

The people we most want to be with	The things we most want to own or experience	The ideas or systems of belief that govern much of our behavior

Because our quality world drives so many of our fantasies, dreams, goals, and actions, a crucial decision that we make is whether we will ground it with a value system that is ethical, balanced, and wise. In this postmodern age in which diverse traditions and systems are honored, such a decision is complicated and difficult. One example is to know where our rights end and the rights of others begin. For some of us, that boundary of self-esteem is treacherous. We either take advantage of others or allow them to take advantage of us. We may do too much for others and not expect them to do for us. Ethical, balanced, and wise quality worlds are the greatest guarantee that we have to build a good life.

TWO CASE STUDIES

ANNA is beginning her second semester of college. Long ago, she chose the dream of attending college and becoming a professional, so she learned how to work hard. Anna carefully created a picture of who she wants to be, and she has tried diligently to match that picture. Although she has had her share of surprises and disappointments about roommates, assignments, and professors, generally she is faring well. She is comfortable on campus and has begun to make genuine friendships, she goes home to see her parents only every five weeks or so, and she seems to have gracefully relinquished the relationships that had so dominated her last two years of high school. Academically, she has found her footing. She has had to change her study habits; now she studies every day. Her grades have stabilized at the C+ to B level, and she has begun serious inquiries about different majors. She plays intramural soccer and has started working 10 hours a week for the student center. She regularly participates in the student organization of her religious denomination. Anna's friends often verbalize that they envy how easily Anna seems to balance academics, friends, family, and other activities. When she hears her friends' comments, Anna feels puzzled, because she is just doing what seems comfortable and right to her. Why do her friends seem to struggle so? They are all talented; they have the same opportunities. Yet they fall prey to procrastination; their decisions often seem like reactions to immediate situations.

Case Study Questions: Do you believe, as the authors do, that the internal pictures we create of the lives we want have powerful influences on how we live our lives? Why or why not? What internal pictures have you created for the life you wish to lead?

JESSE earned a football scholarship, an accomplishment that fulfilled his parents' dreams. They were excited that he was going to college, but even more thrilled that he would play football at the collegiate level. He accepted their vision without question and dreamed of athletic success. However, reality was shocking. He was no longer the star. As a freshman, he was not even a starter. Classes were more difficult than in high school, and he felt he had no time for himself. Academics were forced to a backseat as he strived to succeed on the team. Jesse grudgingly kept the vision of athletic success through two seasons, but he grew to understand that the quality world he wanted included academic as well as athletic achievement. Finally, at the end of his sophomore year, Jesse told his parents the truth. He was uncomfortable in the conflict between athletics and academics and ashamed of his grades. Jesse withdrew into himself the next summer and painfully pondered what he wanted in his life, now and in the future. Gradually, he came to the conclusion that he wanted a sense of freedom to explore new ideas and different types of people. His competitive spirit was still alive, but now it turned to the classroom. He wanted the ability to choose his own priorities, his own actions, his own direction. His quality world was forming as he thought about the college life he wanted to build. He chose to leave athletics and his scholarship, knowing that he would have to find a part-time job for financial support and take student loans to finish school. However, that choice gave him more study time and more energy to focus on academics.

Case Study Questions: Considering his circumstances, did Jesse make the right choice to leave athletics and give up his scholarship? What would you have done if you were Jesse?

Improving Our Quality World

As teachers for many years, we believe an important life skill is our ability to discern and improve our quality worlds. How should such discernment occur? A crucial aspect of any such system is **reflection**, our ability to think deeply and carefully about important issues and their relationship to one another. What follows is one method for discernment, a series of reflective questions in four major arenas of life—**relationships, work, belief,** and **service** (see Figure 1.1).

Relationships. As humans, we are social creatures. Most of us place relationships at the core of our lives. A significant other, family members, friends, colleagues, roommates—these are the people with whom we share our lives. We laugh with them, fight with them, cry with them, celebrate with them, dream with them. There is a tie, a bond, among us. These are the people who know the truth about us, and they love and care for us. We know and do the same for them. Trust and safety are at the center of our quality relationships.

Have you ever asked yourself what are the quality relationships in your life? How closely does the reality meet the dreams and hopes you have for relationships? Where are the differences? Are your visions of quality relationships healthy and hopeful? How do relationships give meaning and purpose to your life?

Work. Across all cultures and all times, people work most of their lives. Work is a major avenue of deriving feelings of productiveness, a basic requirement of a healthy self-view. As a young child, you began working by going to school

FIGURE 1.1   The Four Major Arenas of Life

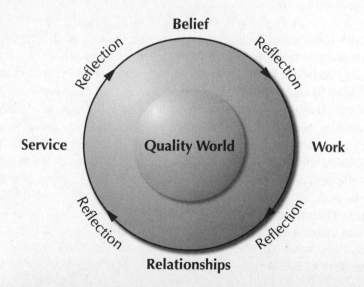

and learning. That was your job in your family, although you probably had chores to do as well. School may still be your primary work, even if now you work at a part-time job that earns you a paycheck. On the other hand, school may take second or third place after family and your job.

At this time in your life, you probably have several visions of work in your quality world. One is the vision of how you wish to be as a college student; in other words, what collegiate experiences do you wish to have? How will you perform collegiate work and what feelings will ensue from your efforts? What subsidiary role does other work play? Another vision is the one you hold of the work you are currently doing. A vision most of you carry is the work you will do after graduation. Remember Anna's clear vision of herself in a professional career. What is your vision of your working career? Where will it occur? What responsibilities will you have? What do you wish to achieve? How does work give meaning and purpose to your life?

Your collegiate work is probably your primary job now. It is important to maintain your professional attitude and work habits at school as well as at work. Show up on time ready to learn, do not leave early, and put forth your best efforts on homework and exams. The work ethic you create as a student will follow you into your career.

Belief. All of us believe in something. Whether we believe in the sacred or the secular, order or chaos, atheism or religion, we all believe. It is human nature to try to make sense of our existence. We rely on our families and our culture to help us find those explanations that fill our quality world. As we move from stage to stage in life, it is healthy to question those explanations. What are your beliefs? What values do you think are important? What beliefs give meaning and purpose to your life?

Service. A basic tenet of human behavior is that we rely on others as they rely on us. We are individuals, but we are also part of larger groups. Thus, some people are willing to work for the common good by participating in service activities. Obviously, volunteer work is a service activity, but there are many others as well. Voting, paying taxes, helping a neighbor or a stranger, contributing to a charity, showing patriotism, obeying community laws—all are service behaviors. Circumstances at particular times in our lives dictate how much or how often we are willing to serve. However, service is one of the core components of a healthy life, so determining a variety of service behaviors gives us many more opportunities. What role does service play in your quality world? How does service give meaning and purpose to your life?

The concept of a quality world may be new to you. We hope you will give it careful consideration, for we believe that if you carefully and thoughtfully adjust the images and feelings that constitute your quality world to a greater congruence with the life you realistically desire to lead, then your motivation to achieve that life will become easier.

The purpose and strategies of this text rest on your ability to choose (and to control) your thoughts, feelings, and behaviors to reach carefully selected goals. We will share how you can increase your ability to evaluate your individual academic situation and plan and execute appropriate action. Becoming a competent student is an individual journey; each of us is a unique learner. Our term for this journey is *academic transformation*.

ACADEMIC TRANSFORMATION

Often we contemplate what it would be like to be different. Our fantasy lives are filled with images of success and acclaim, attractiveness and competence, pleasure and joy—all without effort or cost. The no-man's-land between fantasy and reality is a hard, barren place, but we want to share with you an oasis in that desert. It is possible for humans to transform themselves, in their thoughts, behaviors, and feelings. It is possible for us as students and teachers to transform ourselves, but we must choose carefully exactly how we want to change and what we want to become.

This text focuses on academic transformation—how to become the college student you wish to become—however, the principles and strategies herein will be easily transferable to other areas of life. Our conviction is that truly successful college students are those who do more than make a good GPA; they also have fulfilling personal and social lives, have a clear view of their future professions, develop their physical and spiritual lives, and participate in their communities. Those standards are challenging for any student, and they are accomplished within the academic framework of their lives.

This text focuses on your work as a student. **Academic transformation** is *the process whereby you will carefully assess your current situation as a student, determine specific short- and long-term academic goals based on your values, chart changes necessary to reach those goals, and then make those changes.* Along the way, you must continually evaluate your progress and make the appropriate adjustments; even your long-term goals may change.

It is likely that this time of your life is a time of extraordinarily rapid change. A continual process of reflection, goal setting, accountability, analysis, and adjustment is a good method to support your efforts to become academically successful. Throughout this

The Steps of Academic Transformation

Assess your current academic situation. Consider such things as your academic standing (honor, good, marginal, probation, probationary entrance); scholarship/financial aid requirements; extracurricular activities (athletics, social or subject organizations); residence (oncampus, commuting). Are your learning skills (reading, writing, mathematics, thinking) strong, average, or weak? What is your level of self-confidence? Of stress or anxiety?

Set short- and long-term academic goals based on your values. What are the external forces (finances, family, academic requirements) that affect your academic goals? What are the internal forces—your personal definition of success, your desires for personal and social activities, your search for the best career—that affect your academic goals? Goals should be specific so that you will know when you have reached them. Examples could be a GPA for the term, specific grades in each course, or acceptance into a particular major or program.

Create a list of immediate objectives and an action plan to meet them. Examples of immediate objectives can include reading assignments before class, attending class regularly, and so on. Action plans may include getting enough sleep, going to the library to read and study, using an academic planner to set specific study times, and so forth.

Work to accomplish your objectives. This step is the hardest step. You have to do what you have determined is important. So, use a to-do list every day and mark what you accomplish; encourage yourself to follow your plan; ask friends and family to support your efforts.

Evaluate your progress. At the end of each day, evaluate what you have done and create the to-do list for the next day. Check completed items in your planner and circle any items that were not finished; move them to the next day. What, if anything, is blocking your progress? How can you resolve it?

Make adjustments as needed, and repeat. At the beginning of the next week, take a step back and review. Are your goals and objectives still the same? What challenges have emerged for this coming week? Do you need to seek help from your instructors, study labs or groups, classmates? This time is best used to confirm your accomplishments and chart your tasks for the next week. It is also a good time to reflect on your personal and social goals. How are you?

text we will introduce you to the research, theories, and practices that form the foundation for the steps of academic transformation, and the process will become habitual because you will do it again and again. You may already have strengths in certain areas, such as goal setting, and may want to improve your ability to create action plans. Conversely, you may have the motivation to work hard but have difficulty knowing the best methods of working to meet your goals. The exercises at the end of this chapter will help you begin to master this process. As you read each chapter and complete the exercises, you will increase your mastery.

Exercise 1.2

Strengthening the Transformation

As a beginning exercise in using the six-step process of academic transformation, do the following:

1. Brainstorm a list of at least three goals you would like to accomplish within the next six months. Do these goals meet your values?

2. Give a brief reason next to each item on your list why you want to accomplish it.

3. From this list, create one objective that you could accomplish within the next few months.

4. Set a plan of action (at least three strategies or specific behaviors) to help you complete this objective.

5. Design a method to track the chosen behaviors you are doing.

6. Evaluate your progress weekly for your objective.

7. Make changes and adjustments as needed after you evaluate your progress.

BECOMING AN AUTONOMOUS LEARNER

An excellent example of academic transformation is a student's gradual movement from a **teacher-directed learner** to an **autonomous learner**. Early educational experiences are teacher directed. Teachers expect students to learn by following the teacher's assignments and directions. Students are rarely required to set their own learning goals or deviate from given guidelines. They view the teacher as the source of the right answers, the authority (Weinstein, 1988).

These students write down what the teacher presents, usually word for word. They read the textbook assignment, and they often use rote memory to answer test questions. They depend on the teacher to make connections. The result is that procrastination and boredom are frequent companions.

Whereas this attitude and these behaviors are frequently sufficient for high school, they can be deadly in college. College professors value autonomous learners. Beginning college students often exert real effort in their courses, but when they try hard and use the behaviors that have worked well in the past, they can become confused when the results are disappointing. It is common to hear students say, "I studied harder for that test than I have ever studied before, and I *failed* it! I don't know what to do." They are being called to become autonomous learners, but no professor uses that term. It is a secret password to college success.

An **autonomous learner** is *a person independently competent in a wide variety of academic tasks, able to actively achieve goals based on values, and skilled in self-reflection.* We have identified seven important characteristics of students who are consistently successful in a collegiate environment. As you read the following explanations of the seven characteristics, evaluate how much of each you have already acquired.

1. Autonomous learners have a realistic view of themselves and their academic abilities. Separating fact from fantasy and reality from wishful thinking about ourselves is a major psychological task as we move from adolescence to adulthood. An emotionally healthy and realistic self-esteem is foundational to the effort of reflection, evaluation, and acceptance of our own academic abilities.

Where would you place your academic self-concept?

Fantasy-based ‹——————————————————————› Reality-based

2. Autonomous learners are ethical. A healthy self-awareness leads to a clear understanding of our own values and ethics. Simply believing in a principle is insufficient; living by our values and beliefs is essential to healthy self-esteem. When we are students, academics is our work. Academic honesty and integrity are important components of a successful college career, and they are the method by which we develop our system of professional ethics. If we cheat on college tests or papers, then we are likely to cheat at work.

Where would you place your academic behavior?

Unethical ‹——————————————————————› Ethical

3. Autonomous learners set realistic and appropriate goals for academic achievement. Few abilities are as crucial as that of setting realistic and appropriate goals for any endeavor, and academics is no exception to that premise. A goal can be as large as graduation or a semester GPA, or it can be as immediate as planning to study history for one hour tonight. To set realistic academic goals when there are other legitimate goals in their personal, family, social, work, and physical life is a difficult skill for some college students to master. Balance is the elusive goal for which we strive; the closer we get to balance, the closer we will come to the good life.

Where would you place your ability to set realistic and appropriate academic goals?

Poor ‹——————————————————————————› Good

4. Autonomous learners understand their own learning strengths and weaknesses. To set realistic and effective academic goals, we must know our own learning strengths and weaknesses. For example, if I am a slow reader, then I have to allocate more uninterrupted time to my assignments than my roommate who is a skilled reader. Through accurate academic self-assessment, we can choose the best major, the best semester schedule, and the best learning strategies.

How would you rate your awareness of your learning strengths and weaknesses?

Poor ‹——————————————————————————› Good

5. Autonomous learners use effective learning strategies and adapt those strategies to new situations. Hundreds of learning strategies are available for use, but choosing the most effective way to study a particular subject at a particular time is a skill acquired by reflection and practice. The common metaphor for this skill is a *toolbox,* a reference to the idea that a competent student creates a collection of strategies that she uses appropriately in different situations, depending on her goals, situation, and abilities. You can enhance and expand your current collection of strategies through the various ideas and examples in this textbook.

How would you rate your ability to appropriately vary your learning strategies?

Poor ‹——————————————————————————› Good

6. Autonomous learners manage their behaviors to reach their goals. Having appropriate goals and knowing the best strategies are meaningless unless we do the behaviors to learn. In other words, we have to work at being a student in a timely way. Procrastination and avoidance can destroy academic achievement, so we must learn how to control our own actions.

How well do you manage your academic behaviors?

Unproductive ‹——————————————————————› Productive

7. Autonomous learners use appropriate resources. Teachers, study groups, tutoring programs, library resources, other students, and many other resources exist for any course. Accessing those resources promptly is an important skill.

How effectively do you use resources?

Rarely ‹——————————————————————————› Often

Autonomous Learners

- Hold realistic views of themselves and their academic abilities
- Behave ethically
- Set realistic and appropriate goals for academic achievement
- Understand their learning strengths and weaknesses
- Use effective learning strategies and adapt those strategies to new situations
- Manage their behaviors to reach their goals
- Use appropriate resources

An autonomous learner is also successful in collaborative processes. Modern professional life relies on the abilities of people to work together to solve problems and create effective solutions; thus, learning to participate in learning groups and teams during college will provide effective tools for later success.

CONCLUSION

In this chapter, we have asked you to carefully consider three subjects: quality world, academic transformation, and the autonomous learner. We hope that you will engage in a serious reflection of these concepts as they apply to you through your completion of the guided journal questions following the chapter summary and key concepts. Simply reading an idea has little or no effect on us unless we make the effort to relate that idea to our own thoughts, feelings, and behaviors. Here is your chance to make these concepts meaningful.

As teachers and students, we have come to understand that competency as a college student can be learned. The learning skills in this text grow from what we now understand about our brains—how we learn, know, think. Journey with us as we explore cognitive and behavioral psychology, personality theory, and concepts from philosophy and business.

SUMMARY

- Our quality world begins with the people we want to be with, the things we most want to own or experience, and the ideas or systems of belief that govern much of our behavior. It holds our deepest values and feelings as well as our hopes for the way we wish to live. It is a place where we feel loved and protected.

- Our quality world should be steeped in our value system—one that is ethical, balanced, and wise.

- When we experience hope about a relationship, excitement about an idea, or longing for a possession, we are reshaping our quality world. Reflection is the process we use to continuously evaluate and reshape our quality world. We also use feedback from others we trust.

- The four major arenas of life we reflect on in our quality world are relationships, work, belief, and service.

- Academic transformation is the process whereby you will carefully assess your current situation as a student, determine specific short- and long-term academic goals based on your values, chart changes necessary to reach those goals, and then make those changes.

- There are six steps to academic transformation: assessing your current academic situation, setting short- and long-term academic goals based on your values, creating a list of immediate objectives and an action plan to meet them, doing the work, evaluating your progress, and making needed adjustments.

- The natural progression of moving from being a teacher-directed learner to an autonomous learner is an example of academic transformation.

- An autonomous learner is a person independently competent in a wide variety of academic tasks, able to actively achieve goals based on values, and skilled in self-reflection.

- Autonomous learners have a realistic view of themselves and their academic abilities, are ethical, set realistic and appropriate goals for academic achievement, understand their own learning strengths and weaknesses, use effective learning strategies and adapt those strategies to new situations, manage their behaviors to reach their goals, and use appropriate resources.

KEY CONCEPTS

Academic transformation   Relationships
Autonomous learner   Service
Belief   Teacher-directed learner
Quality world   Work
Reflection

GUIDED JOURNAL QUESTIONS

1. Describe your academic strengths and weaknesses as a learner, particularly in relation to reading, writing, mathematics, and critical thinking. Be as specific as possible by citing previous experiences, courses, and grades. What concerns do you have about beginning this semester?

2. Choose one of the four arenas—relationships, work, belief, service. Describe an example that illustrates a positive aspect you are happy to have in your world. Then describe an example that you believe is not how you want to live. What changes can you make in the second example?

3. What do you envision to be your life's work? Is it different from what you may currently be experiencing? How does (or will) work give meaning and purpose to your quality world?

4. An excellent example of academic transformation is a student's gradual movement from a teacher-directed learner to an autonomous learner. Now that you have read this chapter, define "academic transformation" in your own words. What types of transformation would you consider important for yourself during this period in your academic pursuits?

5. Review the list of seven competencies of an autonomous learner. Which competencies have you successfully achieved? Which are you willing to work toward achieving? Explain.

6. What preparations did you make *before* you came to college that assisted you in being a successful student? What do you wish you had done differently to prepare yourself?

The Last Word

This book began 40 years ago when I walked into a classroom of 20 unsuspecting freshmen who wanted to be successful in college. I had always been a successful student, but at that moment I realized I didn't know how to teach anyone how to do it. Thanks to all those students who went with me down paths of discovery as I figured things out.

—De Sellers

Thinking and Intellectual Performance

I think, ergo I learn.

CHAPTER HIGHLIGHTS

- The Role of Thinking in Study

- Types of Knowledge

- Levels of Intellectual Performance

As we delve into the world of college thinking, we discover complex and challenging theories to guide our development. Autonomous learners develop the capacity to learn and demonstrate their knowledge in widely diverse situations. Many of your college experiences will simulate the work life you desire. Understanding and using your collegiate academic experiences successfully will develop your ability as an autonomous learner.

SELF-ASSESSMENT: Thinking About Learning

College requires you to think and learn at very different levels of complexity. With 5 being "Almost Always" and 1 being "Almost Never," assess your assumptions and feelings about your thinking and learning. Rate each of the following statements honestly by circling the appropriate number. Completing this exercise will help you identify areas of concern you may have as you begin to contemplate more complex learning activities.

	Almost Always		Sometimes		Almost Never
1. I can explore many differing viewpoints on a topic and maintain my objectivity.	5	4	3	2	1
2. I think deeply and thoughtfully about a variety of issues and topics.	5	4	3	2	1
3. I enjoy learning facts, dates, names, and events in courses such as history.	5	4	3	2	1
4. I enjoy learning how to work through a procedure in a math or accounting problem.	5	4	3	2	1
5. I am good at deciding when to use a particular learning strategy as I move from course to course.	5	4	3	2	1
6. I look for or create specific examples to help me understand new concepts.	5	4	3	2	1
7. I prefer to apply (demonstrate, compute, construct, solve) what I am learning when possible.	5	4	3	2	1
8. I am comfortable comparing and contrasting ideas such as two or more theories or historical events.	5	4	3	2	1
9. I find it easy to critique my own work such as a research paper I have written.	5	4	3	2	1

10. I enjoy creating (devising or   5   4   3   2   1
    developing) new ideas based on
    what I have learned in class.

Add up the numbers you circled. Your total score will be between 10 and 50. The higher your score, the more likely you are to be open to thinking and learning at higher levels well beyond memorization. For scores below 30, write or reflect on the items for which you have concerns and consider talking with a trusted friend, a family member, a teacher, a counselor, or an advisor.

THE ROLE OF THINKING IN STUDY

Human learning means *a difference occurs within the learner.* We think differently, behave differently, and/or feel differently as a result of mental activity. Thousands of scholars since ancient times have struggled with **epistemology**, which is *"the philosophical term for the theory of knowledge. It attempts to understand how knowing occurs and to discover its ground, its limitation, its validity and trustworthiness and its relation to truth"* (Hosinki, 1992, p. 150, italics added). One of the goals of this text is to help you develop a comprehensive understanding of the many ways in which learning can be discussed. As philosophers and psychologists try to describe human learning, they usually resort to comparisons. Here are several typical comparisons for human learning used in the last 25 years:

> *Describing mental processes as if the brain were a computer*
>
> *Describing human memory as a filing cabinet*
>
> *Describing study skills as if they were tools in a toolbox*

Each of these metaphors has its advantages and limitations. As you read this text, you may create your own comparisons to help you understand concepts.

Our ability to think is one aspect of our minds, and that ability is different from knowing. We think about the knowledge we have. There are stages of thinking ability (not intelligence) that range from the unreflective thinker to the master thinker (Elder & Paul, 1996). No guarantee exists that a person will become a critical thinker in college; in fact, many graduates are not critical thinkers. Becoming a critical thinker means that a person can routinely use higher-order thinking skills based on reason and evidence, not only in studying but also in life. **Critical thinking** *"is the ability and disposition to improve one's thinking by systematically subjecting it to intellectual self-assessment"* (Elder & Paul, 1996, italics added). Effective study strategies help develop such skills.

An important aspect of critical thinking is the constant ethical concern of being fair:

Fair-mindedness entails a consciousness of the need to treat all viewpoints alike, without reference to one's own feeling or selfish interests, or the feelings or selfish interests of one's friends, community, or nation. It implies adherence to intellectual standards (such as accuracy and sound logic), uninfluenced by one's own advantage or the advantage of one's group. (Paul & Elder, 2001, p. 5)

Becoming fair-minded is challenging because it is so much easier to be the opposite, selfish and shortsighted. To become fair-minded, we must be intellectually humble, courageous, empathetic, honest, perseverant, confident in our reasoning ability, and autonomous (Paul & Elder, 2001). College is a wonderful opportunity to develop these traits if we take the initiative, and college faculty value critical thinking. They will consistently push you to think critically on papers, projects, and exams.

It is easy to let the academic performance demands of tests, papers, and projects limit what we learn and become. Our contention is that because you will spend many hours studying to pass tests and assignments, you might as well seize this opportunity and study to develop your critical thinking skills at the same time. If you do, you increase the likelihood that you will be able to bring your thoughts, emotions, and actions together to reach your life goals and experience fulfillment and a sense of well-being (Paul & Elder, 2001).

Frame your study by thoughtful questions and deliberately push yourself to analyze, apply, and evaluate the information fairly. Search out the assignments and the instructors that will help you develop advanced thinking skills. If becoming a critical, fair-minded thinker is an important goal for you, then you can accomplish it through your undergraduate study.

When we think, we make sense of what is going on—that is, we create meaning. In academic study, we attempt to make sense of a content field, such as history, biology, philosophy, or economics. Each subject that we study represents a distinctive way of thinking about a particular set of questions, and those questions result in the basic concepts of that field. Those concepts provide the underlying unity in the field. Some examples are as follows:

- *mathematics* as the development of a language for quantification

- *algebra* as arithmetic with unknowns

- *sociology* as the study of how the life of humans is shaped by the groups in which they are members

- *physics* as the study of mass and energy and the interrelations between the two

- *philosophy* as the study of ultimate questions and their reasoned answers

- *biochemistry* as the study of the chemistry of life at the molecular level (Paul & Elder, 2001, p. 149)

If we can understand the basic concepts in a field, then we have a much better chance of creating meaningful learning in our daily study. Here are some beginning questions to help you determine such concepts:

- What is the main goal of studying this subject?

- What are people in this field trying to accomplish?

- What kinds of questions do they ask? What kinds of problems do they try to solve?

- What sort of information or data do they gather?

- How do they go about gathering information in ways that are distinctive to this field?

- What is the most basic idea, concept, or theory in this field?

- How should studying this field affect my view of the world?

- How are the products of this field used in everyday life? (Paul & Elder, 2001, p. 152)

Sometimes a good place to find the basic concepts and the logic of a subject is in a good encyclopedia. Your text may also have some introductory material that is useful. Having a clear grasp of the concepts and logic of each course provides you a mental framework in which to direct your learning. That mental framework also helps you understand and remember the material.

Exercise 2.2

What This Academic Success Course Means to Me

Take a few minutes to critically think about this academic success course using the questions we have just mentioned. Next, write a letter to a friend or family member with the purpose of describing this class by reflecting on some of the basic concepts for this course. Be sure to include the reasons you enrolled in the course and what you most hope to gain personally by the end of the term. You may find your syllabus and the Table of Contents helpful to you as you compose your letter. The objective of this exercise is to help you explore the meaning of this class by critically *thinking* about the content.

Introductory courses in a content field typically are more difficult for students than advanced courses because the basic vocabulary, concepts, and logic of the field have yet to be learned. Freshmen and sophomores take many new subjects simultaneously and are surprised by the difficult workload.

All academic subjects are the product of thinking. Thinking creates content. Thinking expresses, organizes, maintains, and expands content. Thinking analyzes and evaluates content. Thinking restructures and transforms content. Whenever you study, you can choose the level of thinking you want and need to use. The deeper your level of thinking, the deeper your level of learning. The fastest way to deepen your learning is to ask questions about the content:

- What is my purpose in studying this content?

- What are my instructor's expectations for my learning this content?

- What are the questions/problems of the content to be considered?

- What concepts are important to those questions/problems?

- What information do I need to explore those questions/problems?

- How can I relate this information to daily life?

Your thinking ability is the cornerstone of your capacity to learn in college, and it will vary from subject to subject. Sometimes you will intuitively ask the questions that lead your study; other times you will need to be much more deliberative and find other sources to help you.

In the following sections, we use a freshman's course schedule to show three important characteristics of college learning: types of knowledge, levels of intellectual performance, and range of difficulty of material.

TYPES OF KNOWLEDGE

CASE STUDY

JENNIFER, a beginning freshman at a local community college, is excited about being in college. During orientation she worked with an advisor and registered for 16 credit hours: English Composition, College Algebra, World History, General Biology (with a lab), and Educational Psychology. Jennifer was a B+ student in a large, urban high school, and she is a little apprehensive about this first semester. She is living in an apartment near campus, but her parents are not far away. In high school she was a competent student, but she rarely felt challenged. Jennifer is eager to do well in college, for she wants a professional career like her parents have.

Like most students, Jennifer has always studied a variety of subjects, but she has never reflected on the differences and similarities between subjects and the demands of each one. Her Educational Psychology professor started the term with a lecture on the three types of knowledge—declarative, procedural, and conditional—that seem to be especially helpful for collegiate learning. Each type varies from the other in three important ways: how we acquire (or learn) that knowledge, how we store that knowledge in our memories, and how we retrieve and use that knowledge.

Types of Knowledge		
Declarative	**Procedural**	**Conditional**
Knowing specific information about something	Knowing how to do something	Knowing when and why to use a particular strategy based on understanding the task and ourselves

Declarative Knowledge

Declarative knowledge is *possessing specific information about something.* Examples of such knowledge are remembering and understanding our name, our social security number, the quadratic formula, four proposed causes of the Civil War, the chemical symbol for sodium, or Einstein's Theory of Relativity. Declarative knowledge is usually facts or theories, but it can also be personal experiences, such as knowing which classes you are taking this semester. For the purpose of academic learning, we focus on declarative knowledge as factual (terminology, specific details) and conceptual (categories, principles, theories, models). In collegiate learning, **factual knowledge** consists of *the basic pieces of information in a particular academic discipline.* **Conceptual knowledge** is *the larger groupings of related ideas*. To create conceptual knowledge, we group factual knowledge into classifications and categories. Then we can use those to create principles and generalizations. Finally, principles and generalizations form theories and models (Anderson & Krathwohl, 2001). In the earlier section devoted to thinking, we discussed the concept of academic disciplines and how each has a unique vocabulary (factual) and set of foundational theories (conceptual). You will build a beginning body of factual and conceptual knowledge in each of the courses you study, and in your major field of study you will build a large and deep body of conceptual knowledge throughout your collegiate years.

Several of Jennifer's classes rely heavily on declarative knowledge: World History and Educational Psychology and the lecture section of her General Biology class. All are full of definitions, data, and concepts, that is, declarative knowledge.

Propositions

Some of the most interesting research in learning has been the investigation of the nature of declarative knowledge and how it is believed we store it in our memories.

Researchers have labeled the basic unit of declarative knowledge as the **proposition**, *one thought or one idea* (Gagné, 1985). For example, the sentence *The courageous student asks a question in class* has three ideas or propositions: the student is courageous, the student is in class, and the student asks a question. As we are reading a textbook or listening in class, we do not consciously think of the single, small ideas that flow and combine into larger and larger units, but psychologists believe that our brains recognize individual propositions and store them as discrete units (schemata) that are linked by meaning. **Schemata** are defined as *mental networks of related facts and concepts that influence the acquisition and understanding of new information* (Slavin, 2003, 2006).

Many study strategies for declarative knowledge use structured and deliberate memory storage and retrieval practice as the primary model for mastery. These strategies attempt to mimic the way in which we believe our brains store and retrieve this type of knowledge. Such strategies help us deeply process our learning to make connections to what we already know. Later chapters describe in detail many of these techniques such as summarizing, visualizing, mapping, networking, diagramming, and creating compare and contrast grids. One other helpful characteristic of declarative knowledge is that college students seem able to acquire and store this type of knowledge quickly, and the more time they allow themselves, the more likely they are to master it at deeper levels.

Although Jennifer is a good reader and has an excellent vocabulary, she is quickly stunned by the amount of reading her instructors expect her to complete in the declarative knowledge classes. In high school, she simply paid attention in class and looked over the material the night before the test, remembering enough to answer the questions the next day in class. However, college texts seem different; she finds that they tend to have much more information and that information seems far more complicated. Upon reflection, she begins to understand that she can remember the factual knowledge, but she is having trouble with the complexity of the concepts. She slowly begins to change her study techniques to pay special attention to the conceptual knowledge her teachers stress. She also chooses to participate in several study groups with other students who have similar learning goals.

Case Study Question: What other suggestions do you have for Jennifer as she continues to explore new approaches to learning declarative knowledge at the college level?

Because our understanding of an idea mandates how our brains store and later access and retrieve that idea for use on a test or on the job, an important study strategy for declarative knowledge is to stop and test ourselves on what we have just been studying. Can we explain it in our own words? Can we give

FIGURE 2.1 An Example of Learning Declarative Knowledge

One method the Roman leaders used to pacify the populace during the first and second centuries, C.E., was large-scale entertainment.	
Strategy	**Example**
Explain it in your own words.	Roman emperors used street festivals, executions, and games (gladiators) to pacify the populace in Rome.
Create examples from your own experience.	Professional sports provide a vicarious experience to release aggression and experience competitiveness.
Think about similar ideas or concepts.	Present-day government programs give services or tax cuts to specific parts of the American public.
Link to prior knowledge.	The movie *Gladiator* shows how the government pacified the general public.
Create questions to test yourself.	Compare methods of how governments influence and control their constituents, with special attention to the Roman government of the first and second centuries, C.E.

examples from our own experiences? A further strategy is to integrate this knowledge into something we already know. How does our prior knowledge relate to the ideas just presented? Can we link this knowledge to something we learned in another class? Does it contradict something the teacher said? The more connections we can make between this new piece of knowledge and other pieces already stored in our brains, the more likely we will remember it when we need it and the more likely we will really understand it. (See Figure 2.1 for an example of learning declarative knowledge.) No one had taught Jennifer to read and study in these ways, so she struggles during her first semester.

Most declarative knowledge presented to college students is in words, through either lecture or text. Yes, effective teachers and writers also use graphs, charts, and tables, but the major message is in words. So the task of the student is to take the words and do something with them to achieve meaning.

Procedural Knowledge

To know how to do something is different from knowing about something. When we *know how to do something*, such as read, add fractions, create an income

statement, or write a marketing case study, we have **procedural knowledge**. When we use procedural knowledge, either physically or mentally, we are actively creating a result. Generally, acquiring procedural knowledge means learning a skill. An example would be the ability to add fractions. A simplistic overview of the steps of that ability contains the determination whether like denominators exist; if not, the conversion of all denominators to one common term; then the conversion of numerators to the appropriate units; then the adding of the numerators (but not the denominators); and, finally, the reduction of the resulting fraction.

Productions

Psychologists have labeled the *process of knowing how* as **productions** (Gagné, 1985). A production flows in a logical, systematic sequence, something like a flow chart that is often used in designing computer programs. When we are first learning a production, each step comes slowly. We may make errors in the sequence—omitting, inserting, or transposing steps. Our work is conscious and slow. But something happens as we practice the task. We become faster and more accurate, and, most important, we do not have to devote much of our conscious minds to the task. Doing the task becomes automatic.

Understanding or meaning plays as important a role in learning procedural knowledge as it does in learning declarative knowledge. If we only memorize a production, a rule, or a procedure without understanding it, we are unable to adjust to a slightly changed situation or problem. We just follow rules blindly and are helpless when we are confronted with changes. However, if we understand the production and why it is structured the way it is, then we can often apply the production to new situations.

Jennifer is taking two primarily procedural knowledge courses this term: English Composition and College Algebra. The lab section of General Biology is also somewhat procedural. In high school, Jennifer did fairly well in mathematics because there were frequent homework assignments, quizzes, and exams. She had many opportunities to practice problems, and most of the high school quizzes relied heavily on memory. Her first College Algebra test was a shock, for the instructor combined several procedures into one problem. Sheer memory no longer worked; she had to understand the procedures to be able to solve the problem.

Procedural knowledge cannot exist without the appropriate declarative knowledge. For example, our knowledge of what a fraction is and what

FIGURE 2.2   An Example of Learning Procedural Knowledge

Learning how to write a persuasive essay	
Strategy	**Example**
Participate as much as possible when learning the new procedure.	When reading/studying sample essays, mark the structure of the persuasive argument.
Work extra problems and exercises to "overlearn" the material.	Choose three possible topics about which you have strong feelings and brainstorm a rough outline for each.
Practice over periods of time (work a little every day).	Brainstorm on one day, search the Web on the second day, choose a topic and create an outline on the third day, write a rough draft on the fourth day, and edit the final copy on the fifth day.

properties it has (declarative) pairs with knowledge of how to reduce a fraction (procedural). Psychologists believe that the two types of knowledge are stored closely to each other in our brains, again hypothesizing that meaning is the link.

For Jennifer, learning (acquiring) procedural knowledge is quite different from learning declarative knowledge. Because she has difficulty understanding the concepts of procedural knowledge classes such as math or accounting, the key to success is an ongoing effort. Excellent class attendance and participation, supported by a large quantity of homework exercises, are the beginning steps. Teachers rarely give (and students rarely do) enough homework exercises to truly master a production; therefore, successful students usually work extra problems until the process (production) seems easy, automatic, and fast. (See Figure 2.2 for an example of learning procedural knowledge.) Because acquiring a production is most likely to happen by practicing over a long period of time, procrastination and the resultant cramming are deadly for this type of learning. It is almost impossible to learn procedural knowledge at the last minute. Jennifer quickly adjusted her study techniques in College Algebra by working more problems every day and attending tutoring sessions, so her performance on the second test improved.

Case Study Question: What other suggestions do you have for Jennifer as she continues to explore new approaches to learning procedural knowledge at the college level?

Procedural knowledge requires time and practice to acquire. It is an active process that yields a product. Although it is slow in the beginning, it becomes rapid, accurate, and automatic. If we understand the process, we will be able to apply it in new situations.

Conditional Knowledge

Conditional knowledge—*knowing when and why to use particular strategies*—is the third type of knowledge directly related to academic learning. When we understand the nature and the requirements of an academic task such as a test or project, we are using conditional knowledge. When we are aware of our own learning strengths and weaknesses and adjust our studying accordingly, we are using conditional knowledge (Anderson & Krathwohl, 2001). (See Figure 2.3 for an example of using conditional knowledge.) Much of this text is about acquiring the most appropriate strategies for collegiate learning. Students with highly developed conditional strategies are successful learners; they are both efficient and effective. They are able to thoughtfully maximize their abilities, whether they are in the classroom, a

FIGURE 2.3   An Example of Using Conditional Knowledge

Preparing for my first World History exam	
Strategy	**Example**
Know different strategies for different tasks.	Review note cards, all notes and the PowerPoint notes from the instructor. Write practice essays. Study with a partner.
Understand why you should use certain strategies.	Creating and reviewing note cards will help with memorizing the terms, dates and concepts. Writing practice essays will help with comprehension and analysis of the information. This will also help sharpen writing skills. Studying with a partner will help fill in gaps in learning and provides a way to reinforce already learned material.
Know how to regulate your study.	Plan extra study time the week before the exam and schedule a time to meet with another student from the class to review the material.

study group, or private study. Such students know what memory techniques are most suitable for a science class; they use the appropriate note-taking techniques for a lecture class that uses objective testing; they use specific types of strategies to prepare for an essay exam; they organize their study time to competently master accounting procedures; they control external distracters to their concentration by manipulating their study environment. We believe that conditional strategies involve more than just the knowledge of when and why to use certain strategies; they also involve the knowledge of how to understand and control our own behavior. It is not enough to know what to do to reach our goals; we must be able to regulate our behavior so that we do what we need to do when and how we need to do it. This cluster of skills is difficult to master, but we have been helping students like Jennifer accomplish that task for many years.

Jennifer continues to expand her understanding of the many ways in which college academics differ from high school learning. She has increased her cognitive strategies (conditional knowledge) by utilizing different approaches for her declarative and procedural courses. She is coming to understand both her strengths and her shortcomings as a college learner. Now she needs a clearer understanding of the levels of intellectual performance she must master in college.

Case Study Question: What other suggestions do you have for Jennifer as she continues to determine when and why to use particular strategies (conditional knowledge) to learn declarative and procedural knowledge at the college level?

Exercise 2.3

Using Declarative, Procedural, and Conditional Knowledge

Match the type of knowledge to the correct activity. Completing this activity will facilitate your understanding of the three types of knowledge.

A. Declarative knowledge

B. Procedural knowledge

C. Conditional knowledge

1. _____ Practicing a problem using the Pythagorean theorem

2. _____ Explaining the law of supply and demand

3. _____ Memorizing musical symbols

4. _____ Selecting a note-taking format for sociology class

5. _____ Comparing behavioral psychology with cognitive psychology

6. _____ Giving a persuasive speech

7. _____ Creating sample test questions to study for a biology exam

8. _____ Memorizing the state capitals of the United States

LEVELS OF INTELLECTUAL PERFORMANCE

There are several levels of intellectual performance—not different subjects or even different kinds of learning tasks, but different levels of mastery of one concept or one set of data. The primary contributor to this approach was Bloom (1956). He posited six levels, each with direct applicability to the academic setting. Bloom envisioned a stair-step model, with each successive level dependent on the one(s) below, and that model is still taught today to people entering the teaching profession. Recent scholars (Anderson & Krathwohl, 2001) have revised Bloom's model to include a more intensive reflection of recent theoretical models of learning. In this text, we use much of the revised model so that we can investigate more closely the center point of collegiate learning—the necessity of understanding the meaning of academic material if we wish to retain and use it.

Figure 2.4 provides a matrix using the revised **Bloom's Taxonomy**.

Remember

The entry point to learning academic material is to remember it—that is, to remember it long enough to be able to think about it. Most of us take this skill

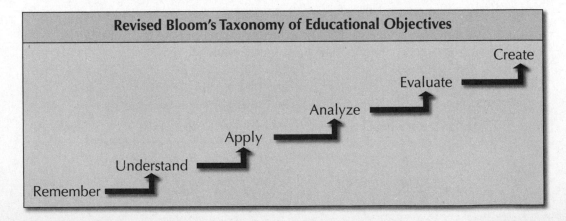

Revised Bloom's Taxonomy of Educational Objectives

Create

Evaluate

Analyze

Apply

Understand

Remember

FIGURE 2.4   Matrix Using the Revised Model of Bloom's Taxonomy

Level	Definition	Sample Verbs	Examples
Remember	The ability to recognize or recall an idea, a fact, or an occurrence in a form similar to the original presentation	Define, describe, identify, label, list, match, name, state	Reciting "The Raven" by Edgar Allen Poe
Understand	The ability to construct meaning from the literal message in a communication	Classify, describe, discuss, explain, give, interpret, paraphrase, summarize	Explaining the meaning of Poe's "The Raven"
Apply	The ability to use understanding of ideas correctly and appropriately in a new situation	Apply, demonstrate, determine, compute, construct, solve	Labeling the differing rhyme schemes in Poe's "The Raven"
Analyze	The ability to break the material into its constituent parts and detect the relationships and organization of those parts	Analyze, categorize, compare, contrast, diagram, discriminate, distinguish, infer, outline, separate, subdivide	Comparing and contrasting Poe's "The Raven" with "Serenade"
Evaluate	The ability to render a value judgment based on criteria and standards	Appraise, conclude, critique, decide, defend, interpret, judge, justify, recommend	Writing a critical analysis of Poe's "The Raven"
Create	The ability to create a new product from the ideas or materials understood	Compile, compose, create, design, develop, devise, hypothesize, invent	Creating a poem with meter and rhyme scheme similar to Poe's "The Raven"

for granted until we realize that we have just spent 30 minutes reading a textbook and cannot remember what we have read. The same phenomenon can happen in a classroom when we are listening to a lecture. We have to attend to the information and hold on to it if it is going to become something we will keep. Marking a text and taking lecture notes are two methods of holding on to academic material. Future chapters on cognitive learning theory and strategies give many strategies to help you remember academic material.

Remember is *the ability to recognize or recall an idea, a fact, or an occurrence in a form similar to the original presentation* (Bloom, 1956). Note that the definition denotes two types of remembering—recognition and recall. When we see an item and are able to match it with something we have seen before, we are recognizing it. Many test questions require this type of remembering. However, there is a more complicated form of remembering. If we are asked a question about some piece of factual knowledge, and we can spontaneously pull that information from our memory, then we are recalling it.

Understand

Students frequently resort to memorizing without understanding and are then lost when professors ask them to use or evaluate the information. Although memory is necessary, it is insufficient for collegiate learning. The foundation of collegiate learning is to **understand**, *the ability to construct meaning from the literal message in a communication.* Understanding is a complex phenomenon, and researchers have hypothesized many different stages of this ability (Anderson & Krathwohl, 2001). However for the purposes of this text, we will use the original definitions created by Bloom in 1956 because we believe they are the best suited for students. He believed that we are able to translate, interpret, and extrapolate the information remembered when we understand (Bloom, 1956). In this text, we use *comprehend* and *understand* interchangeably.

To acquire comprehension may take much more attention and effort than simple remembering requires. We begin to examine this complex level of knowledge by using an example from Jennifer's course in educational psychology, the concept of multicultural education. She has always been able to remember factual knowledge, but she is struggling with understanding the complexity of the concepts in this course.

Understanding usually begins with a concept or idea that is worded in either abstract or concrete terms. Most textbooks present a concept in abstract terms, such as the following example of a definition of multicultural education: "all students, regardless of the groups to which they belong, groups such as those related to gender, ethnicity, race, culture, social class, religion, or exceptionality, should experience educational equality in the schools" (Banks, 1993a, p. 24, as cited in Woolfolk, 1998, p. 163).

The first step to understanding is to **translate** *an abstract idea into specific examples.* When Jennifer reads the assignment, she creates several specific examples of what would constitute educational equality for people of different groups, then she reflects on the definition of exceptionality and thinks of an example of that idea. Often the most powerful method of translating an abstract concept into a specific example is to use a personal

Understand

Step 1	Translate a concept into specific examples.
Step 2	Explain in your own words the relationship between the concept and the examples.
Step 3	See connections and make predictions.

memory that exemplifies the concept, so she reflects about an incident that had happened in her middle school science class when some of the students were gifted in science and others were not. Another example of translation occurs during the lecture when her college instructor presents a concept in concrete form first, then expects his students to move from that example to the abstract idea. His lecture begins with a story of a specific child's experience in a fifth-grade classroom. Jennifer's ability to translate that specific incident into an abstract statement of the concept imbedded in the example demonstrates her mastery of the first step of understanding.

The next step to understanding is the ability to **interpret** or **explain**, *to articulate the difference between the concept and a specific example, to tell about the idea in your own words* (Bloom, 1956). In our example, Jennifer would explain the core concept of educational equality. How would she explain this idea to someone from another country? Or another century? Does this concept mean that all children should have the same educational experience? Grappling with a concept is not an easy matter, so she begins to ask herself many questions. Her competency in explaining a concept lies in her ability to communicate the idea in her own words, without simply repeating the words used by the text or the professor.

The third step to comprehending is to **extrapolate**, *the ability to see connections between two or more identified ideas or to make predictions based on the understanding of the ideas* (Bloom, 1956). In many circumstances, our ability to simply ask *What if . . . ?* may help us extrapolate the information. In the case of our example of multicultural education, some simple questions would help us understand this concept, such as *What if funds are limited?* or *What textbooks would we need?* or *What if teachers do not have sufficient knowledge to . . . ?* It is not necessary, or practical, to examine all possible questions; usually one or two forays of extrapolation are sufficient to understand the concept solidly.

Apply

When we understand a concept or idea, then we can begin to use it in a variety of intellectual activities. To **apply** is *the ability to use understanding of ideas correctly and appropriately in a new situation* (Bloom, 1956). The most obvious example of application would be a case study. If Jennifer were given a description of a specific school curriculum, would she be able to recognize whether it followed the principles of multicultural education or not? Although our example is declarative knowledge, many application levels of college learning occur with procedural knowledge classes such as mathematics, accounting, and statistics. In understanding, "the emphasis is on the grasp of the meaning and intent of the material. In application it is on remembering and bringing to bear upon given material the appropriate generalizations or principles" (Bloom, 1956, p. 144).

Analyze

Another level of knowledge, **analyze**, is the focus of much college testing. It is *the ability to break the material into its constituent parts and detect the relationships and organization of those parts* (Bloom, 1956). Our example of multicultural education lends itself to many variants of analysis. An obvious analysis would focus on the different components that would have to exist for such education to occur, such as curriculum, materials, and teacher training. However, many other kinds of analysis are also possible. If you can analyze, then you can compare and/or contrast both within and outside the concept. Jennifer could describe the similarities (comparison) and the differences (contrast) between two different curricular proposals or three different texts with reference to this definition of multicultural education. She could trace the development of a multicultural education program in a school district.

Evaluate

The next level of knowledge is **evaluate**, *the ability to render a value judgment based on criteria and standards* (Bloom, 1956). An important aspect of evaluation is a critical reflection on both the internal logical consistency of a process or product and the external validity of that same product or process.

Evaluation assignments are quite common in the advanced courses in your major. Sometimes they involve group work and group presentations. In our example from educational psychology, Jennifer could be asked to review a middle school curriculum by the criteria presented for multicultural education and rate that curriculum with her rationale. She might be asked to defend the school's decision to create an honors program for gifted students or a tutorial program for athletes during a school budget crisis.

Create

The highest level of knowledge, **create**, is often the most exciting of all the levels. Originally titled *synthesis,* it is *the ability to create a new product from the ideas or materials understood* (Bloom, 1956). One of the most common creative assignments is to design a new example of a concept or an idea. An assignment might require that Jennifer write a fifth-grade history curriculum unit that would meet the premise of this concept. She could also be asked to infer three problems that could occur when such a curriculum would be proposed to a school board.

A practical note: Applying this theoretical model of intellectual performance is not always simple. We often stop and evaluate results at various points in the learning process. Such evaluation may motivate us to retrace our steps and begin to think about a topic in a different way.

Using the Taxonomy

An important academic skill is to identify the level of knowledge expected in different classes by different professors because the desired performance mandates the study strategies required for that level of mastery. In simple terms, you use different study strategies for an essay test at the analysis level than you do for a problem-solving test on the application level. Successful students vary their class notes, their study notes, their study times, and their test preparation according to the level at which they will be tested.

Exercise 2.4

How Do You Learn at Each Level?

For practice using the revised Bloom's Taxonomy, use any chapter you have already read from this textbook to complete this exercise. After reviewing the chapter, provide an example of how you could use each level of the taxonomy in learning a portion of the chapter's content. We have given you an example for the first level. Completing this exercise will help you understand how to use the taxonomy as a study tool.

The chapter I have selected is Chapter _____.

Remember	I could create note cards to help me memorize the important terms.
Understand	_____
Apply	_____
Analyze	_____
Evaluate	_____
Create	_____

Exercise 2.5

Determining Levels for Test Questions

Review an old test (preferably a college exam—especially one from a declarative knowledge–based course). For each question, determine the level of intellectual performance required according to the revised Bloom's Taxonomy. This exercise can be completed on most any type of exam (multiple choice, true/false, essay, and so on). Completing this exercise will help you see how different questions can test you at very different levels of thinking.

CONCLUSION

In this chapter, we have given you some complex and important concepts that undergird successful academic performance. We will use these concepts repeatedly to demonstrate which study strategies will lead to the best performance in differing courses, assignments, and so forth. In this chapter and throughout the text, we will encourage you to understand yourself as a learner and to strategically use your time and talents to achieve your academic goals.

The most important word to remember is THINK. We expect you to think. Your professors expect you to think. Your future employers expect you to think. Think about your subjects; think about the profession you will be joining; think about yourself as a learner.

SUMMARY

- Thinking is not the same as knowledge. We think about the knowledge we have.

- Critical thinkers use higher-order thinking skills based on reason and evidence. It involves the process of evaluation or categorization based on previously stored standards.

- Becoming fair-minded is an essential element in critical thinking. It entails treating all viewpoints alike without our own predispositions and biases.

- When we think, we make sense of what is going on—we create meaning. We must create meaning from the concepts we learn in our different courses.

- The deeper your level of thinking, the deeper your level of learning. Asking questions about the content of your courses deepens your learning.

- Human learning means that a difference occurs within the learner. Academic learning is that set of knowledge and skills that our society expects as a result of school experience.

- There are three types of knowledge: declarative, procedural, and conditional.

- Declarative knowledge is possessing specific information about something. The basic unit of declarative knowledge is the proposition, one thought or one idea.

- Schemata help us recognize individual propositions, and the use of these mental networks helps us connect new information with prior knowledge.

- Strategies for learning declarative knowledge include explaining in your own words, creating examples from personal experiences, thinking about similar ideas or concepts, linking to prior knowledge, and creating practice test questions.

- Procedural knowledge is knowing how to do something, and a production is the process of knowing how. Productions flow in a logical, systematic sequence.

- Strategies for learning procedural knowledge include participating as much as possible when learning the new procedure, working extra problems and exercises to "overlearn" the material, and practicing over periods of time.

- Conditional knowledge is knowing when and why to use particular strategies based on understanding the task and ourselves.

- The use of conditional knowledge involves knowing different strategies for different academic tasks, knowing why to use certain strategies, and knowing how to regulate study behaviors based on personal learning strengths and weaknesses.

- According to the taxonomy, there are six levels of intellectual performance, each successive level being more complex and dependent on the one(s) below.

- Remember is the ability to recognize or recall an idea, a fact, or an occurrence in a form similar to the original presentation.

- Understand is the ability to construct meaning from the literal message in a communication.

- Apply is the ability to use understanding of ideas correctly and appropriately in a new situation.

- Analyze is the ability to break the material into its constituent parts and detect the relationships and organization of those parts—the ability to compare and contrast.

- Evaluate is the ability to render a value judgment based on criteria and standards.

- Create is the ability to create a new product from the ideas or materials understood.

KEY CONCEPTS

Bloom's Taxonomy (Revised) of
educational objectives:
remember, understand, apply,
analyze, evaluate, create

Conceptual knowledge

Conditional knowledge

Critical thinking

Declarative knowledge

Epistemology

Extrapolate

Factual knowledge

Fair-mindedness

Human learning

Interpret/explain

Procedural knowledge

Productions

Propositions

Schemata

Translate

GUIDED JOURNAL QUESTIONS

1. What are several ways in which college learning differs from high school learning? If you have been in the workforce, how does college learning differ from job-related learning?

2. What is the difference between knowing, thinking, and critical thinking? Of the courses you are taking this term, in which ones will you need to fully develop critical thinking skills? In which will you have the most difficulty being fair-minded and open to new ways of thinking?

3. Of the courses you are currently enrolled in, which are the most and least enjoyable? Analyze your answers based on the type of knowledge each class primarily involves (declarative, procedural, conditional). Many classes may be a combination of the three. Do you see a trend in which type of knowledge-based course you are most comfortable with taking? Explain.

4. As you learned in this chapter, your college instructors will require different levels of intellectual performance. Using the taxonomy, list each of your courses. What do you predict to be the highest level of intellectual performance required for each class? Support your answers with concrete examples.

5. How do you learn material for a course that requires you to understand material such as sociology or psychology? Include in your answer several examples of learning strategies.

6. How do you learn material for a class that requires you to apply material such as accounting or mathematics? Include in your answer several examples of learning strategies.

7. How do you prefer your instructors to present the material (lecture, class discussion, PowerPoint slides, computer-assisted instruction, group work, and so on) in a declarative knowledge–based course? In a procedural knowledge–based course? Why are these your preferences?

The Last Word

Learning something new is always an exciting ride for me. In that way, I am perpetually childlike. I invite you to this perspective—just for today—get excited about learning.

—De Sellers

Learning in Class

But I slept through class in high school.

CHAPTER HIGHLIGHTS

- Your Job as a Student
- Range of Difficulty of Material
- How to Learn in Class

By the time you get to college, you have been a student for at least 12 years. You made each transition between levels: preschool to kindergarten, kindergarten to elementary . . . but the shift to college is often the hardest. One of the reasons is that you are simply expected to be an autonomous and competent learner. Easier said than done, even if you worked hard in high school.

SELF-ASSESSMENT: Skills for Success

Preparing adequately for class, listening intently, and taking good notes are essential skills for college success. With 5 being "Almost Always" and 1 being "Almost Never," assess your skills for success. Rate each of the following statements honestly by circling the appropriate number. Completing this exercise will help you identify concerns you may be experiencing about these skills.

	Almost Always		Sometimes		Almost Never
1. I assess the difficulty level of each of my courses and revise my study strategies accordingly.	5	4	3	2	1
2. I can identify subjects where learning comes naturally compared to those where I have to work hard.	5	4	3	2	1
3. I read and/or complete assigned material before class.	5	4	3	2	1
4. I keep my attention focused during the entire class period.	5	4	3	2	1
5. When listening to a lecture, I can recognize the most important points.	5	4	3	2	1
6. I vary my note-taking to fit different types of courses.	5	4	3	2	1
7. I take organized and legible notes so I don't have to recopy them.	5	4	3	2	1
8. I review my lecture notes before the next class.	5	4	3	2	1
9. I use a partner to help me fill in missing gaps in my notes.	5	4	3	2	1
10. I am satisfied with my current abilities to learn in class.	5	4	3	2	1

Add up the numbers you circled. Your total score will be between 10 and 50. The higher your score, the more likely you are to be skilled in preparing for class, listening, and note-taking. For scores below 30, write or reflect on the items for which you have concerns and consider talking with a trusted friend, a family member, a teacher, a counselor, or an advisor.

YOUR JOB AS A STUDENT

In college, your job as a student seems deceptively simple. You register for classes, get the syllabus and look at the requirements, show up in class, study for the exams, and move on to the next semester. If it appears to be so simple, why do more than 60% of students entering college fail to graduate? The answers are complex, but decades of research and inquiry yield clear results.

- College is harder. The expectations of professors are high, and the subjects are much more demanding.

- The responsibility for learning and performance is *yours*. No excuses, no rationalizations, no rescue.

- Students' lives today are much more complicated. Many have to work one or two or even three jobs to support themselves. Most have to cope with the fast-paced, technology-driven, overinvolved, overcommitted demands of life in the twenty-first century. All this contributes to stress and anxiety.

- Seductions that take you away from learning abound. Whether it is connecting with new friends or old, social networking, gaming, partying, health and fitness activities, all require thoughtful management to contain.

As you look back over these factors, reflect about your own circumstances. What are the complicating factors in your life?

This chapter begins with an analysis of what makes some courses more difficult than others. Then we move swiftly into presenting most of the crucial study strategies you need to implement for in-class learning early in the semester. Be prepared to sit up and take notice.

RANGE OF DIFFICULTY OF MATERIAL

Why are some topics easy to learn and others difficult? The difficulty of academic content varies dramatically in college across three dimensions: the inherent difficulty level of the content; the manner and method of presentation;

> **Range of Difficulty**
>
> - **Content difficulty:** How difficult is the material?
> - **Quality of presentation:** How well is the material presented?
> - **Intuitive–formal continuum:** How intuitive or formal is the material for me?

and the skills, learning preferences, and prior knowledge of the learner. Successful learners assess the difficulty level of their courses and vary their study strategies accordingly.

Content Difficulty

The first dimension—the inherent difficulty level of the content—is important to acknowledge. Some subject areas are simply more complex than others; they require a more formal intellectual process. Higher levels of thinking require more complex vocabulary. An example is differential calculus, which is more difficult than algebra. Assignments in research methods in psychology tend to be more complex than social psychology. Anatomy and physiology are more difficult than botany. Organic chemistry is more difficult than inorganic chemistry. Tax accounting is more difficult than general accounting. And so on. Collegiate courses are not equal in their content difficulty. Experienced students carefully schedule such difficult courses; they try to take them in long semesters and often try to enroll in only one or two such difficult courses in a term. Even if students are interested and talented in the courses, these difficult courses tax them.

Quality of Presentation

The second dimension of difficulty is the manner and method of presentation. A good writer or a good lecturer can present material in an understandable format. The reverse is also true; poor writing or lecture skills can muddle a presentation and make the content difficult to learn. Many textbooks are badly written; they give the reader little help in discerning which ideas and facts are most important. On the other hand, some textbooks have a plethora of learning aids—introductions, graphs, definitions, summaries, questions, illustrations, and the like. And many teachers post PowerPoint presentations, outlines, and handouts on a web-based course management system.

College students realize that some of their instructors are knowledgeable in the content field but may not be expert teachers for beginning students. Poor or inappropriate teaching styles can include inarticulate speech, lack of clear examples, disorganized lectures, too rapid delivery of information, and reluctance to entertain questions or alternate points of view. When such a mismatch occurs, the responsibility for learning is on the student. If the information for a course is poorly presented, then experienced students initiate efforts to secure outside sources, such as tutors, supplemental readings, and study groups.

Another difficulty arises when the material was created in a different time or culture. Art from another time or place can be difficult to understand. Translations are harder to read than originals; you are reading the ideas once removed. If the writing occurred in another century or culture, you have to make an imaginative leap to read as if you were from that time and place. Primary sources (those writings in which the author is the originator of the thought) are more exciting, and often more difficult, to read than secondary sources (those writings in which the author writes about the thoughts of others). Almost all textbooks are secondary sources. You are more likely to read primary sources in literature and philosophy courses.

Intuitive–Formal Continuum

We learn all the time, but academic learning is different from other learning. The difference between learning the plot of a movie and learning the political philosophy of Machiavelli is vast. The content may be inherently more difficult, and the presentation challenging or clumsy, but an individual learner's interests, skills, preferences, and prior knowledge can also dramatically affect how difficult a particular course may be for that student. We call this dimension of the range of difficulty the **intuitive–formal continuum**. The easier and more natural a learning situation is for us, the more intuitive it is. The situation may seem easy because we bring life experiences that relate to the topic, because we have already learned many things related to the new material, or because we have a talent for that type of mental process. We may have a deep interest in the subject or we may simply be curious. Whatever the reason, we can just go with it. The teacher's explanations seem clear, and we frequently think about the material outside of class. There is little or no anxiety, and we are often eager to learn. The readings seem easy, and we believe that they are easy because we are interested. The truth is probably the opposite; we become interested because it seems easy, natural, and intuitive. We will study the material, trying to remember certain definitions or facts, but night-before cramming seems to be sufficient. Generally, in intuitive learning situations, we do not have to make any specific effort to understand; understanding just seems to happen naturally.

By contrast, in a formal learning situation, the material seems so difficult and confusing that it is easy for our minds to wander from the lecture or the text, and we become bored. The boredom is often rooted in how hard it is for us to achieve understanding. Formal learning situations demand energetic, purposeful strategies and formal reasoning processes to make understanding easier. It is as if we are swimming upstream against a strong current. We may have to read

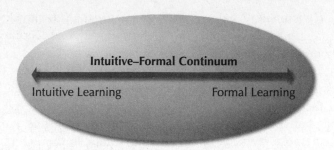

the book before class (and again afterward), sit close to the front of the class-room, use a formal note-taking system, and ask questions. We may have to study that subject every day, preread and outline the chapters, use a study guide, and find other students with whom to form a study group. The deliberate activity level is high because the result of our efforts should be understanding. If we cannot understand the material, what we may memorize does us no good, now or in the future. One encouraging note is the more successful we are in a formal learning situation, the more likely the subject will gradually move to the left on the continuum and become easier to us.

CASE STUDY

JAMAIL is an entering freshman in a community college. He enrolled in World Civilization and General Chemistry with a lab. He quickly realized that World Civilization was an intuitive course for him. He had liked history in high school and read many extra biographies; he often watched the History Channel. His college history teacher was a good lecturer and the required readings were long but interesting. Jamail had to learn how to take college notes quickly and how to answer complicated analysis test questions, but generally his study skills of reading and his class attendance adjusted to the college level rapidly. On the other hand, General Chemistry was instantly intimidating. Even though he had studied basic Chemistry in high school, this professor lectured rapidly, and the numerous terms and concepts seemed unfamiliar and confusing. The textbook was worse. Within three weeks, Jamail knew he was in trouble. He went to the campus tutoring program several times a week, joined a study group, and spent long hours going over the text and his notes. His efforts helped him barely pass the first test, but he knew that this formal learning situation would be his biggest challenge in the term.

Case Study Questions: What advice or counsel can you offer Jamail to help him feel more secure in Chemistry? In addition to the learning strategies he has already adopted, what suggestions can you offer?

Case Study Questions: What has been your biggest academic challenge? Be specific. Explain how you felt during the challenge. What learning strategies did you implement? What could you have done differently?

The more formal and difficult a learning situation is for us, the more deliberate our learning strategies need to be in order for us to be successful. Many students fear one course or another because they have struggled in that subject before. Their own anxiety and worry can sabotage a new effort. We are convinced that if students carefully plan how they will approach the subject, they can be successful.

Exercise 3.2

Range of Difficulty of Your Classes

Choose the two most difficult courses you are taking this semester and answer the questions by marking an "X" on the continuum. Then complete the statement listed below. This exercise will help you assess the range of difficulty of two of your courses. It will also help you brainstorm strategies to help you become successful in these courses.

Course #1 _____

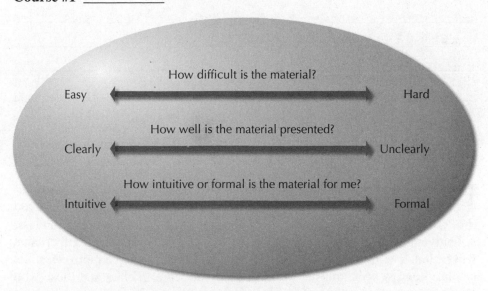

How difficult is the material?
Easy ←——————————→ Hard

How well is the material presented?
Clearly ←——————————→ Unclearly

How intuitive or formal is the material for me?
Intuitive ←——————————→ Formal

Based on my ratings, I predict I will need to use the following learning strategies:

_____ _____

_____ _____

_____ _____

Course #2 _____

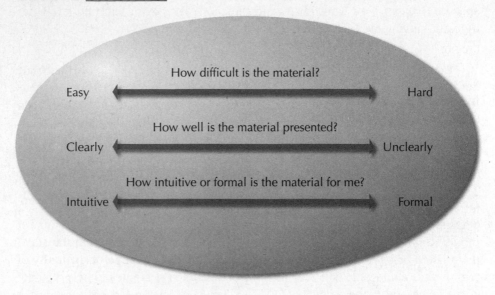

Based on my ratings, I predict I will need to use the following learning strategies:

_____   _____

_____   _____

_____   _____

HOW TO LEARN IN CLASS

In four years of college you will spend almost 2,000 hours in classrooms listening to lectures and participating in class discussions. At least 80% of class time is lecture (Armbruster, 2009). If you master the skill of learning in class, not only will you be more successful academically, but your college experience will be much less stressful because studying out of class will be more effective.

It is easy to spot students who know how to learn in class and those who clearly do not. Pretend you are from another century or planet and watch a typical undergraduate class. How many students arrive well before the instructor or wander in 10 or 15 minutes late? Head toward the back of the room or insist on sitting in the first two rows? Sink gratefully into a seat and are immediately asleep or take notes attentively? Stay tuned in to their music or remove the headphones? Participate in class discussion or focus on text messaging?

Make no mistake. The purpose of a college class is to advance your learning in that course. The ideas that are presented, explained, and developed are not always duplicated in the text or on the course website. When you learn what you should in class, your study time can then focus on the outside readings and exercises instead of on the material you should have already mastered in class.

Listening and Note-Taking

There are few learning activities that are more cognitively demanding than taking notes during a college lecture. "Students must listen to the lecture, select important ideas, hold and manipulate these ideas in working memory, interpret the information, decide what to record, and then write it down" (Armbruster, 2000, p. 176). Educational research clearly shows that the completeness of lecture notes is positively related to academic achievement (Armbruster, 2000); in other words, the more complete our notes are, the more likely we are to be successful in that course. "The bottom line is that the real value of taking notes is to have them for review" (Armbruster, 2000, p. 179). Curiously, another person's notes are usually not very helpful. What seems to matter is that we do the work to listen, select, hold, interpret, decide, and write. Succinctly, the task is difficult but important for academic success in order for you to have the materials you need to study for tests.

Passivity is your greatest enemy when you sit in class. You must find a way to engage in what is happening in the classroom. Class learning is more than simply transcribing the instructor's notes into your notebook or your laptop. It is more than remembering the stories and jokes the instructor uses as illustrations and forgetting the main ideas. It is more than watching slides or computer displays. Becoming competent in note-taking takes most college students one or two semesters.

Good in-class learning requires good listening. We can have the ability to hear, but not the ability to listen. Real listening is hard work. As children and adolescents, we usually develop the ability to *tune out* rather than *tune in*. Social networking has also become an enormous distractor for deep listening. So, deep listening may initially seem like climbing a steep hill. It requires the following:

- **INTENT.** If we intend to listen and understand and keep reminding ourselves of our goals, then we are likely to get more information.

- **READINESS.** Being physically and mentally prepared for class helps. Fatigue, hangovers, and internal emotional upsets can keep us from listening. Reading *before* we go to class dramatically enhances our ability to listen deeply.

- **RECORDING.** Whether we take traditional notes, use a laptop, print out guided notes from the course website, or some other method, creating a written record of what we hear helps us listen and understand.

- **CONNECTION.** The more we link what the instructional message is to what we know or believe/disbelieve or experience, the more we will retain.

Your learning strategies should vary in lecture, problem-solving, discussion, and distance education classes. What follows is a brief description of these types of classes and an introduction to several of the respected note-taking techniques. But first, we provide a list of useful note-taking strategies for most types of college courses.

Good Note-Taking Strategies

Good note-taking strategies develop with time and practice. The criteria are always whether the strategies help you learn what you need to learn. Obviously, strategies should vary from class to class and from student to student. Here are some general strategies that we recommend:

- Get enough sleep the night before classes.

- Attend all lectures.

- Arrive early with the right materials.

- Sit toward the front of the room.

- Date the first page of your notes each day.

- Use a heading to label the notes.

- Write in pen on one side of the paper (pencil fades).

- Use phrases, not sentences.

- Create your own symbols and abbreviations.

- Write down the main ideas, supporting details, and examples.

- Gently bring your mind back to the subject (when it wanders).

- Write down what the instructor emphasizes through pauses, repetition, summarization, and energy.

- Look for and mark relationships between the concepts.

- Review the material before the next class session and continue the review process several times each week.

Lecture Classes

Lecture classes differ dramatically in size, from 25 to 250 to 500 students. In lecture classes, you create study notes that, when combined with your outside sources, should constitute your learning resources. Those notes should not replicate the book, but, instead, they should comprise a record of the main points of the lecture (there are usually five or six), relevant facts to support those points, examples that illustrate those points, and explanations of difficult ideas. Listen for concepts and facts you did not find in the readings.

The next section presents several note-taking methods for lecture classes: guided notes, Cornell notes, T-notes, discussion.

Guided Notes

Increasing numbers of college teachers manage their courses through a website. An advantage for them and their students is that they can post PowerPoint slides, lecture notes, or outlines online and expect students to bring printed copies to class. These guided notes—lecture outlines with room for you to record key points and examples—provide a strong organizational base for your notes, and research indicates that "guided notes improve all measures of note quality" (Armbruster, 2009, p. 233). See Figure 3.1 and Figure 3.2 for examples of instructors' guided notes posted online.

FIGURE 3.1 An Example of Guided Notes Using a PowerPoint Handout

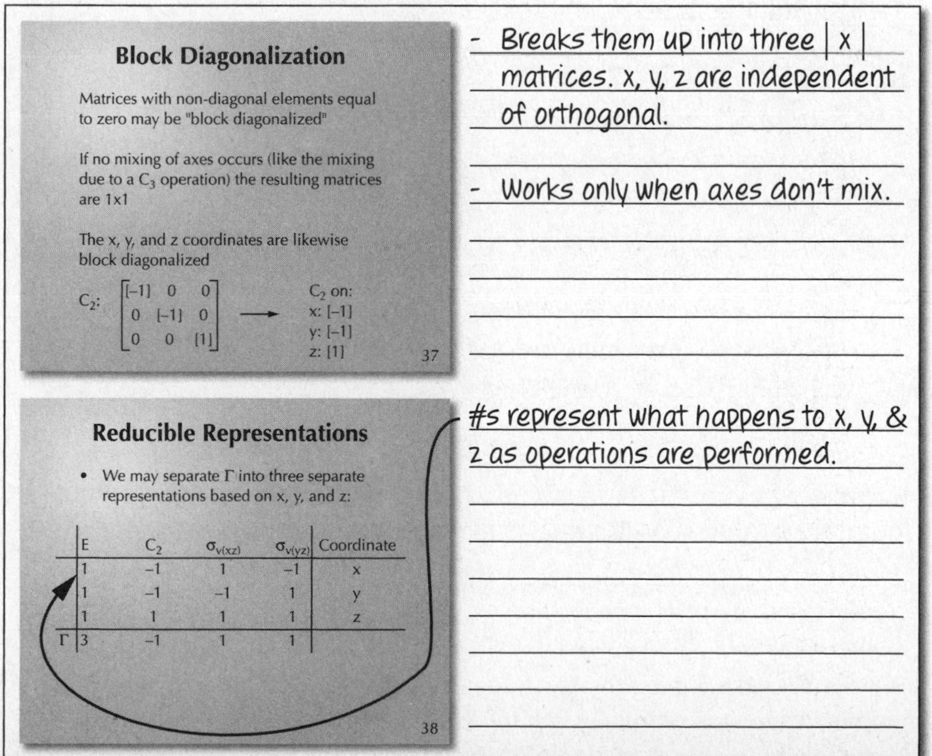

FIGURE 3.2   An Example of Guided Notes Using an Instructor's Outline

Chantal Washington   October 3
Perry's Theory of Cognitive Development

Cognitive Theory* – intellectual & ethical development of college
students[†]

I. Students' developmental tasks are to:
- become academically competent
- learn to develop satisfying friendships & relationships
- become indep. of parents & authorities
- choose career & lifestyles
- examine values & beliefs

II. William Perry (1970)
- worked in Harvard U's Bureau of Study Counsel
- encountered personality differences
- became aware that what were thought to be personality
  differences were developmental patterns

III. Perry's Theory
- identified 9 stages individuals progress through, each
  becoming more cognitively complex
- stages are sequential
- 9 stages are presented in 4 categories for simplification:

- Commitment
- Relativism
- Multiplicity
- Dualism

*This font indicates teacher-generated text posted on an online course web site for students
 to print before class.

[†]This font indicates student-generated notes taken on the outline during class.

Advantages of this system are numerous:

- Printing and planning for a lecture in advance increases both intent and prior
  knowledge. It is especially helpful when students preview the material.

- The notes present the larger picture of the concepts of the course material.
  Thus, students can focus on the interrelationships of the concepts as well

as capturing the relevant factual information. The result is that active learning and more critical thinking during class is possible.

- Study groups are more effective because they have a common starting foundation of material that is routinely referenced.

Although guided notes are popular among students, there are major pitfalls:

- Students report that class attendance is more difficult, as they can persuade themselves not to go to class because they have the outline notes (Armbruster, 2009). Yet class attendance is more efficient because what you learn there you do not have to learn on your own, and professors frequently lecture on material that may not appear in the text or outline. College tests reflect deeper information that is often only minimally shaped by the outlines, so the guided notes alone are insufficient.

- Students may mistakenly take a passive role in class and choose to rely on the outline and listening. Memory based on listening alone without the creation of notes tends to be weak.

Exercise 3.3

Guided Notes

Practice taking notes from one of the following guided note-taking formats for at least two class sessions using the guidelines listed below.

BEFORE CLASS:

- Select one or more of the following formats:

  a. *Instructor's PowerPoint Lecture Slides.* Access the course website and choose the printing option that best fits your note-taking needs (e.g., number of slides per page, lines for note-taking, and so forth). It is easiest to add additional notes in class when you print three PowerPoint slides per page.

  b. *Instructor's Outline for the Lecture.* Access the outline on the course website, but increase the amount of blank space under the headings and then print a copy.

  c. *Instructor's Lecture Summary, Lecture List of Topics, or Lecture Class Notes.* Access any of these, but again, provide some space so that you can add additional information. You instructor is expecting you to fill in the gaps during the lecture.

- Glance over the pages to familiarize yourself with the topics to be covered in class.

- Compare the guided notes that you have accessed to the material you read or completed for class. This will help you see the bigger picture of the upcoming lecture.

DURING CLASS:

- Check off or highlight points on the guided notes as your instructor covers them.

- Add additional notes to the guided notes. This is the most important step!

- Decide quickly if you need to construct your notes in a formal note-taking structure like (e.g., Cornell or T-notes to be introduced next in this chapter).

- Implement the Good Note-Taking Strategies previously covered in this chapter.

AFTER CLASS (AS SOON AS POSSIBLE):

- Fill in any gaps to make your notes more complete and legible (you might consider comparing your notes with a classmate's notes).

- Type the notes you have taken into your instructor's electronic outline, especially if your handwriting is poor.

- Review any PowerPoint slides or other information posted to the course website *after* class, and check to make sure the notes you took during class are complete.

- Determine main ideas from the notes and write possible questions that might appear on the exam.

BEFORE THE NEXT CLASS SESSION:

- Review your notes at least once before the next class session.

Cornell Notes

Created over 40 years ago at Cornell University by Walter Pauk (1997), this system requires dividing note pages into three sections: the note-taking section, the cue column, and the summary area. This method works well for mostly lecture-based classes (especially those declarative courses with facts, details, and examples). It is an organized method for recording, revising, and reviewing notes.

To create a page for Cornell notes, draw a vertical line two and one-half inches from the left edge of the paper; end the line two inches from the bottom of the sheet. Then, draw a horizontal line two inches up from the bottom of the page. Also include your name, date, and the page number at the very top, on the left or right side. Paper in this format is available from most college bookstores in loose-leaf, spiral, and tablet form.

Once you have taken your notes, read over them and fill in any gaps to make your notes more legible. Then, determine the main ideas from the notes and write questions in the cue column. Using a plain sheet of paper, cover up the notes in the right-hand column. Read the questions you created and then recite aloud the answer. Check your answer by removing the plain sheet of paper. Repeat the sequence until you have mastered the material. After your initial review, write a summary statement (a couple of sentences) for each full page of notes in the summary area. See Figure 3.3 for an example of notes taken using the Cornell system.

FIGURE 3.3   An Example of Cornell Notes

Jared Schultz	9-30
Karl Marx	
p. 13	
What is Marx's reasoning?	- Constant drive for new markets. - Creation of new and insatiable needs.
What makes one's life his own?	- The recognition of one's morality as the necessary condition of authentic living.
What is authenticity?	- Authenticity is morality. - The creation of the culture of fantasy, the eclipse of time.
When was Freud's synthesis?	- Freud's synthesis was between enlightenment and romanticism.
What is the importance of the shift?	- Shift to psychogenic from organic understanding of mental disease to understanding of psychogenic. - Discovery of the unconscious. - Expansion of the sexual. - The future of illusion.
Marx's reasoning is the constant drive for new markets & the creation of new & insatiable needs.	
According to Marx authenticity is morality.	

Pauk believes that it is important to review notes as soon as possible, at least before going to sleep. He stresses the importance of getting a global view of the notes while trying to retain the details. To do this, he encourages students to reflect by asking, "What's the significance of these facts or ideas? What principles are they based on? How can I apply them to what I already know? How do they fit? What's beyond these facts and ideas?" (Pauk, 1997, p. 209).

In an extensive review of research on lecture note-taking, Armbruster (2000) reported that students typically record fewer than 40 percent of lecture ideas (one study reported as little as 20 percent) and that students tend to record fewer notes during the latter part of a lecture. The research is also adamant that the quality and quantity of notes are both important; the more complete the notes are for review, the greater the potential for learning. How students prefer to learn can also influence learning. Some students tend to learn more from the actual note-taking process (as they organize and find relationships while writing the notes), whereas others tend to learn more while they review the notes. Thus, the pressure on college students is to be active and involved learners in the classroom as well as to become expert and flexible in the skill of reviewing their notes outside of class.

Exercise 3.4

Cornell Notes

Practice taking notes in the Cornell format from a lecture class for at least two class sessions using the following guidelines:

BEFORE CLASS:

- Draw a vertical line two and one-half inches from the left edge of a sheet of paper; end the line two inches from the bottom of the sheet (look for preprinted wide-margin paper at your college bookstore).

- Draw a horizontal line two inches up from the bottom of the page.

DURING CLASS:

- Take notes in the right-hand column as you would normally.

- Leave the cue column on the left blank except for brief notations to emphasize potential test questions, key terms, significant facts, and so on.

AFTER CLASS (AS SOON AS POSSIBLE):

- Fill in any gaps to make your notes more legible or type the notes you have taken if your handwriting is poor. Integrate your notes into your instructor's electronic outline if posted on the course website.

- Determine main ideas from the notes and write questions in the cue column.

BEFORE THE NEXT CLASS SESSION:

- Cover up the notes in the right-hand column using a plain sheet of paper.

- Read the questions you created and then recite the answers aloud.

- Check your answers by removing the plain sheet of paper.

- Repeat the sequence until you have mastered the material.

- After your initial review, write a summary statement (a couple of sentences) for each full page of notes in the summary area at the bottom of the page.

Invite another student (one who is familiar with this note-taking system) to read over your notes and give you feedback. This exercise will strengthen your note-taking skills and aid you in learning lecture material.

Problem-Solving Classes

The purpose of problem-solving classes is simple: class time is used to solve problems and to discuss the process of doing so. The strategy for taking good notes in such a class is to write down not only the problem but also the verbalization of the steps. In other words, write down each step and then explain what was done in your own words. The sequence of steps is crucial. Math, accounting, economics, finance, computer programming, statistics, logic, and case study-based courses are all examples of problem-solving classes.

T-Notes

Introduced in 1983 to assist college students, T-notes, created by Archie Davis and Elvis Clark (1996), are a way to organize and learn different types of lecture information. Similar to the Cornell method, the T-notes system is also a method to record, revise, and review notes.

To use this system, begin by dividing a page of paper by drawing a large "T." Extend the top of the T from the left margin to the right margin, leaving a space of one and one-half inches across the top of the paper. Extend the leg of the T down the center of the page, beginning from the top line to the bottom of the page. Above the T, center the title of the lecture or major topic. Also include your name, date, and page number at the very top of the left or right side.

As you encounter lecture information, divide the information between the two columns. For example, if you are given a term to learn, place the term on the left side of the T and the definition and examples on the right side. Or, if you are to learn a visual such as a diagram, draw the diagram to the left of the T and the explanation to the right. See Figure 3.4 for an example of T-notes.

FIGURE 3.4   An Example of T-Notes for Learning Terminology

Bibiana Alvarado 1–23	
Add and Multi Principle	
p. 6	
- Variable	Represents a value; x, y, c
- Equation	Problem $x + 3 = 6$, $a^2 + b^2 = c^2$
- Expression	$x + 3$, c^2, $a^2 + b^2$
- How do we determine value of variable	Solve for the variable
- Evaluate	Substitute / "plug-in"
- Like terms	$2x, 5x; 15zy, .05zy$
- Unlike terms	$2x + 5xy$ $3xy + 7zy$
- Distributive property	$a(b + c) = ab + ac$
- Addition principle	For any real #s a, b, c $a = b => a + c = b + c$
- Multi principle	For any real #s a, b, c $a = b => ac = bc$
- Using both +/− principles together	ID variable +/− terms as needed simplify/combine like terms −/÷ to isolate variable simplify answer

T-notes are especially useful for learning procedures such as those common in mathematics or statistics. For example, if you are learning an algebra equation, place the formula on top of the T. Then write the steps to solving the equation to the left of the T and examples that correlate with the steps on the right of the T (see Figure 3.5 for an example).

FIGURE 3.5   An Example of T-Notes for Learning an Equation

Rod Hill   2–11

The Quadratic Formula

p. 25

$$x = \frac{-b \pm \sqrt{b^2 - 4ac}}{2a}$$

X represents the solutions of: $ax^2 + bx + c = 0$	Ex 1: Solve $5x^2 - 8x + 3 = 0$
Steps:	(Already in stand. form) $a = 5, b = -8, c = 3$
1. First must find standard form of equation	Using quad form:
2. Then should try and factor — if it is not possible, then use the quad formula	$$x = \frac{-(-8) \pm \sqrt{(-8)^2 - (4)(5)(3)}}{2(5)}$$
3. Determine values for a, b, c and substitute into formula: $$x = \frac{-b \pm \sqrt{b^2 - 4ac}}{2a}$$	$$x = \frac{8 \pm \sqrt{64 - 60}}{10} = \frac{8 \pm \sqrt{4}}{10}$$ $$x = \frac{8 \pm 2}{10}$$
4. The solutions of any quadratic equation can be found by using the quad formula (ALWAYS!)	So, $$x = \frac{8 - 2}{10} \quad \text{or} \quad x = \frac{8 + 2}{10}$$ $$x = \frac{6}{10} \quad \text{or} \quad x = \frac{10}{10}$$ So, $$x = \frac{3}{5} \quad \text{or} \quad x = 1$$ Thus, the solutions are 3/5 & 1

T-notes are designed to be used as a self-test system similar to 3×5 index cards; however, the advantage is that you do not have to rewrite the information but simply cover any part of the T to self-test.

Exercise 3.5

T-Notes

Practice taking notes in the T-note format for a problem-solving class (math, accounting, science lab) for at least two class sessions using the following guidelines.

BEFORE CLASS:

- Divide a page of paper by drawing a large "T." Extend the top of the "T" from the left margin to the right margin, leaving a space of one and one-half inches across the top of the paper. Extend the leg of the "T" down the center of the page.

DURING CLASS:

- Above the "T," write the name of the procedure or topic.

- As you encounter lecture information, divide the information between the two columns. List the steps used to complete the procedure to the left of the "T" and examples to the right.

AFTER CLASS (AS SOON AS POSSIBLE):

- Fill in any gaps to make your notes more legible.

BEFORE THE NEXT CLASS SESSION:

- Cover up the notes on either side of the "T" using a plain sheet of paper.

- Recite aloud the answers.

- Check your answers by removing the paper.

- Repeat the sequence until you have mastered the material.

Invite another student (one who is familiar with this note-taking system) to read over your notes and give you feedback. This exercise will strengthen your note-taking skills and aid in learning problem-solving material.

Discussion Classes

Discussion classes are often great fun, but students frequently leave class without any notes. That behavior is dangerous because we rarely remember concepts unless we write them down and go over them, even if we have been interested in the discussion. In this type of class, the professor usually summarizes a main point when the discussion ends. Listen for those summaries and record them. Discussion notes tend to be shorter, and they usually do not follow any particular structure. Ideas are important here, not details. Sometimes a good strategy is to meet quickly with another class member after class and compare notes. Before exams, brainstorm possible test questions in a study group. See Figure 3.6 for an example of discussion notes and possible test questions.

FIGURE 3.6   Example of Discussion Notes and Possible Test Questions

Sandy Chang
    11–28   Discussion on Social Stratification
    p. 89

- Social Stratification?

     System by which a society ranks categories of people in a
     hierarchy.

- 4 principles of Social Strat:
    ① Char. of society–not simply a function of individual diff.
    ② Persists over generations.
    ③ Varies in form.
    ④ Rests on widely held beliefs.

- Davis-Moore Thesis:
    - Positions that are most important (for society) and that require
      talent and/or training must be the most highly rewarded.
    - Most highly rewarded positions should be those that are
      functionally unique & on which other positions rely.

- Social Strat (An explanation by Weber)
    - Model of Class Structure.

POSSIBLE TEST QUESTIONS:

① Describe social stratification. Be sure to include the 4 principles of
    Social Strat.
② According to Weber, what are the 6 social classes?

Distance Classes

A significant change in higher education has taken place in the past 25 years. Distance education has evolved through four generations of structure, although all four are still used. Distance education provides instruction when students and instructors are separated by physical distance but connected by technology.

The simplest distance education programs are correspondence courses in which students study independently and send their lessons and tests electronically or by mail. The next level in complexity are those courses with video and/or audiotapes and, perhaps, some audio broadcasts during which students can ask questions. The third generation uses the Internet for one- and two-way videoconferencing, email, chat rooms, and so forth. Some schools have recently begun to offer fourth-generation multimedia (multiple forms of communication such as audio and video) and hypermedia in which students participate in teleconferencing over the Internet; have access to a multitude of online sources such as tutorials, course materials, and online databases; and "collaborate over e-mail and within chat rooms" (Caverly & Peterson, 2000, p. 306).

An important characteristic of both the third- and fourth-generation distance education programs is whether the students interact with each other in real time (synchronous) or in delayed time (asynchronous). Distance education using technology such as telephone, television, satellite, Internet-based chats, or a virtual online environment such as Second Life®, are **synchronous**, meaning that the students and instructor can communicate together at the same time (also referred to as "real time"). Communication that does not occur in real time between two or more people is referred to as **asynchronous** learning such as an Internet-based forum, discussion board, blog or wiki (The University of Oklahoma Website, 2009).

Students attracted to distance learning course formats may be working full-time, deployed in the military, living in rural areas, enrolled at more than one institution, retraining for their career, or simply retired and wanting to increase the quality of their life with further education. To be successful, these students are

- self-motivated and enjoy learning in these types of virtual environments;
- self-regulated and self-disciplined with little trouble sticking to a schedule;
- comfortable communicating through writing;
- committed to working in isolation and not needing instant feedback;
- readily able to access the required technology and to use it properly (The University of Oklahoma Website, 2009).

To learn successfully in such situations, students must analyze the circumstances and create the appropriate notes for study. Although there are arguable advantages of flexibility for the individual's circumstances, the disadvantages of solitude and ample opportunity for procrastination may make distance education coursework more difficult than traditional classroom study. Dropout rates are 15–20 percent higher for online courses than for traditional courses (Winograd & Moore, 2003). In distance education, students need to have strong time management and online research skills as well as the ability to self-direct learning. To counteract this difficulty, some teachers are setting firm time guidelines for module and lesson completion.

Exercise 3.6

A New Vocabulary

Can you define the following terms or phrases? If not, do a quick Internet Google search for each. Newer forms of virtual learning environments have already been invented since this book was published. Can you add two or three terms and definitions to this list? This exercise will increase your virtual learning literacy.

- Blended or hybrid course
- Blog (or web log)
- Chats (or virtual chats)
- Computer-assisted instruction
- Course management system (or learning management system)
- Databases (for doing library research)
- Discussion board
- eLearning (or E-learning)
- Listservs
- Podcasting
- Social networking (Facebook, Myspace, Second Life, Twitter)
- Virtual learning environments
- Vodcasting
- Whiteboards
- Wikis

CONCLUSION

Becoming a skilled note-taker in a college class is an important step toward becoming an autonomous learner. This auditory and organizational skill directly relates to becoming a professional person who has numerous tasks to manage independently for a wide range of clients or supervisors. Each class session is an opportunity, so we hope you will be courageous and try many of these new techniques.

SUMMARY

- Sixty percent of students entering college today fail to graduate because (a) college is harder, (b) the students bear the responsibility for learning and performing, (c) students' lives are more complicated today, and (d) there are more distractions today vying for students' time.

- Experienced students will be able to identify the more difficult content courses and will carefully schedule no more than one or two such courses each term.

- The intuitive–formal continuum affects how students approach classes with less- than-ideal instructors or textbooks. Students' interests, skills, preferences, and prior knowledge can also affect how difficult a particular course might be. The easier and more natural a learning situation is, the more intuitive it is.

- In a formal learning situation, students must employ purposeful, deliberate strategies such as reading the book before class, sitting close to the front of the classroom, using a formal note-taking system, asking questions, studying the subject every day, outlining the chapters, using a study guide, and forming a study group with other students in the class.

- The completeness of lecture notes is positively related to academic success in that course.

- In-class learning requires good listening, which entails intent, readiness, creating a written record of what is heard, and connecting.

- Good note-taking strategies develop with time and practice.

- Class notes should comprise a record of the main points of the lectures, relevant facts, examples, and explanations of difficult ideas.

- Learning resources are a combination of study notes and outside resources.

- Guided notes are teacher-generated lecture notes, outlines, or PowerPoint notes with room for students to record key points and examples.

- Cornell notes require dividing the paper into three sections: the note-taking section, the cue column, and the summary area. This system allows students to write questions in the cue column that correspond with the notes in the note-taking column and summarize material in the section along the bottom of the page.

- Designed to be used as a self-test system, T-notes are aptly identified because students draw a "T" on the note-taking paper. One column is used for terms and diagrams, and the other column is for corresponding definitions and explanations.

- T-notes are most effective in problem-solving classes, such as math, accounting, statistics, and logic. This format encourages students to write down not only the problem, but also the verbalization of the steps and their correct sequence in the next column.

- When taking notes in discussion classes, students should listen for and record the professor's main point summaries, bearing in mind that ideas, not details, are what is important.

- To be successful in distance classes, students must be (a) self-motivated and enjoy learning in a virtual environment, (b) self-regulated and self-disciplined with little trouble sticking to a schedule, (c) comfortable communicating through writing, (d) committed to working in isolation and not needing instant feedback, and (e) readily able to access the required technology and to use it properly.

KEY CONCEPTS

Asynchronous

Content difficulty

Cornell notes

Discussion classes

Distance classes

Good note-taking strategies

Guided notes

Intent, Readiness, Recording, Connection (IRRC)

Intuitive–formal continuum

Lecture classes

Listening

Note-taking

Problem-solving classes

Quality of presentation

Range of difficulty

Synchronous

T-notes

GUIDED JOURNAL QUESTIONS

1. Explain how well you adapted your learning when previous courses encompassed extremely difficult course content.

2. At some point in your past education you have had a lackluster high school teacher or college instructor. In other words, this person should have taken a different career path. Explain how well you adapted to the instructor's poor quality of presentation.

3. List three activities (such as hobbies) in which you believe you have intuitive skills and background knowledge. How do you think you acquired such intuition for each of these activities? List three academic courses in which you believe you have intuitive skills and background knowledge. How do you think you acquired such intuition for each of these courses?

4. What is your favorite type of class—lecture, discussion, or problem solving? Explain why using specific examples.

5. Think about the classes that are easiest for you to take notes in and those that you find to be the most difficult. What are the differences in these classes? What can you determine from these differences?

6. Describe your current methods of taking notes and studying from lectures. Now that you have read this chapter, how do you think the Cornell and T-note systems will be useful to you?

7. Relate the experiences you have had with distance education or virtual learning environments. Explain why these types of learning environments were easier or more difficult for you. What were the advantages and disadvantages to taking these courses? Freely address any of the terms that you defined in Exercise 3.

The Last Word

The information in this chapter alone would have saved me countless hours of ineffective and even wasted study time my freshman year. My grades were good, but I paid a high price to earn them.

—*Carol Dochen*

Learning Outside Class

Outside of class?!? The brochure didn't say anything about this.

CHAPTER HIGHLIGHTS

- Essential College Learning Resources
- Learning from Textual Sources
- Learning from Solving Problems or Case Studies
- Learning from Writing
- Learning from Individual Projects
- Learning from Peers
- Learning from Academic Networking

Understanding, not memory, is the foundation of college learning. The trick is to learn to understand, then memorize what is important. To **study** is to *apply the mind so as to acquire understanding and knowledge.* Research tells us that if we understand the concepts of the material we study, then we are better able to remember and use that information in other ways (Bransford, Brown, & Cocking, 1999). We tend to understand something by being active in the learning process. Simply listening to a lecture or reading a chapter in a textbook may not be enough. If we begin to demonstrate, discuss, manipulate, or teach the information, our comprehension and learning increase dramatically.

We have already discussed the different types of knowledge—declarative (factual and conceptual), procedural, and conditional—as well as the levels of intellectual performance (remembering, understanding, applying, analyzing, evaluating, creating). By considering these factors as we shape our study methods, we are much more likely to excel in our performance on tests, projects, and papers. In this and future chapters, we will model many ways to do just that.

Exercise 4.1

SELF-ASSESSMENT: Skills for Success

Developing effective reading techniques and learning from a variety of sources are essential skills for college success. With 5 being "Almost Always" and 1 being "Almost Never," assess your skills for success. Rate each of the following statements honestly by circling the appropriate number. Completing this exercise will help you identify concerns you may be experiencing about these skills.

	Almost Always		Sometimes		Almost Never
1. I can identify the primary ideas in a reading passage.	5	4	3	2	1
2. I am able to concentrate while I read.	5	4	3	2	1
3. I monitor my comprehension while I read.	5	4	3	2	1
4. I easily learn new vocabulary.	5	4	3	2	1
5. I seek help from outside sources or others when I get confused by what I am reading.	5	4	3	2	1
6. I complete the practice problems and exercises in my textbook.	5	4	3	2	1
7. I write a rough outline before I begin a writing assignment.	5	4	3	2	1
8. I complete writing assignments a day or two before the due date to allow time for revisions.	5	4	3	2	1
9. I enjoy learning from hands-on experiences such as class projects.	5	4	3	2	1
10. I put my full effort into out-of-class learning opportunities.	5	4	3	2	1

Add up the numbers you circled. Your total score will be between 10 and 50. The higher your score, the more likely you are to be skilled at learning from a variety of collegiate resources. For scores below 30, write or reflect on the items for which you have concerns and consider talking with a trusted friend, a family member, a teacher, a counselor, or an advisor.

ESSENTIAL COLLEGE LEARNING RESOURCES

There are six major methods that students use to learn academic information outside the classroom: reading textual sources both in print and electronic versions, solving problems, writing, doing individual projects, working with peers, and creating/using academic networks. Students who are adept at using all methods and wise about when and how to use them are academically literate. Such abilities are a good example of conditional knowledge.

LEARNING FROM TEXTUAL SOURCES

Most academic knowledge is represented in words—millions upon millions of words. Professors swim adeptly in words, but sometimes students feel they are drowning. Most students are willing to read if they know how to extract the meaningful knowledge from the sources, but it is easy to be intimidated by the size and complexity of college texts. Most professors expect students to read and will deliberately test on assigned readings, even if the topic has not been discussed in lecture.

Students enter college with a wide range of reading abilities. Some have been avid readers since childhood; others rarely read, except for immediate information. Some enjoy reading; others despise it. Research tells us that successful students use a wide range of strategies (Mulcahy-Ernt & Caverly, 2009). We urge you to use this section to review your own attitudes and skills and then choose the techniques that seem helpful. Here we will define academic reading, i.e., reading for understanding rather than reading solely for personal information or entertainment. We will look at the enormous variety of academic textual sources, the construction of context, and a deliberate study method to increase your ability to read for understanding. Along the way, we will also look at ways of increasing your concentration, comprehension monitoring, and vocabulary.

Mortimer Adler (1902–2001) was a popular educator and author. Of the many ideas he championed, the foremost is the importance of critical reading as a foundation of a free society. He believed that being a good reader leads us to listen and talk well—all skills that lead to clear thinking. Adler (1940) defines **reading** as *an intensely private and complex activity or skill in which the reader catches (understands) every sort of printed communication.* He continues, "Reading a book is a kind of conversation. You may think it is not conversation at all, because the author does all the talking and you have nothing to say. If you think that, you do not realize your opportunities and obligations as a reader" (p. 235). It is our opportunity to understand the author's message, and our obligation to critically evaluate it.

In order to "catch" academic text, we have to work hard. The more active reading is, the better understanding it yields (Mulcahy-Ernt & Caverly, 2009). Reflect on the levels of intellectual performance in Bloom's Taxonomy. Memory is the lowest level. We have to remember to understand. Understanding is the point at which reading ends and study begins. We have to understand before we can apply knowledge or analyze it or evaluate it.

Many studies of successful college readers (Pressley and Afflerbach, 1995, and Zimmerman, 2002, in Mulcahy-Ernt & Caverly, 2009) show certain clear attributes. When these successful students read academic text, they do the following:

- Use a **forethought phase**. They analyze the instructor's assignment and the author's purpose. They set goals and select strategies. They motivate themselves by recalling feelings and beliefs from other similar circumstances.

- Complete a **performance phase**. They read and control their attention. They continually monitor their comprehension. If they lose understanding, they quickly reread or revert to fix-up strategies. If they understand the text, then they deliberately add to or change their existing knowledge.

- End with a **reflection phase**. They evaluate whether they met their goals set earlier and analyze their successes and failures. Then they encourage themselves to use the successful strategies in the future (based on Zimmerman, 2002).

Academic Textual Sources

An astonishing array of academic textual sources exists, both in print and electronically. Here are some of the structures you will find as undergraduates:

- **Survey text**—usually a lengthy book that provides an introductory overview of an academic field such as sociology or communications. It is usually highly structured with outlines, graphics, headings, and summaries. Vocabulary specific to the field abounds, and the content is ordered either conceptually or chronologically. Such a text usually has multiple authors, so the tone tends to be bland and impersonal. Recently, publishers have begun offering an online version of the text at a small additional charge. It is a wise decision to purchase that and other supplemental materials, such as study guides, workbooks, and so on.

- **Reference text**—a source for a lab science or an applied course such as accounting or economics. Contains massive amounts of data, both factual and conceptual. Be sure to purchase any supplemental materials offered by the publishers.

- **Conceptual text**—a book organized around key concepts. Highly readable with many examples and applications. Such texts usually focus on a theme within an academic discipline and may be used in a variety of courses in applied fields such as business, psychology, or communication.

- **Problem-centered text**—various lengths, but at least 50 percent of the text is problems or case studies. Highly structured with the processes of problem-solving defined and delineated. Commonly used in education, health sciences, and social sciences courses.

- **Selected readings**—a collection of essays, articles, and poetry related to a given field. The writings may be excerpts from larger works. Often the authors are writing about their own ideas, rather than the ideas of others. The intended audience of each individual reading varies from professionals in a specific field to the general public. Selected readings are used for class discussion, personal reflection and journaling, and writing.

- **Literature**—whether entire works or portions, these readings tend to be challenging because of level of content, structure, vocabulary, context, and historical significance. The readings tend to be short, but highly sophisticated, with demanding vocabulary. Sometimes, they span centuries and have been translated from other languages. Both characteristics increase difficulty. Advanced foreign language courses use literature readings in that language.

- **Research articles**—professional, highly structured reports that present analyses of scientific experiments. Intended audience is typically professionals within that field so articles are usually published in specialized journals. These articles are found through electronic databases when you are researching specific topics.

Increasing Prior Knowledge

A powerful method of increasing our ability to read is to have prior knowledge about the content in our mind *before* we begin to read. A definition from

Mulcahy-Ernt and Caverly (2009) of **prior knowledge** is *the student's famil-iarity with the topic and his/her reading ability.* Note that all three types of ac-ademic knowledge—declarative, procedural, and conditional—are part of that definition. Familiarity with the topic is declarative (factual and concep-tual knowledge); reading ability is procedural knowledge (know how to read) and conditional (knowing what strategies to use to reach the purpose). Some-times college students simply do not have such knowledge. The solution to the dilemma is to locate information about the topic and structure that infor-mation in your mind so that you will have a place to put (connect) the new content as you read it. Each type of textual source requires a different type of prior knowledge.

- **Survey and conceptual texts.** These are the most common texts for undergraduates. The deliberate structure allows for an efficient construction of prior knowledge by using techniques called pre-reading, surveying, or skimming. Two levels of pre-reading exist: the entire book and a specific chapter. At the beginning of the term, examine the overall plan of the book by skimming the table of contents, the preface, and the appendices. The preface should tell you why the authors wrote this book in this way. Choose a middle chapter and look carefully at the structural aids—outline, headings, definitions, graphics, pictures, summaries, questions, sidebars. They should be consistent throughout the book.

   When you sit down to read a chapter, spend five to ten minutes creating your context. Look at the chapter title, introductory outline, and chapter summary. Read the summary twice. Now, think about what you have seen. What is the primary question this chapter is answering? What do you already know about this question? What interests you about this question? Now you are ready to read.

- **Reference texts.** These massive and complicated texts require a more intensive pre-reading. Do the same initial preview of the book. Spend the time to learn the structure of each chapter. Locate the graphic presenta-tions (flow charts, hierarchies, maps) as they frequently present the major concepts. Work through each section of the chapter, using the presented case studies and completing the problems. Most chapters will require two or three work sessions.

- **Selected readings.** Sometimes these texts have short introductions to each reading. Read and reflect before class discussion. Oftentimes, reflective questions follow each reading; use them to shape your reflection.

- **Literature.** The best gift to yourself is to first experience literature as art, without a practical thought about upcoming tests, and then return to study the text. The other choice is to pragmatically gather the information from outside sources to construct your context. The Internet will rapidly give you basic information about the work, including its significance, cultural background, and author biography.

- **Research articles.** Almost all articles provide an abstract, a complete summary, at the beginning. Highly compacted, we suggest you read it twice before reading the article.

- **Problem-centered text.** Such texts are essentially manuals. Locate your assigned problems or cases, then read related text in that section before working problems. The temptation is to avoid the written material and simply use the problems.

As you can see, we take this issue of creating a context in which to read and study quite seriously. In a way, it is similar to an athletic warm-up in which you get your body ready to exercise. By creating a context, you are essentially building a relevant body of prior knowledge, something to which to attach the new information. You are warming up your brain to accept new information in a meaningful way, thus increasing the likelihood you will remember that information.

A Study Method to Increase Understanding

After warming up, you begin to read the text. Your brain should be in active mode, looking for the explanations, answers, and information your survey has revealed. Because survey, conceptual, and encyclopedic texts are the norm for many students, the following processes are our suggestions for this step.

Read section by section. Use the headings to help formulate questions about the material as you read. The purpose is to make you less passive and more active in the reading process. Questions will provide you with a purpose for reading as you search for answers. In these texts, the primary structure is the paragraph.

Identify the primary idea(s). When we read well, we find and interpret important words. The primary idea or ideas will begin to emerge as you preview and use the headings and ask and answer questions while reading a subsection. Usually the primary idea occurs within the first or second paragraph of a subsection of text. Another method to determine the main idea is to turn the heading into a question. You can then read to answer that question.

Read before marking. Read the first subsection without marking anything. Stop and think. When you find a primary idea, mark it by underlining or highlighting, or annotate key words and phrases in the margin. What in that subsection is important about the primary idea? Are there important definitions or identifications? You may find one or two or three items to mark or

FIGURE 4.1   An Example of Student-Marked Text

Ethnic and Racial Differences

Ethnicity is used to refer to "groups that are characterized in terms of a common nationality, culture, or language" (Betancourt & Lopez, 1993, p. 631). We all have some ethnic heritage, whether our background is Italian, Jewish, Ukrainian, Hmong, Chinese, Japanese, Navajo, Hawaiian, Puerto Rican, Cuban, Hungarian, German, African, or Irish—to name only a few. **Race**, on the other hand, is defined as "a category composed of men and women who share biologically transmitted traits that are defined as socially significant," such as skin color or hair texture (Macionis, 2003, p. 354). Depending on the traits you measure and the theory you follow, there are between 3 and 300 races. In effect, race is a label people apply to themselves and to others based on appearances. There are no biologically pure races (Betancourt & Lopez, 1993). In fact, as you saw in Chapter 4, for any two humans chosen at random, an average of only .012% (about one hundredth of one percent) of the alphabetic sequence of their genetic codes is different due to race (Myers, 2005). Still, race is a powerful construct. At the individual level, race is part of our identity—how we understand ourselves and interact with others. At the group level, race is involved with economic and political structures (Omi & Winant, 1994).

Sociologists sometimes use the term **minority group** to label a group of people that receives unequal or discriminatory treatment. Strictly speaking, however, the term refers to a numerical minority compared to the total population. Referring to particular racial or ethnic groups as "minorities" is technically incorrect is some situations, because in certain places, such as Chicago or Mississippi, the "minority" group—African Americans—is actually the majority. This practice of referring to people as "minorities" because of their racial or ethnic heritage has been criticized because it is misleading.

Source: Excerpted text used by permission from Woolfolk, A. (2007). *Educational Psychology*. Boston: Pearson, p. 168.

annotate, but be selective, for if you mark or annotate too much, the process becomes useless. If you are reading an electronic version of a text, use the marking system available in the same way. See Figure 4.1 for an example of textbook marking.

Continue the process.   Work through each subsection, back and forth, reading . . . thinking . . . marking or annotating. As you work, be sure to look over any charts, graphs, or boxed inserts. These graphic aids will help you understand the ideas, as will completing any of the exercises included within the chapter. Work for 15 to 20 minutes then get up and take a 5-minute break. Then go back to work.

Review. Review as soon as possible—we recommend within the first day or so of reading the material. You may want to create review strategies, such as chapter review cards, mapping, study guides, or test preps to aid your review (see Chapter 6). Try to explain out loud what you understand from the text. Continue to briefly review the material until test time.

The end result of a productive study session is twofold: you have an understanding of the main ideas of the text reading, and you have a marked or annotated text that will help you prepare for exams. The markings are yours, your choices; that is why it is useful to buy unmarked or minimally marked texts. What other people have marked will not help you.

Reading other types of textual sources such as selected readings and research articles is quite different from the five-step process described above for reading survey, conceptual, and encyclopedic texts. If the reading is complex and difficult, be prepared to read it several times. In this type of reading, each sentence is important. There are few or no headings. Especially in philosophy, multiple readings are essential.

If you are reading complex literature from another time and another language, you may want to locate a simple plot line and list of characters that you can print and keep with you as you read. The original intended audience usually knew the characters and the plots as well as you know your favorite TV show, so the author could assume that prior knowledge.

Good Reading Strategies

- Make sure you have all the assigned print materials, in either paper copy or electronic version.
- Set aside time to read when you are alert. Decide whether you need to read the material before or after the lecture.
- Choose what you are going to read and how long and make a deliberate intention to learn.
- Find a place that supports your concentration with minimal distractions.
- Preview the material to be read to help assess your memory.
- Read to understand the material; then mark the primary points or take notes on them.
- Practice rehearsing and explaining what you understand.
- Reread sections that are confusing or ask for help.
- Set aside time in your schedule to review your reading material for each class.

Improving Concentration, Comprehension, and Vocabulary

Many college students improve their reading concentration, comprehension, and vocabulary during their first year in college. Using many of the strategies we have been discussing should improve all your reading skills. However, you may realize that you need intensive work on one or more of these skills. The following sections give some strategies in all three areas. (For more specialized help, go to your campus reading or learning centers, which offer diagnostic testing, tutoring, computerized instruction, and reading improvement courses.)

Sharpening concentration

If you have poor concentration or are a gifted daydreamer, if your mind wanders each time you pick up a textbook, the cure is ruthless. Study in 10-minute sessions. Study earlier in the day, not late at night. Fatigue is the enemy, so be sure you are sleeping enough. Read the chapter one subsection at a time. Turn the heading into a question and when you find the answer, write it down. Hold yourself accountable for every minute you are looking at the page. If you have to stand up and hold the book, do so. After each 10-minute session, test yourself on the material (note how many paragraphs you read while concentrating). Look over those paragraphs and quickly recall the most important points. Continue with this procedure and finish reading the first subsection.

Daydreaming is a habit; so is concentration. Get in the habit of concentrating when you are looking at a text. Each time you realize that you are daydreaming, pull your mind back to the information on the page.

Several sensible strategies to improve reading concentration are to set specific goals (*I will read and understand the first 10 pages of Chapter 7 in the next hour*), to read purposefully to meet those goals, and to choose the best time of day to read. Take a 5-minute break every 20 minutes. These actions help develop a positive attitude.

Two types of distractions can impinge on concentration when we study: external and internal. External distractions concern the place you study: Is it orderly or chaotic? Quiet or noisy? Comfortable or crowded? Look at your environment for study. What changes do you need to make to support your study concentration? Internal distractions include boredom or active dislike for the subject matter, personal problems or worry, and feelings of fatigue and being overwhelmed. Using goals and self-talk may help you to overcome such distractions, but if serious personal problems exist, we recommend that you speak with a campus counselor.

Exercise 4.2

Internal and External Distractions

Complete the grid in Figure 4.2. This exercise will aid you in identifying and eliminating distractions that interfere with your learning.

FIGURE 4.2 Self-Analysis of Internal and External Distractions

Internal Distractions	Check all that apply	Describe the problem	Plan to correct the problem
Negative reactions to noise (your feelings and self-talk)			
Daydreaming			
Personal problems and worries			
Boredom			
Anxiety/dislike for subject			
Awesomeness of study task			
Fatigue			
Other			
External Distractions			
Study area			
Auditory distractions			
Visual distractions			
Furniture/work space			
Lighting			
Temperature			
Other			

Monitoring comprehension

Good readers are continually aware when they understand the material and when they do not. They routinely reread when necessary, locate primary ideas, and infer implied primary ideas. They identify supporting details, recognize patterns of organization, rephrase ideas into their own words, reread difficult sections, and create sample questions. If you are struggling with comprehension, then stop at the end of a text section and reflect how well you have understood the material. Can you recall the main ideas? The underlying premise is that we hold ourselves accountable to understand the material. If you cannot understand after reading, go back and reread. If you still do not understand, ask for help. If you are lucky enough to have a study guide for the text (a quick Google search will tell you if one is in print), use it to organize your efforts by going back and forth between the guide and the text. Instructional CDs and online study guides can also help.

Exercise 4.3

Monitoring Your Comprehension

To learn to monitor and increase your comprehension, select a reading assignment in one of your textbooks for a lecture-based class (this exercise is unsuitable for math, literature, or philosophy texts). As you do this exercise, use your most powerful concentration strategies, trying to control both external and internal distractions.

1. In two or three minutes, look over the chapter title, the main headings within the chapter, and any introductory or summarizing material. Answer the following questions: What is the author's main purpose in this chapter? What are the main ideas? What is the structure of the information presented?

2. Divide the chapter into sections; it is usually a good idea to use the primary or secondary headings as the dividers. Read or study each section using the following strategies:

   • Look at the section heading and turn it into a question. You will be reading to answer that question.

   • Look for the general definition or primary idea of the section's topic in the first two or three paragraphs and mark it by underlining, highlighting, or bracketing.

   • Read or study each paragraph. What information is the author giving? Why is he or she giving it? Place a check mark beside the paragraph if you can answer both questions and an "X" if you cannot.

- At the end of the section, stop, reflect, and attempt to relate the information to the section title and the main idea. Look at any paragraphs you marked with an "X." Do they make sense now? If so, cross out the "X." If not, write down questions to ask your instructor.

- Mark one to four important ideas, facts, or conclusions you believe you should remember.

- As you finish each section, on your own paper write a short summary statement of what you believe to be the most important ideas of the section.

Developing vocabulary

Another type of reading difficulty is the lack of a collegiate vocabulary. If every tenth word in your freshman English reader is unfamiliar, you need to do specific vocabulary development. The fastest method is to go online or to the campus learning center and study Greek and Latin roots and prefixes. Another is to consult a dictionary *regularly*. Make vocabulary cards, write sentences using new words, and become a wordsmith, a craftsman with language. Reading will greatly aid your vocabulary development. Persistence is the key; if you can truly learn one new word each day, your vocabulary will grow as your intellectual abilities grow.

If there is new vocabulary to learn, make flash cards with the word on one side and the definition on the other. Some students find it extremely helpful to add an image to each flash card—especially those students who learn visually. To use this method, think of an image that represents the information and then draw the image using stick figures or symbols. The actual process of thinking about an appropriate image will facilitate your memory. Flash cards also work for identifications and grouped items (types, characteristics). Carry them in your backpack or pocket and practice them several times a day.

LEARNING FROM SOLVING PROBLEMS OR CASE STUDIES

Learning from homework problems is much more than simply getting the answer. We have to learn the process so well that we are able to use it in other situations. Math, accounting, economics, and statistics are the most common procedural courses through which critical learning occurs through solving problems or exercises. We have said that learning procedural knowledge takes many repetitions spread out over time. That fact is a primary underpinning of the basic strategy for this type of learning: Work problems promptly and often. Here are some suggestions:

- Begin homework problems as soon as you can after class. Do not delay.

- Work hard from the first day of class. It is difficult to catch up if you get behind, and cramming does not help.

- Be persistent. If you get stuck, take a short break and then go back to the problem.

- Talk aloud about what you are doing to solve the problem, as if you were teaching someone else.

- Many texts give answers to the questions the teacher does not assign. Use those for practice.

- If there are workbooks or study guides, use them diligently.

- If you are confused, seek help immediately. There are tutors, labs, study groups. Ask a classmate who is doing well in the course for help.

- Overlearn. By that we mean practice more problems than assigned.

Because we tend to learn better in one mode over another, we learn better either through words or through quantitative symbols such as numbers and letters. It is wise to use our strongest mode of learning as the primary way we approach a problem, then translate solving that problem into the other mode. T-notes can be quite helpful in using both modes to solve problems.

LEARNING FROM WRITING

Writing assignments are a particular type of project that some students find difficult, but writing is one of the most important methods in learning how to think critically. Most collegiate writing is about formulating an argument and defending it, a skill you will use throughout your professional life. Here are some suggestions:

- Determine the purpose and structure of the assignment as well as the format for presentation.

- Set a timetable allowing for brainstorming, drafting, rewriting, editing, and preparing final copy. Good writers usually finish the rewriting stage at least 48 hours before the due date so that they can bring a clear mind to the editing and preparation stages.

- If you think best by talking, then ask a friend to listen as you generate the concepts for your paper.

- Once you have chosen an idea, write a rough outline of your argument.

- Start writing. Many writers start in the middle, then they keep adding other sections. You can always write the introduction last.

- Rewrite into a coherent document.

- During editing, look carefully for the errors you frequently make and correct them. Sometimes, if you read the last sentence, then the next to last sentence, then . . .; you will see grammatical errors more easily.

- Double check that your presentation meets every criterion that the instructor has set.

A common form of performance anxiety is called "a writer's block." It occurs when a person is afraid to start the writing process and can become a serious issue. If you have suffered from this sort of anxiety, please see the Appendix entitled "Overcoming Specific Academic Anxieties."

LEARNING FROM INDIVIDUAL PROJECTS

Since the mid-1990s, college teachers have begun to assign many more projects to undergraduate students because employers are demanding the skills that result from those experiences. Expect to receive individual projects in many classes, especially in your major field of study. Such experiential learning can be quite powerful if your involvement is high. Individual projects often involve public presentations using some form of media.

Successful students report the following behaviors in individual projects:

- Projects and experiments always take longer than expected. Begin early.

- Be sure that you completely understand the assignment. Ask questions in class; go to the professor during office hours. Can you explain the assignment to someone else?

- Collect all the materials you will need as soon as you can.

- Set a timetable to complete the project 24 hours before it is due. Use specific goals for each part of the project—research, learning from sources, presentation.

- Practice your presentation so that your timing and any visuals are coordinated.

- If you are distributing handouts or other materials, make sure to have enough copies.

- Prepare printed presentation for the instructor, if required.

LEARNING FROM PEERS

Another powerful form of learning is to learn from other students. Many cultures use this as a primary form of learning; however, Western culture has come to it more slowly. Colleges now provide numerous opportunities for you to learn from peers, including tutoring labs, structured learning groups, test review, and group projects. Explore all your options early in the term and determine the times, places, and circumstances of tutoring labs and any learning groups that are led by experienced undergraduate or graduate students. It is a good idea to investigate those before you need the help.

If you want to establish an effective study group, choose two other students who share your desire for success (three is the magic number for a group). Set a specific time, place, and topic. A good place is a study room in the library. Expect everyone to have completed the initial study of the material and to bring questions to the group. Compare notes from the lecture across the group. A study group can become a test review group. Focus the discussion on two points: the unanswered questions about the material from the lecture and assigned readings, and the predicted questions for the next test.

A lively, competitive interaction in a group will help everyone's learning. Debate the issues or quiz each other. Assign topics and let each person "teach" for five minutes. If you have been unwise enough to include a lazy person or a leech, eject him or her from the group. Older, returning students are good additions to a group because they are usually highly motivated and willing to work hard.

Test review groups may also be organized and led by your instructors or teaching assistants. We strongly suggest that you complete all the readings and assignments before you attend and take all your materials. These sessions are usually so valuable that it is wise to adjust your schedule so that you can attend.

Another type of learning from peers is a group project. These are required portions of a course and usually count heavily toward your grade. Instructors often issue grades not only on the final product of the project, but also on how well the team works together. Here are some suggestions on being successful in such a project:

- Show up to the first meeting and decide if you want to be the leader or a team member. The leader usually works harder in a group effort.

- Be sure that you understand the assignment and decide what part of the project you want to do and assertively ask for it.

- Scheduling and coordinating meetings are often difficult for groups. Suggest that members use social networking (email, blog, and so forth) to communicate.

- Suggest a specific timetable for the project.

- Set your timetable for your portion of the project.

- Meet regularly with your group to collectively work on the project.

- Complete your portion of the project in a timely fashion and communicate it to your peers.

One of the most uncomfortable situations is a team member whose irresponsible behavior jeopardizes the project. Do not delay assertive confrontation with that person. The team leader should lead that confrontation, but the group should also participate. Go to the instructor if the group cannot reach resolution.

LEARNING FROM ACADEMIC NETWORKING

The personal use of electronic media for social networking is growing exponentially throughout the world's cultures, and nowhere faster than on college campuses. We like a new term, **academic networking** (D. C. Caverly, personal communication, July 16, 2009), defined as *using the benefits of social networking to interact with peers, faculty, and support services toward the purpose of improving academic performance*. Academic networking is currently used for two purposes: communication and learning. In communicating with instructors and collegiate staff, remember that college faculty and staff members have strong expectations about how you communicate. They expect respect, courtesy, and time to respond to your questions and/or requests. Few of them are available 24/7, so do not be surprised if the request you send on Saturday afternoon does not get answered until Monday or even later in the week. In some classes you will have the opportunity or even be required to use social networking (e.g., blogs, texting, virtual environments), so consider how often and to what extent you feel comfortable interacting with faculty members using these channels.

Students are by far the most current users of academic networking. They create threads and discussions on networks such as Facebook to clarify confusing concepts, debate topics covered in class, and to create study groups. They also post inquiries about homework problems so that other students (as well as tutors, graduate assistants, and faculty members) can respond. By the time this book is published, we predict academic networking with be considerably more advanced and widespread.

CASE STUDY

BENNY is a second-semester freshman with above average intelligence and a formal diagnosis of attention deficit hyperactivity disorder (ADHD) and a medical prescription. In high school, his parents and his girlfriend gave him structure to help him be organized. His social skills are excellent, and he usually finds time to spend with his friends. Although he excels in math and science, he is doing poorly in English and history. Benny has difficulty concentrating and focusing on reading assignments, and he also finds his class notes hard to decipher. He has legal accommodations for extra test time and early access to course syllabi and assignments, but he often does not do his readings and forgets to complete some of his assignments. He is not as consistent taking his medication as he was in high school.

Case Study Questions: Based on your reading and experience, what actions would you recommend Benny to initiate? In what areas should he seek help and from whom?

CONCLUSION

Studying is not just reading and memorizing, although it encompasses both. Remember that studying is applying the mind so as to acquire understanding and knowledge. It is the work of a student. Most study skills books tell students to study two hours for every hour of class. Not a bad average, but it is an average. Some courses will require four hours for every hour of class and some will require 30 minutes. The two-for-one average will usually yield average grades. Unlike high school, it takes effort even to make Cs; As and Bs are much harder to achieve.

Studying is like any job. With time, effort, and attention, you can learn to do it well. By practicing studying, you will be able to master the most powerful skill in the human arsenal: the ability to understand.

SUMMARY

- There are six major methods available for use to learn academic information outside the classroom: reading textual sources, solving problems, writing, doing individual projects, working with peers, and creating and/or using academic networks.

- Studying is not just reading and memorizing. It is applying the mind to the material so you are able to comprehend and use the knowledge.

- Reading has been defined as an intensely private and complex activity or skill in which the reader catches (understands) every sort of printed communication.

- Successful college readers have three attributes in common. They use a forethought phase, complete a performance phase, and end with a reflection phase.

- There are seven primary types of academic textual sources: (1) survey texts, (2) reference texts, (3) conceptual texts, (4) problem-centered texts, (5) selected readings, (6) literature, and (7) research articles.

- Each type of textual source has its own unique characteristics and purposes that must be understood in order to try and understand the message being conveyed.

- A powerful method of increasing one's ability to read is to have prior knowledge in mind before beginning to read. Prior knowledge is the reader's familiarity with the topic and his/her reading ability.

- Steps in reading a textbook include previewing, using the headings, identifying the primary idea(s), reading before marking, continuing the process, and reviewing.

- To sharpen your concentration, set specific goals, read purposefully, choose the best time of day to read, and take breaks.

- Two types of distractions can impinge on concentration when we study: external and internal.

- To improve comprehension, you should reread when necessary, locate primary ideas, identify supporting details, recognize patterns of organization, rephrase ideas into your own words, reread difficult sections, and create sample questions.

- To increase your vocabulary, study Greek and Latin roots and prefixes and consult a dictionary regularly. Remember, the more you read the more your vocabulary will develop. Creating visual vocabulary note cards is an effective strategy.

- Solving problems is a good way to learn procedural knowledge. Working problems at the end of each chapter and resources such as study guides, labs, study groups, and tutors are all useful.

- Writing is one of the most important methods in learning how to think critically, especially when formulating and defending arguments.

- Individual projects are common in college, appeal to students who like hands-on learning, and often involve making a public presentation using some form of media.

- A study group is a good resource for most classes. Three is the magic number of participants, yet the key is the people who form the group.

Look to study with others who are motivated, come prepared, and are at or slightly above your level of comprehension.

- Academic networking, using the benefits of social networking to interact with peers, faculty, and support services to improve academic performance, is rapidly expanding how students communicate and learn in college.

KEY CONCEPTS

Academic networking	Reading
Developing vocabulary	Reflection phase
Forethought phase	Sharpening concentration
Group projects	Solving problems/case studies
Individual projects	Study
Monitoring comprehension	Study groups
Peers	Textual sources
Performance phase	Writing
Prior knowledge	

GUIDED JOURNAL QUESTIONS

1. Describe your current methods of reading and learning from your textbooks. Now that you have read this chapter, how do you think the reading suggestions will be useful to you?

2. Reflect on when you are able to concentrate the most on your reading. Is there a pattern for the time of day, surroundings you are in, subject matter? What can you determine from the results of this reflection? Explain and give examples.

3. What approaches have you used in the past (or will begin to use) to monitor your comprehension as you read difficult college textbooks? Explain.

4. College classes require more intensive and in-depth study strategies. What techniques will you implement to achieve success in your current courses?

5. Envision how your writing skills will become more highly refined with more experience. What specific steps of the writing process would you like to gain more mastery?

6. When speaking or writing, do you have difficulty formulating an argument and defending it? Explain fully. Discuss several previous or current courses that required such skills.

7. What must take place to make a study group effective? A group project? Describe your previous experiences with peer learning.

8. Describe your personal use of social networking tools. How do you envision electronic media affecting higher education in both positive and negative aspects?

The Last World

The ability to read well has served me all my life; it is the foundation of my independence as a professional.

—*De Sellers*

Academic Learning and Neural Development

My, what big dendrites you have.

CHAPTER HIGHLIGHTS

- Brain Learning Theory
- A Descriptive Model of Academic Learning
- Increasing Our Academic Learning and Memory

We possess the most complicated machine in the world—our brain. Understanding its capabilities and possibilities, as well as its quirks, helps us harness its power.

Did you know that human brains are getting larger over time? Our great-grandparents' brain weighed about four ounces less than ours! Each and every second of our lives, several billion bits of information pass through our brains at speeds up to 250 miles per hour (Benesh, Arbuckle, Robbins, & D'Arcangelo, 1998). As we learn more about the brain, we learn more about how to learn. Educational psychologists and biologists are combining knowledge and theory to give us new insights into how our minds grow, change, and learn.

SELF-ASSESSMENT: Learning and Memory Skills

Your memory is one of your most important survival tools for college. As information increases each year, you are expected to learn more in your college experience than others before you. With 5 being "Almost Always" and 1 being "Almost Never," assess your learning and memory skills. Rate each of the following statements honestly by circling the appropriate number. Completing this exercise will help you identify areas of concern you may have about your ability to learn and remember effectively.

	Almost Always		Sometimes		Almost Never
1. I can pay attention during most class lectures when I make the effort.	5	4	3	2	1
2. I generally get enough sleep to be able to concentrate when I read and study.	5	4	3	2	1
3. I am keenly aware of when I do not understand the material I am reading/ studying or the problems I am trying to solve.	5	4	3	2	1
4. I practice repeating a concept or a skill over and over to reinforce my learning.	5	4	3	2	1
5. I use a variety of methods when learning material (read it, write it, say it out loud, explain it, and so on).	5	4	3	2	1
6. I learn by connecting new information to knowledge I've learned in the past.	5	4	3	2	1
7. I can remember names, dates, and places (facts).	5	4	3	2	1
8. I can remember theories, events, and processes (concepts).	5	4	3	2	1

9. I tend to misplace things   5   4   3   2   1
    when I don't make a point
    to remember where I've
    put them.

10. Forgetting is a problem for   5   4   3   2   1
    me, even when I read,
    study, and attend class.

Add up the numbers you circled. Your total score will be between 10 and 50. The higher your score, the more likely you will feel confident about your learning and memory skills. For scores below 30, write or reflect on items for which you have concerns and consider talking with a trusted friend, a family member, a teacher, a counselor, or an advisor.

BRAIN LEARNING THEORY

In many ways, we are just beginning to know how our brains learn. Existing theoretical explanations of how we learn include the following:

- **Physiological**—the physical construction and processes of the brain. For the first time, we can look inside a working brain and begin to understand how it works.

- **Information processing**—the flow of information (data) into the brain and what the individual does with that information in terms of learning and memory. In simple terms, the process converts sensory input (vision, sound, and so forth) into symbols (words, concepts, images) and then processes those symbols so knowledge can be held and retrieved.

- **Constructivism**—the concept that individuals construct meaning from information based on their perceptions, beliefs, experiences (Woolfolk, 2007).

- **Emotional experience**—"Emotions produce chemicals that enter the brain and physiologically affect the synapses and, consequently, the brain's ability to think, learn, and remember" (Smilkstein, 2003, p. 86).

Until recent years, how our brains learn (the physiological process) has been only hypothesis. Now, modern technology illuminates many

of our learning processes. We are discovering that our brains have inborn characteristics that include

- motivation to learn.
- imagination and creativity.
- problem-solving ability.
- tendency to seek patterns.
- logic and reason (Smilkstein, 2003, p. 71).

Important principles for academic learning emerge from both the physical
and theoretical research. As you study this chapter, concentrate on how these
principles can work for you in your life as a student. Making the connections
between theory/research and practical applications empowers you to become an
autonomous learner.

We have about 100 billion **neurons** (*brain nerve cells* or gray matter) in
our brain. Each neuron has a body and from that body grow *fibers* called
dendrites (see Figure 5.1). Each neuron also has *one long fiber* called the

FIGURE 5.1   The Neuron

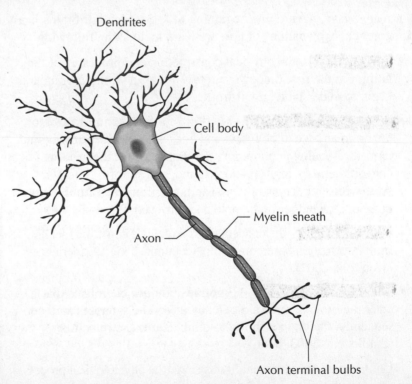

FIGURE 5.2   Neuron and Glial Cells

Glial
Cells

Neuron

axon covered by glial cells that produce **myelin** (*white matter sheathing*). Glial cells have many functions in each stage of life. "One of their most important functions is to increase the speed of conduction in neurons" (Garrett, 2009, p. 32). For academic study, the important function is that glial cells "contribute to the development and maintenance of connections between neurons" (p. 33) (see Figure 5.2).

At the end of each axon is a tiny bulb called a **terminal** (*connection point*) filled with *chemicals* called **neurotransmitters**. Terminals allow dendrites and neurons to communicate with each other; this *communication* is called a **synapse** (Garrett, 2009; Smilkstein, 2003) (see Figure 5.3).

> The brain's gray matter and white matter are responsible for memory, thinking, reasoning, sensation, and muscle movement. Scientists have mapped the various regions of the brain that correspond to different functions and specialized neural circuitry. . . . These regions and circuits manage everything we do and experience, including falling in love, flossing our teeth, reading a novel, recalling fond memories, and snacking on a bag of nuts. (Small & Vorgan, 2008, p. 5)

FIGURE 5.3   Synapse

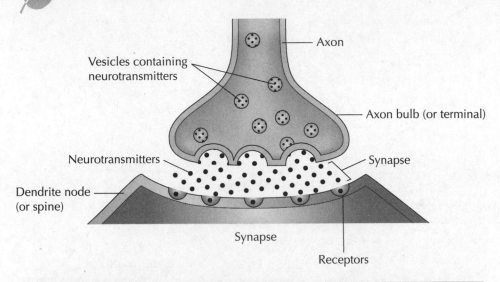

Exercise 5.2

Make a Fist

One of the first steps in enhancing your memory is to have some understanding of how your brain learns. This exercise will help you visualize a nerve cell and the growing of dendrites.

Make a fist with your right hand. Your fist represents one neuron (brain cell). Now slowly begin to extend each finger. Each finger represents a dendrite. Now make a fist with your other hand and slowly begin to extend each finger. Finally, make one finger from your left hand almost touch a finger on your right hand. When one finger almost touches another, you have now represented two nerve cells connecting (a dendrite connecting to another dendrite). Your two fingers (dendrites) almost touching each other represent a synapse and your hands each represent a network of neurons.

The brain is in a constant state of change. When we practice those connections (synapses) by study and repetition, the neural network as a whole can grow and adapt (see Figure 5.4). Such capability is plasticity, *the ability of the brain to be modified*. The number of possible neural connections is greatest at age two; then the brain begins a dramatic simplifying and reduction process because too much information coming in will overload the system. Circuit pruning, a natural process, is *the elimination of excess neurons and synapses* (Garrett, 2009, p. 73). By adolescence, the capability of neural connections has

FIGURE 5.4   Neural Networks

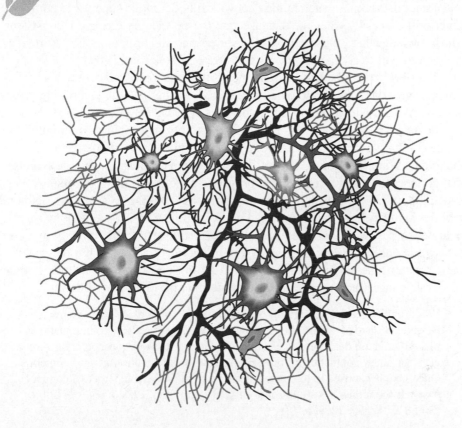

shrunk 60 percent (Small & Vorgan, 2008). While pruning continues throughout maturity, the capability to create neural connections stabilizes. Thus, the adult brain is efficient, small enough to focus and function, large enough to learn.

Most researchers agree that the more active our brains are, the more dendrites, synapses, and neural networks we have. Our brains interact with the environment, the setting or circumstances of our lives. If the environment is enriched with many interesting items and ideas, then our brains will be active. If the environment is impoverished, then our brains will make fewer neural connections because we have built fewer dendrites.

A definition of **learning** that emphasizes the physical aspects of our brains is *a form of neural plasticity that changes behavior by remodeling neural connections* (Garrett, 2009, p. 371). As we learn, neurons connect with each other into networks. Although we can think about these networks in an abstract way, researchers are unable to create them in realistic ways, even using the most powerful computers. Each of us has neural networks that are so large and so complicated that they far exceed what we can imagine. Neural networks are being intensely studied by biologists, psychologists, philosophers, engineers, and computer scientists because such human network functioning is superior to computer functions, especially when the data used are messy, incomplete, and inconsistent. The knowledge that we use networks to understand and remember is important as we look to build a competent set of study strategies (Garrett, 2009).

The plasticity of the human brain means that it has evolved over tens of thousands of years as new technologies (fire, wheel, written language, printing press, and so on) occur. However, no technology has ever had the effect on the brain that computer technology has had. The digital revolution, a binary communication system built on a transmitted code of pluses and minuses, is the perfect match for the human brain. "Our brain's neural circuits—axons, dendrites, and the synapses that connect them—are biologically primed to function digitally" (Small & Vorgan, 2008, p. 13). The result of this revolution is that our brains are changing more rapidly than they have ever changed. For those of us who use technology several hours each day, we experience **continuous partial attention**, *staying aware of everything but rarely focusing on any one thing*. For example, if we keep attending to instant messaging while we are studying and listening to music, then academic concentration and learning and memory become more difficult.

> When paying partial continuous attention, people may place their brains in a heightened state of stress. They no longer have time to reflect, contemplate, or make thoughtful decisions. Instead, they exist in a sense of constant crisis—on alert for a new contact or bit of exciting news or information at any moment. Once people get used to this state, they tend to thrive on the perpetual connectivity. It feeds their egos and sense of self-worth, and it becomes irresistible. (Small & Vorgan, 2008, p. 18)

Multitasking and continuous partial attention are different. In **multitasking**, we have *several tasks we want to accomplish simultaneously in order to save time*. For example, we may exercise and watch TV or study while we are washing our clothes. But, continuous partial attention creates heightened stress in our brain as we try to attend to many sources of information. It is the multiple sources of information and our constant awareness of them that damages attention, making it incomplete and discontinuous. Research points to both negative and positive results from continuous partial attention. The negative results are

- mental stress/burnout—feelings of fatigue, irritability, distractedness
- lowered ability to concentrate (symptoms similar to attention deficit disorder)
- decreased ability to learn deeply
- lowered interpersonal communication skills

Over time, this new form of mental stress impairs learning, leads to depression, and alters those parts of the brain that control mood and thought. An important result of research shows that sleeping for at least one hour counteracts some of the effects of continuous partial attention (Small & Vorgan, 2008). Other breaks from technology, such as exercise and being with friends, should also help. We can deliberately spend more time interacting with people in person, not digitally. Positive results include the following:

- Reacting more quickly to visual stimuli, both real and virtual.

- Highly developed neural circuitry to search and sift through large amounts of visual data.

- Performance of some mental tasks becomes more efficient (Small & Vorgan, 2008).

You can begin to control the health of your brain by attending to its exposure to technology and the effects of that exposure. If you are using technology more than eight hours each day, practice turning it off for an hour or so and letting your brain rest.

The development of computers in the 20th century helped us grasp some basic facts about learning, and theorists originally believed that the human brain functions like a computer. That concept was the earliest idea of information processing theory, but the theory has become a much more complicated one that stresses the development of cognitive processes. The crux of current thought is that we construct meaning from the data that flows to us and, from that meaning, construct our memories.

On the other hand, research also indicates that heavy users of the data blitz seem to develop "neural circuitry that is customized for rapid and incisive spurts of directed concentration" (Small & Vorgan, 2008, p. 21). In other words, some people who use multiple electronic devices many hours each day improve their ability to search and locate specific information quickly and accurately. How can we get the best of both worlds? The strategies and techniques in this text specifically develop focused attention, comprehension, and recall as the data blitz swirls around us. Pay close attention to determine which strategies will help your learning.

Exercise 5.3

Enriching Your Learning Environment

- An "enriched" learning environment facilitates the growth of dendrites and an "impoverished" environment inhibits growth. Describe how you envision an enriched learning environment compared with an impoverished learning environment.

- What suggestions do you have for your current instructors to create a more enriched learning environment to facilitate dendrite growth? How can you enhance your own learning (create an enriched environment) to facilitate your growth of dendrites? This exercise will help you identify ways to enrich your learning environment.

A DESCRIPTIVE MODEL OF ACADEMIC LEARNING

Current psychological concepts about academic learning are complicated and often confusing. On one hand, each of us has a lifetime of experience in learning; on the other hand, how we learn seems mysterious. Because the theories about human learning and the research undergirding them are so complex, we have created a relatively simple model that integrates the primary principles of each theory for use in this text.

When we reflect on our own learning, some basic elements become clear. What follows is our description of what we believe is the academic learning process; the description is based on our reflection, current psychological and neuropsychological research and theory, and common sense. The primary model we explore is the dual-store of memory (Figure 5.5) that posits three components of memory: a sensory register, a short-term or working memory, and a long-term memory. This basic structure comes from information processing theory, but we will include elements of the other three theoretical approaches: physiological, constructivism, and emotional experience.

FIGURE 5.5   The Dual-Store Model of Memory

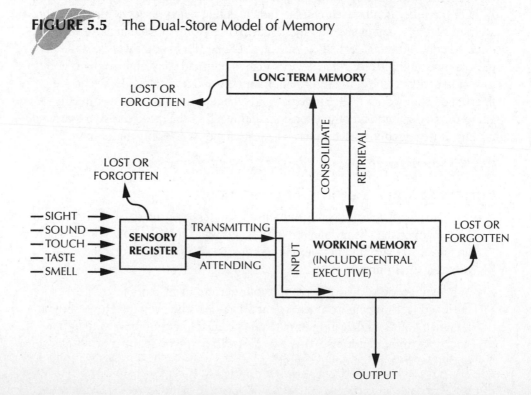

Dual-Store Model of Memory

Academic learning becomes possible when our **sensory register** (*sight, sound, touch, smell, taste*) grabs a signal from our environment. A signal may be the teacher's voice in a lecture, the print from a textbook, a graph written on the board, the image from a picture. The act of our *sensory register intentionally focusing on and grabbing the signal* is called **attending**. At that moment, two other parts of our brain are active.

First, the part of our consciousness in the working memory that directs our sensory register to attend to the signal is the **central executive,** and its *functions include controlling the flow of information from the sensory register, processing it for consolidation in the long-term memory, and retrieving it from that same long-term memory*. The central executive concept interests educational psychologists because that part of the learning process is what study strategies (conditional knowledge) improve. This model also suggests that there are automatic auditory and visual systems that help maintain the information while the central executive function is working (LeFrançois, 2000). Along the way, this central executive system is also thinking (comprehending, selecting, comparing, creating). Such a workload is amazing, yet we do it continually.

Second, our long-term memory, including declarative, procedural, and conditional knowledge, is immediately available. We not only have the ability to recognize or read the language used, but we also have the ability to know if the information (signal) is familiar or unfamiliar. So, from the very first moment, many parts of our brain are operational. Part of being a successful learner is being able and willing to attend to the signal. During our waking hours, we are always paying attention (our minds are constantly consumed with thoughts), but we may not be paying attention to the right signal, especially during academic learning. If we deliberately intend to learn, we increase the likelihood that we will learn. Our ability to attend to academic signals varies, but we can increase that ability by specific concentration strategies.

Sensory Register

In the dual-store model, the sensory register is believed to have unlimited capacity for all the environmental information that we are capable of sensing, and that information is held for a few moments in the form in which we sensed it (visual: less than one second, auditory: two to four seconds). In those moments, we have neither understood nor interpreted the information. In academic learning, we must attend to the information that we are trying to learn so that we can move it to our working memory. At the same time, we are discarding all the other information as if it were junk mail. The most important aspect of attention for academic learning is that usually we "cannot attend to or otherwise learn from two complex situations at the same time" (Ormrod, 1999, p. 187), so we must purposefully attend to the academic information if we are to learn it. As we stated earlier, continuous partial attention, the result of long-term technology use, hinders academic concentration, so it will be important to notice when you need to focus on academic information and step away from multiple technologies.

Research has shown that we pay greater attention to information if the size or intensity is exaggerated; if it is unusual or incongruous; if it has emotional or personal significance (Ormrod, 1999). Academic information usually does not come to us in these forms, but we can incorporate these characteristics in our study strategies to help us remember. Examples include creating an action story or a bizarre image to remember material or connecting a personal memory or experience to the material you are learning.

Working Memory

The information goes from the sensory register to the working memory, where it is held for less than 20 seconds. *The part of our conscious mind that thinks* is called the **working memory**. Interestingly, research indicates "that much of the information consolidated in working memory is consolidated in an *auditory* form, particularly when the information is language based" (Ormrod, 1999, p. 189). The capacity of our working memory is amazingly small. Miller (1956) explains that the capacity is the magical number seven plus or minus two (7 ± 2); in other words, we can hold about seven items of information in our working memory at one time. Those seven items of information are usually chunks of information, not individual letters or numbers. Five to nine items seem sufficient, even in difficult academic learning, and expert students easily combine pieces of information (chunking) into larger and larger chunks.

It is here in the working memory that we understand new information. It is here in the working memory that we think. As soon as we understand something or create a new idea or connection, then our central executive function decides whether it is important to remember it. If we understand the information correctly, then we can consolidate it in the appropriate neural networks. If we do not understand it, then we cannot connect it to the appropriate networks in our long-term memory.

Consolidation, *the act of organizing information and placing it into the long-term memory*, is a deliberate act, and there are many methods especially suited for collegiate learning. A crucial part of consolidation is the practice of retrieving the information. So we consolidate and retrieve, consolidate and retrieve, each time growing the dendrites and creating larger neural networks. Most information in the long-term memory, especially that related to academic learning, is consolidated semantically, that is, by meaning. For example, all the information about a topic such as brain learning is consolidated as connected neural networks.

If we experience and practice new information, then the appropriate dendrites, synapses, and neural networks increase. The larger the network, the more we can remember and use that knowledge. Such effort also increases the likelihood that we will build related networks and related consolidation for this information, thereby increasing our chances of remembering the new information (Smilkstein, 2003). Ideally, our retrieval process becomes automatic and easy because we have built rich and varied networks. When we are asked to perform that information or use it in a new way, we are able to do it quickly and accurately.

The more ways we input and practice material, the larger the networks become. In other words, if we recite aloud, write items down, explain to someone else, or create colorful study aids, the networks will be larger and more reliable. If we use multiple ways of learning, then both the number and the variety of networks grow (Smilkstein, 2003).

Long-Term Memory

Long-term memory differs dramatically from working memory. First, **long-term memory** *seems to have an infinite capacity and indefinite duration*. Age, disease, and injury can cause dendrites and neural networks to die, but for most of us, the duration and stability of our long-term memory is quite remarkable. Four important insights about long-term memory come from the theoretical approaches:

- Information consolidated in our long-term memory becomes knowledge (dendrites and neural networks).

- Long-term memory is usually constructed knowledge; that is, our working memory selects, organizes, and manipulates the information before storing. Thus, we construct what we learn and remember.

- Pieces of knowledge are usually consolidated with related pieces of knowledge in neural networks; that is, the organization of our long-term memory is primarily based on meaning (Ormrod, 1999).

- Emotional experience can greatly affect learning, either positively or negatively.

We have billions of pieces of knowledge already consolidated, primarily in **schemas**, *neural networks grouped by meaning*. The more we know, the

FIGURE 5.6   Characteristics of the Dual-Store Model

	Sensory Registers	Working Memory	Long-Term Memory
Capacity	Unlimited	Extremely limited (7 ± 2)	Infinite
Duration	Fleeting (1–4 seconds)	Extremely short (<20 seconds)	Indefinite
Storage mode	Same as signal	Auditory	Meaning

Source: Ormrod, J. E. (1999). *Human Learning*. Upper Saddle River, NJ: Merrill/Prentice Hall.

more we can learn because we have created more networks. As you progress in your studies, you will discover that you are creating an ever-increasing body of knowledge. See Figure 5.6 to review the characteristics of the dual-store model.

Declarative knowledge is consolidated in networks as explicit memories, that is, memories that we can consciously access. There are many types, including **episodic memory** (*events*), **factual memory** (*facts*), **autobiographical memory** (*information about yourself*), **spatial memory** (*location of the individual and objects in space*), and **semantic memory** (*knowledge about the world, rules, and principles that can be verbalized*) (Garrett, 2009; LeFrançois, 2000). Much of collegiate learning is declarative knowledge, especially factual memory and semantic memory.

Procedural knowledge (how to do something) is consolidated in networks as implicit memories. In other words, once we have thoroughly mastered a particular process, we will remember how to do the process but struggle to verbalize each step because we usually cannot remember them. Academic learning that is procedural will eventually become automatic, almost unconscious, after extensive practice (e.g., certain math or accounting functions).

Applying the Model

The realization that we will be expected to perform on tests and projects determines much of the academic learning process. Such realization is good, because students are inundated by so much information in each course that it is impossible to learn everything. Professors shape and narrow the content by their lectures and the required readings or problems. Students must continue the narrowing process as they look at the content and begin to organize what they need to remember, what they need to understand, what they need to apply, and so forth. The level of learning needed (the revised Bloom's Taxonomy); the awareness of one's own learning strengths and weaknesses; the competing demands of other courses, work, and family—all contribute to the consolidation and retrieval practices chosen for study.

INCREASING OUR ACADEMIC LEARNING AND MEMORY

As you read these strategies, reflect on your own learning strengths and weaknesses. Which strategies already work for you? Which look promising?

Attending

Every day we are bombarded with an enormous variety of signals from our environment, particularly those that are technological. As students, we are also bombarded by hours of lecture, hundreds of pages of print, and many classroom discussions. We can only learn academic information if we attend to it. Here are the ways that successful students manage their academic attention:

- Make the deliberate intention to pay attention and to learn the information, rather than daydream. If you drift away, gently bring yourself back to the task of attending. Research supports that intentional learning is more successful (Ormrod, 1999).

- Get enough sleep and exercise so that your body will support attending.

- Just before a lecture, look back over the notes you took before. When you are reading, quickly look back at the preceding chapter. In other words, activate the appropriate neural networks from your long-term memory.

- Use more active strategies if the material is difficult or boring to you. For example, sit at the front of the room or sit at a desk or table to study. Ask questions as you read. Or explain the material to someone. Be energetic in the learning process.

- Avoid distractions. If sitting next to friends disrupts your learning, move. Turn off the social networks. Clear your desk or study table of anything that promotes daydreaming. Go to the library and study in a place separated from noise or movement.

- Take notes during presentations, even discussions, and mark print while reading. Doing such an activity helps to hold your attention to the task.

- Use retrieval cues as you learn new information (e.g., reminding yourself of how something you are learning is similar to something else, or providing context for the material). Create your own cues while you are learning. The cues act as hooks to help you remember. The cues will help you locate the consolidated memories.

Some of us are primarily visual learners; that is, we learn best by seeing pictures, charts, graphs, and words. Some of us are primarily auditory learners; that is, we learn best by hearing information and explanations (Smilkstein, 2003). It is important to recognize our strengths, but also to compensate for our weaknesses. As college learners, we do not have to passively accept a learning environment. Instead, we can get information in other modes that accommodate our learning strengths to enrich our own learning environments.

Understanding

Understanding, the concept from Bloom's Taxonomy, is the core skill of collegiate learning. In ideal circumstances, it is easy to understand data or concepts when we attend to them, but some circumstances are not ideal and we have great difficulty. The greatest temptation is to just memorize and hope to pass the test. However, memorization without understanding means we do not use meaning to consolidate the information in the appropriate neural networks, so even if we remember it long enough for a test, we will not be able to use that information later. There are three cardinal rules for understanding collegiate material.

• *Continually search for meaning as you attend to new information.* The search for meaning occurs through patterning. Your brain needs to find and connect the new information to something similar. **Comprehension monitoring** means *the continual awareness we have of our own understanding as we learn something new.* All of us routinely monitor our understanding of conversations and instructions and ask people to repeat what they have said when we do not understand. When we study academic material, it is important that we are aware when we do not understand so that we can take action immediately. Such monitoring of academic learning is not as easy as monitoring in our daily lives, especially if we have created a habit of not expecting to understand tough academic material.

• *Make sure you really understand the material.* The most powerful method of determining whether you are comprehending a particular set of material is to engage in a mini performance. In other words, test yourself before you face a teacher's test. The first step of understanding is translation—changing from one form of representation to another. For example, can you translate details into concepts *or* concepts into details; can you paraphrase (put into your own words)? The best method is oral; translate out loud, to your study partner, your roommate, the wall, if necessary. What can you say without consulting your lecture notes or the text? If you cannot say much, if you simply repeat or recite the message, or if what you say does not really make sense, then you are not comprehending at a level necessary for college.

If you have already developed good comprehension monitoring when you are learning, celebrate that skill. If you have not developed such skills, then consider frequently stopping and checking how much you understand. Doing so will slow your studying temporarily, but it is the only way to improve this skill. Use study questions from the text to help you monitor. Turn the topics from the lecture into questions. Acquire the habit of question-and-answer as you study your notes (the Cornell system helps with this technique) or print material.

Most college teachers presume that your abilities in comprehension monitoring and understanding are competent. Frankly, many do not recognize comprehension problems and believe that students who are having trouble are simply not trying. Comprehending collegiate material requires intent, skill, effort, and determination. It is routine in college to read and reread, to ask for help, and to struggle with difficult and complex material.

As we presented in Chapter 2, understanding has three steps: translate, interpret or explain, and extrapolate (see connections and make predictions). In all cases, understanding is active; we have to do something with the information. In practical terms, the first step is to review your notes or the print material. Does seeing it again help your comprehension? If not, what other sources could help? A conference with the instructor? A tutor? A study group? A fellow student? Other print explanations in the library or on the Internet?

• ***Do whatever you have to do to understand the material.*** (The realization that you do not really understand the material calls this principle into play.) Such work is hard and takes effort and time. Students often struggle with how much time and effort is required. You may discover you have to study four or five hours for every class hour in a difficult subject just to be able to understand the material.

Consolidating (Building Dendrites) and Retrieving

The stark reality of collegiate learning is that there is far more information in any one course than we can reasonably learn, much less remember. From the first

---

**Methods of Increasing the Reliable
Consolidation and Retrieval
of Academic Learning**

- **Intention:** Make the deliberate intention to remember particular information for a specific purpose.
- **Effort:** Put energy and intensity into retrieval practice.
- **Structure:** Carefully choose the appropriate structure to consolidate and retrieve the information.
- **Multiple modalities:** Use the modalities that work best for you and for the material.
- **Meaningful connections:** Connect what you are learning with prior knowledge, information from other courses, and personal experience.
- **Practice:** Do this again and again and again.

---

lecture to the last moments before a test, our primary learning strategy is to understand the material so that we can determine what parts we need to carefully consolidate and retrieve to perform adequately both in the course and beyond. In other words, every time we write something down from the lecture or mark the text, we are continually sifting through the information and selecting what we believe is important. Students are often shocked that college faculty are far less directive than their high school teachers were. The reason is simple: one of the skills college students are expected to master as undergraduates is the skill of determining what is more important for a specific purpose and what is less important for that same purpose. Over time, most students usually learn how to direct their own studies.

As we move from understanding to deliberate consolidation/retrieval practice for performance, we process the course information over and over again. We select the content that we believe is important, we organize or elaborate that information, and we practice it until we are ready for performance. From summarizations to note cards to graphic organizers to matrices, we use methods of selection, elaboration, and practice. Remember, the more time we spend on the material, the more thoroughly (deeply) we will learn it. A similar premise that was used for understanding—*Do what you have to do to learn the material*—applies here: *Do what you have to do to accurately remember or understand or apply or analyze . . . the material.* Learning strategies take time. Pick the most effective, but also the most efficient, techniques for your needs.

The accuracy of what we choose to consolidate and retrieve is crucial. If we are thoughtful about what and how we learn, then our academic performance is likely to be competent. If we make errors in our understanding or with the memory devices we use, then we will consolidate and retrieve inaccurate or incomplete information. Replacing the inaccurate memory with an accurate one is much harder than simply learning the information correctly the first time.

CASE STUDY

LINDSEY, a sophomore business major, is generally a competent student, but she has hit a major roadblock in her first required economics course—a D on her first test. A conference with her instructor quickly reveals that she missed almost all the application questions. As she and her instructor talked, Lindsey realizes that she has a general understanding of the concepts and theories but she did not know them well enough to apply them in a new problem set, even though she was able to memorize definitions. She has three weeks until the next test.

Case Study Questions: What do you believe Lindsey should do in class to understand the material for the next economics test? What should she do outside of class to reach the application level? What campus resources could help her strengthen her understanding in order to apply this knowledge to new problems that will appear on the exams?

Forgetting—Causes and Remedies

Certain types of forgetting occur in the working memory and long-term memory. Because the capacity of the working memory is short, information may simply disappear (decay) before it is processed and deliberately consolidated in the long-term memory. Additionally, the working memory has an extremely limited capacity, so old information may be displaced by new information. Another kind of forgetting is when previous learning may interfere with the acquisition of new information (LeFrançois, 2000). Memory theorists refer to these three explanations of forgetting as decay, displacement, and interference, respectively. Failure to consolidate and retrieve information accurately also contributes to forgetting.

An important contribution from Craik and Lockhart (1972) is the following concept: *how thoroughly (deeply) we process information determines whether we retain it or forget it*. Effective learning strategies seek to intensify and deepen the processing of information so that there is a greater guarantee that it will be consolidated in the long-term memory in such a way that it can be retrieved. Meaning is the great key for this strategy, for if we understand the information and deliberately process it by translating, explaining, or inferring, then we have practiced retaining it and intensified its power.

Think of an air-traffic controller who controls departing and arriving aircraft, weather information, security information, and numerous other data systems. Like the air-traffic controller, the central executive naturally organizes information that comes to it (chunking), but it can also learn to organize academic information using specific methods to facilitate and enhance retrieval. These methods include mapping, outlining, graphic organizers, elaborations, memory systems, note cards, matrices, flow charts, time lines, and networks. Knowing which ones to use and when to use them effectively depends on your conditional knowledge (e.g., personal preferences, content, expected level and type of performance, prior knowledge and skills, and goals). In the next chapter, you

Common Causes and Remedies of Academic Forgetting

Decay—information disappears from working memory before consolidation.

Remedy—choose important information and deliberately practice consolidation and retrieval.

Displacement—New information replaces old information in the working memory.

Remedy—Link new information to old and practice both.

Interference—Prior information in long-term memory blocks consolidation of new information.

Remedy—Link old information to new and practice both.

Failure to consolidate—Poor or no consolidation strategies are used.

Remedy—Deliberately connect new information to prior knowledge and practice.

Failure to retrieve—Unreliable association between new information and prior knowledge means new information has not been stored where it can be readily found.

Remedy—Use spaced and frequent practice to build reliable retrieval.

will have the opportunity to learn and practice many of these methods.

The last type of forgetting is when we cannot retrieve the information that is consolidated in our long-term memory. Whereas personal experiences are so powerful that we remember them readily without any intent or practice, academic learning rarely has that impact. Deep processing and deliberate practice create the multiplicity of neural networks that support retrieval. The more modalities (e.g., auditory, visual, verbal, symbolic) we use in practice, the more powerful the practice will be. When we practice remembering, our working memory is accessing our long-term memory, finding the information, and pulling it into conscious thought. That cycle is the retrieval cycle, one we must do again and again to perform the information reliably.

CONCLUSION

We began this chapter talking about the extraordinary machine each of us has—our brain. Research is finally showing us its amazing capacity, and there are few academic fields today more compelling. As a college student, you drive this machine and test out its limits every day. We believe that if you thoughtfully incorporate academic strategies, you will be pleased with the improvement in your learning. Stay tuned for all the advances to come in your lifetime!

SUMMARY

- The brain is constantly changing. The term *plasticity* represents that learning organizes and reorganizes the brain.

- Learning is the growing of dendrites.

- The brain has 100 billion *neurons* (brain nerve cells). Each neuron has the ability to grow fibers called *dendrites*. Dendrites and neurons can communicate with each other through synaptic terminals and create neural networks.

- Circuit pruning is the elimination of excess neurons and synapses.

- A definition of learning that emphasizes the physical aspects of our brain is *a form of neural plasticity that changes behavior by remodeling neural connections.*

- No technology has ever affected the brain like computer technology has, which can cause a state of *continuous partial attention*—staying aware of everything, but rarely focusing on any one thing.

- Continuous partial attention can have both positive and negative results, but brain health can begin to be controlled by attending to its exposure to technology and the effects thereof.

- Multitasking is trying to accomplish several tasks simultaneously to save time.

- Human memory can be viewed through the theoretical explanation of the dual-store model, which consists of the sensory register, a short-term or working memory, and a long-term memory component. Also included in this model is the concept of a central executive.

- Attending is when the sensory register grabs information from the environment.

- The most important aspect of attention for academic learning is that usually one cannot attend to, nor learn from, two complex situations simultaneously.

- The part of our conscious mind that thinks is called the working memory.

- Consolidation is the deliberate act of organizing information and placing it into the long-term memory. A crucial part of consolidation is the practice of retrieving the information.

- Long-term memory, which seems to have an infinite capacity and indefinite duration, is where consolidated information becomes knowledge.

- Declarative knowledge is consolidated as explicit memories, while procedural knowledge is consolidated as implicit memories.

- A simple model of learning has three stages: attending, understanding, and consolidation (storage) and retrieval, each having multiple strategies for better implementation.

- There are six methods for increasing the reliable retrieval of academic learning: intention, effort, structure, multiple modalities, meaningful connections, and practice.

- As the learner moves from understanding to deliberate consolidation/retrieval practice for performance, the course information is practiced over and over again.

- Because the accuracy of what the learner chooses to consolidate and retrieve is crucial, academic performance is likely to be competent when the student is thoughtful about what is learned.

- There are five explanations of forgetting: decay, displacement, interference, failure to consolidate, and failure to retrieve accurately.

- Strategies such as mapping, outlining, graphic organizers, elaborations, memory systems, note cards, matrices, flow charts, time lines, and networks are all ways to organize academic information that facilitates and enhances retrieval, thus minimizing forgetting.

KEY CONCEPTS

Attending
Autobiographical memory
Axon
Brain learning theory
Central executive
Circuit pruning
Comprehension monitoring
Consolidation and retrieval
Continuous partial attention
Dendrites
Episodic memory
Factual memory
Forgetting
Glial cells
Learning (physical aspect)

Long-term memory
Multitasking
Myelin
Neurons
Neurotransmitters
Plasticity
Schemas
Semantic memory
Sensory register
Spatial memory
Synapse
Terminal
Understanding
Working memory

GUIDED JOURNAL QUESTIONS

1. Think of one thing you have learned to do well outside of school or college. It can be a hobby, sports activity, driving, playing music, and so on. Think back to before you knew how to do it. Now, write about the entire learning experience, from learning to mastery. In your answer, reflect on the three stages of learning: attending, understanding, and consolidation (storage) and retrieval.

2. Describe your experience with continuous partial attention (staying aware of everything, but rarely focusing on any one thing). Give details and examples.

3. What does it mean to have an enriched learning environment? An impoverished learning environment? Describe a time when you experienced each of these.

4. What is meant by brain learning theory? Describe the many aspects of this theory and relate them to your own learning.

5. Describe a past learning experience using the dual-store model. You may choose either a successful or unsuccessful learning experience. Be as specific as possible, and relate as much of the model as you can to your experience.

6. Describe a time when your emotions affected a particular memory in a positive manner. Then describe a time when your emotions affected a particular memory in a negative manner.

7. Think about a time when you had trouble learning and retaining academic information. Which of the "forgetting" causes addressed in this chapter help to explain your experience? What remedies could you now implement to avoid the same mistakes?

8. You are helping your friend, Sam, study for an exam in history. He tends to learn the material fairly well, but has a hard time retrieving the material for the exam. Having read this chapter, you now know that intention, effort, structure, multiple modalities, meaningful connections, and practice can help your friend. Convey to Sam specific examples as to how he could incorporate these methods to improve his retention on his next history exam.

The Last Word

Why is it that my strongest memories are those that I most want to forget?

—*Russ Hodges*

Preparing for Performance

Lights, Cameras, Action!

CHAPTER HIGHLIGHTS

- Defining Academic Performance

- Predicting Academic Performance

- Three Approaches to Academic Learning

- Simple Study Techniques

- Advanced Study Techniques

We have been learning all our lives, so in some ways it seems peculiar to become self-conscious about this process we have been doing for so long. However, academic learning is different from other kinds of learning. The intention of academic learning is that we demonstrate our understanding and use of new information through a stylized set of performances: quizzes, tests, papers, reports, projects, presentations. Our performances then receive an evaluation in the form of a grade by experts (teachers). The recently renewed practice of internships follows the same model, with the evaluation done by supervisors in the field. One premise behind this elaborate evaluative system is that if we demonstrate competent performance, then we have *learned* the material and we will be able to use it in the future—that is, in our professional, personal, and civic lives. The second premise is that in the process of learning and performing, we will learn how to think analytically and evaluatively.

Thus, academic learning is inextricably tied to a specific kind of performance. It is neither a casual nor happenstance process. The first task of students is to determine the specific academic expectations of a teacher: what is to be learned and how will that learning be demonstrated? The second task is to determine what we bring to this learning situation: what skills and content do we already possess? The third task is to determine how we need to acquire the information and how we should practice performing it. All these tasks require accurate and conscientious reflection.

Exercise 6.1

SELF-ASSESSMENT: Preparing to Perform Academically

Throughout your college career, you will be faced with many varied opportunities to demonstrate your understanding and use of new information. With 5 being "Almost Always" and 1 being "Almost Never," assess your ability to prepare effectively for tests, papers, projects, and so on. Rate each of the following statements honestly by circling the appropriate number. Completing this exercise will help you identify areas of concern you may have about your ability to prepare for academic performances.

	Almost Always		Sometimes		Almost Never
1. I match my learning strategies to the level of learning (taxonomy) required to perform well on tests, papers, projects, and presentations.	5	4	3	2	1
2. I predict and create sample test questions and answers to help me learn material.	5	4	3	2	1
3. I use mnemonics (memory tricks) when memorizing lists or concepts.	5	4	3	2	1
4. I create note cards to help me memorize, understand, and/or analyze material.	5	4	3	2	1
5. I create one- to two-page summary sheets over my lecture and/or textbook notes.	5	4	3	2	1
6. I use color (ink/highlighters/ note cards), pictures, maps, and/or diagrams to help me organize and analyze material.	5	4	3	2	1

7. I begin work on papers   5   4   3   2   1
   and reports early enough
   to edit my work before
   turning in final copy.

8. When I need help writing   5   4   3   2   1
   papers and reports, I know
   when and where campus
   writing assistance services
   are available.

9. I am comfortable working   5   4   3   2   1
   alone or in small groups
   on course projects.

10. I practice giving   5   4   3   2   1
    presentations (with visual
    aids if required) multiple
    times before making the
    final presentation.

Add up the numbers you circled. Your total score will be between 10 and 50. The higher your score, the more likely you will feel confident about your ability to perform academically. For scores below 30, write or reflect on the items for which you have concerns and consider talking with a trusted friend, a family member, a teacher, a counselor, or an advisor.

DEFINING ACADEMIC PERFORMANCE

We come to college for many reasons, but the primary focus is that we will learn—that is, get an education—and thus become a different person. Many of you will go on to complete programs and graduate. If you choose to achieve a baccalaureate degree, you should differ dramatically from the person you were when you entered college. As a graduate you should have

- a specific set of declarative knowledge (theories, principles, concepts, data) and procedural knowledge (skills) in your major and minor fields.

- an increased ability to learn independently.

- the ability to reason, problem solve, and think critically about a wide range of subjects.

- a recognition of the primary principles necessary to understand our culture, including history, government, philosophy, literature, science, and the arts.

- a system of personal ethics.

Colleges and universities use several methods to ascertain that you have these characteristics before graduation. The most common are required courses and exams.

Academic performance is *the demonstration of our understanding and use of new information through a stylized set of performances: quizzes, tests, papers, reports, projects, presentations.* Assessment can be done by an instructor, a peer, an outside expert, instructor evaluation of participation, objective tests, essay tests, projects, presentations, performances, creative works, papers, portfolios, field work, group process, student critiques, student reflections, reports, journals, and so on. Institutions are recognizing that collaborative projects and internships are also important to professional development. Most of these formal processes are graded, but many opportunities are never directly graded, such as leadership or participation in student organizations, volunteer service, attendance at campus lectures, and performances.

A few campuses are now using portfolios, an intensive method of monitoring each student's progress toward graduation. Portfolios are collections of student work. Students and their instructors choose papers, projects, and tests that represent the best academic work of a year. Some schools ask students to add to their portfolio each year. Even if your school does not require portfolios, you may wish to create one just for yourself, especially for work you complete in your major and minor fields.

Grades

Grades are the primary means of ascertaining whether you have met (grades A, B, C) or have not met (grades D, F) the criteria for graduation. College grading is much different from high school; instructors have a great deal of autonomy. Whether it is an essay test or an English theme or a group project, experienced teachers know quickly what grade is deserved. Even multiple-choice tests are designed to reflect particular levels of mastery. A major responsibility of faculty is to determine what the appropriate standards for each field are. What follows are descriptions of commonly held standards for college grades. Read these carefully, because they are the criteria most of your instructors use each time they grade your work.

A-level work standards. Consistent mastery of the subject matter, including key concepts and vocabulary, and frequent, insightful questions about the material; commitment to careful and accurate critical thinking using appropriate premises and language from the subject field.

B-level work standards. Competent mastery of the subject matter, including key concepts and vocabulary, but little insight; reasoning ability is competent, but rarely creative.

C-level work standards. Inconsistent competency with the subject matter and unclear reasoning; some knowledge and use of basic concepts and principles.

D-level work standards. Poor understanding of basic concepts and vocabulary using primarily rote memory, unclear and illogical reasoning.

F-level work standards. Little or inaccurate comprehension of the basic concepts of the subject; incompetent reasoning and poor intellectual performance (Paul & Elder, 2001, pp. 173–175).

We realize that some instructors and some institutions have lower standards than the ones that we have articulated. However, we believe that these standards are a fair representation of American higher education.

Exercise 6.2

Grading Yourself and Your Teachers

This exercise will help you compare the criteria for earning good grades as a student with the criteria of being a good teacher.

1. Using the grade-level work standards just discussed, determine a grade level for yourself in **each** of the courses you are taking. Explain your choices.

2. Can these same work standards be used to grade your *teachers?* Why or why not?

3. What are the attributes of an A teacher? How do these differ from a B or C teacher? Do any of your teachers deserve the grade of D or F? Explain.

PREDICTING ACADEMIC PERFORMANCE

How can we perform competently, or even brilliantly, if we do not know the criteria? The answer is that we cannot; yet many students enter the learning and studying process without serious and accurate prediction of what they need to understand and how they must perform that understanding. Prediction is an interesting business because we are rarely 100 percent accurate in any area, and academics is no different. As we stated at the beginning of this book, the course syllabus is the first opportunity that the instructor has to state intentions and expectations. Syllabi contain the structural requirements of a course: what type of performances and the relative importance of each. Equally important are the qualitative criteria (the standards) that the instructor will use in evaluating each performance, but these are rarely stated overtly in the syllabus. If our expectations of how we will be evaluated are accurate, then our learning and study can be focused and efficient. How can we discern what our instructors' value? In the following sections, we discuss some things you can do and questions you should ask yourself each time you receive an assignment for a test, project, paper, or speech.

What Is the Content?

The question *What is the content?* encourages you to look at the scope of the material to be covered on the test. The syllabus is the first place to look, because often teachers will carefully explain the content covered in each assignment.

For a test. Make a list of all the major topics covered in the syllabus and the lectures. Are there additional topics in assigned readings? Has your instructor grouped or organized them? Has your instructor prepared a study sheet as a handout or on the Internet? Can you organize them logically? Which are the most important? The least important? Make a set of note cards or a list of all the technical terms and definitions.

For a project. What is the tangible outcome or product (e.g., written paper, oral presentation, multimedia, artwork, computer application, performance)? What is the purpose or question that the project should address? What are the limits imposed by the assignment? If the assignment is written as a handout or on the Internet, read it carefully and mark all the key words.

For a paper or speech. What is the thesis? Is it the appropriate scope (narrow/broad) for the length of the paper or speech? What source materials are needed? If the assignment is written as a handout or on the Internet, read it carefully and mark all the key words.

What Is the Level of Learning Needed?

One of the most powerful learning strategies is to study a subject at the level of learning you will be asked to perform. If you can accurately predict the level of a test, project, paper, or speech, then you can design your study so that you practice performing at that level. For example, if the content of a literature test involves comparing/contrasting two novels, then you can organize your study accordingly and practice writing short paragraphs comparing and contrasting the plots, characters, settings, significance, and so forth. The box at right is a reminder of the revised Bloom's Taxonomy, or the level of learning, discussed in Chapter 2.

> **The Revised Bloom's Taxonomy of Educational Objectives**
>
> Create
> Evaluate
> Analyze
> Apply
> Understand
> Remember

For a test. Keep in mind that objective questions start at the remembering level but generally range through understanding to application; short-answer questions start at the remembering level but usually require understanding; procedural classes such as economics and accounting require the application level for most questions; and essay questions tend to require the higher levels of the taxonomy—analysis, evaluation, and creation. Will sample test questions be available on the instructor's website, in textbook study guides, at review sessions, or in campus libraries? Some instructors are direct about the level of performance they expect; others use more subtle hints in offhand comments, such as *You need to be able to show me you understand these concepts* or *You'll have to give concrete examples of these principles.*

For a project. The level of learning is crucial. Should your project simply demonstrate that you understand a concept or should it demonstrate that you can apply it, analyze it, evaluate it, or create something new? Consider talking with your instructor individually to determine whether you clearly understand the level required. If the project is to be done by a group, make sure the entire group has agreed on the level to be demonstrated.

For a paper or speech. Remember that you will be functioning at the creation level. Assuming you will use analysis and evaluation to produce your work, how will you use your sources to produce an original work?

Prediction is a collegiate skill that develops slowly. The more careful you are in paying attention to these issues and then deliberately designing your learning and study strategies according to your predictions, the more successful you are likely to be. For example, if you are preparing for an essay test in introductory philosophy, and the instructor tells you that 25 percent of the test will be definitions and 75 percent will be three essay questions, you know that you need to master the content at the analytical level. So you might predict some questions and try to answer them or form a study group that discusses and debates the major points covered in the lectures.

Exercise 6.3

Predicting Exam Questions

Predicting and creating sample test questions are valuable methods to assist your learning. Select a declarative knowledge–based course for which you are currently studying for an upcoming exam and answer the following questions. Completing this exercise will assist you in using prediction to prepare for an exam.

- Will you be tested by multiple-choice, true/false, matching, fill-in-the-blank, short answer, essay, or a combination of several of these testing modes?

- What do you predict will be the highest level of learning that you will be expected to master?

- What are 5 to 10 sample questions at the appropriate learning level that reflect the predicted testing mode?

THREE APPROACHES TO ACADEMIC LEARNING

The premise of academic performance is that we will demonstrate our understanding of the information we have learned. Teachers and students often fail to communicate accurately on this point. Students sometimes determine that the only performance level needed is simple memorization, a recitation of data without any broader understanding. This level of learning, *remembering* from the taxonomy, is the ability to recognize or recall an idea, a fact, or an occurrence in a form similar to the original presentation. Although important as an initial step in academic learning, simple memorization is extremely limited.

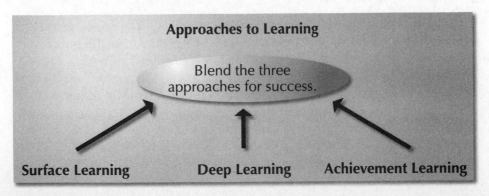

Surface Learning

When we approach learning from the viewpoint that we simply have to answer so many questions to pass the test to meet the requirement and thus stay out of trouble, "learning then becomes a balancing act between avoiding failure and not working too hard" (Entwistle, 1990, p. 685). **Surface learning** describes an approach to academic learning in which *students are motivated by extrinsic or outside rewards, not their own desire to learn about the subject.* Students who engage in surface learning

- believe that the material being studied is boring, useless, or irrelevant.
- see assignments as demands rather than opportunities.
- focus on the literal aspects of the information rather than its meaning or significance.
- rely on rote memorization to prepare for performance.
- avoid making personal connections to the material or its implications.
- worry about failure.
- resent the time necessary for studying (adapted from Entwistle, 1990).

Both cynicism and anxiety foster surface learning (Entwistle, 1990) because both tend to push us toward using only memorization instead of learning the material at the other levels of the taxonomy—understanding, application, analysis, evaluation, and creation. Time pressures and our thoughts about assessment measures can increase our anxiety and lead us away from meaningful learning.

Deep Learning

Deep learning is dramatically different from surface learning in that *students are motivated to learn deeply to satisfy their own curiosity.* Students who engage in deep learning

- believe the material being studied is interesting and potentially useful.
- see assignments as opportunities.
- focus on the underlying meaning of the material.
- relate their understanding to their prior knowledge by reading and discussion.
- think about the information and create hypotheses about how it relates to other topics and subjects.
- find learning emotionally satisfying (adapted from Entwistle, 1990).

Sometimes students who want to learn deeply respond well to the collegiate atmosphere, and other times they become cynical and depressed if they feel no one, including teachers, shares their values. To be successful in school, they have to learn to meet practical deadlines and occasionally settle for less than the perfect outcomes they desire. The most important choice for such students is the choice of department and instructors. A major advisor who shares their philosophy is also helpful.

Achievement Learning

A third type of learning seems to be occurring more frequently in recent decades. **Achievement learning** occurs when *students are motivated by the ego enhancement that comes as a result of high grades and academic awards.* Students who engage in achievement learning

- see high grades as important.
- are competitive in academic settings.
- meet formal academic requirements carefully, such as time, length, and topic.
- use time strategically.
- value their self-discipline and systematic learning habits.
- concentrate on learning the material that the teacher views as important and avoid other material that might not help their grade.
- like highly structured courses and need little interaction with teachers.
- enjoy the external attention of success and the internal feelings of self-accomplishment (Entwistle, 1990, p. 686).

Students who view learning as a vehicle for achievement often choose this road early in life, even in primary school. They pragmatically use both surface and deep learning to meet their ego needs.

These three extreme models of learning highlight a major dilemma in American higher education. Many collegiate faculty passionately believe in the deep-learning approach; it is the way they prefer to learn and it is usually the way they study within their own field. They often want their students to learn in the same way. Deep learning is an idealistic model, and it works for a few people all of the time and for many of us some of the time. Learning that way can be exhilarating; it is the flow experience that we talked about earlier. However, we may be so entranced by the intellectual journey that we do not pay attention to the specifics we are required to meet.

Deep learning in every course does not seem to be a practical choice for many students, especially those who struggle with balancing work schedules, organizational commitments, or family responsibilities. The shortcomings of surface learning are only too obvious. Although we may pass a quiz based on surface learning, we have little or no permanent learning. Essentially, we walk away from the learning experience with nothing but a grade. Achievement learning does give us permanent and usable knowledge, but it allows little room for creative intellectual exploration and for experiencing the intrinsic joy of learning. The choices we make in the type of learning we do in college matter. College is a serious and expensive business. How can we blend all three types of learning to create the right path for each of us?

CASE STUDY

SUSAN is an energetic woman in her thirties who is married with two elementary school age children. She reentered community college this year to complete a degree in environmental studies and is taking three courses: Physical Geography, College Mathematics, and Political Science/Government. Susan is highly motivated to do well in school because she wants to pursue a graduate degree, and her early years in college yielded mediocre grades. Her family encourages her, but her husband has to work overtime frequently, and one of her children is struggling in school. Occasionally, her mother comes over to help out with the children, but that usually happens only once a week. Susan is a competent student, but she has to work hard for her grades. She feels she is continually juggling demands from many different sources. She is motivated to make good grades, not only for her own need to achieve but also because her family is sacrificing for her to return to school. Her target GPA for this term is a B average (3.0). As an older student, she believes this is her chance to prepare for a professional career.

We asked Susan to reflect on her course load this term and determine what mode of learning would best suit each course. Here is a summary of her reflections:

Physical Geography

This course is important to my major; they call it a foundational course, and my advisor told me that I need to master this material because it will be used in numerous junior- and senior-level courses. The material is complex and technical, with long vocabulary lists. I know I will have to do a lot of memorization just to learn the terminology, but I will also have to understand how to use all those terms and concepts. My learning mode in this course must be deep to make a solid B in this course.

College Mathematics

As long as I work consistently in math, I can be competent on the tests. This course is required for my major, and it is important because some of my advanced courses and the graduate courses I plan to take require that level of mathematical skill. I'll never be a mathematician and I don't get really excited by math, but I can do this work. My learning mode in this course will be achievement, and I will strive to make a B.

Political Science/Government

Well, this course is required for everyone. Most of the students will be freshmen and sophomores. I've heard it's a large lecture course with mostly multiple-choice tests. I haven't been that interested in government or history or courses like that, but maybe some of the information on elections will be okay. Frankly, I'll do what I have to do, but my learning mode will be surface, unless I get interested in some topic. I'll try for a B but will take a C if I have to. If I have extra study time, I won't put it into this course.

Case Study Questions: What approaches to academic learning (surface, deep, achievement) has Susan determined would best suit each course? How might these different approaches affect her attitude, the amount of time she allocates, and the study strategies she chooses to use in each course?

Exercise 6.4

Your Approach to Learning

How often do you use surface, deep, and achievement learning? Just as Susan reflected on her courses, reflect on your courses this term and determine what mode of learning you are using for each and why. This exercise will help you evaluate appropriate learning modes for your courses.

SIMPLE STUDY TECHNIQUES

As you look at all the examples, we recommend that you experiment with the different formats for material you are currently studying. The examples move from the simple to the complex, from the lowest level of learning, *remembering,* to the upper level, *analysis.*

How can I remember all of these dates for history?

Write all of them down in chronological order and create a time line. Label each event and star the three most important. Start by practicing those three in order several times, and then begin to add the in-between dates. If you're really creative, make up a story about the most important dates. Sometimes dates already are associated with something familiar, such as an address, phone number, the grade you were in and the corresponding year, a movie title.

How can I learn foreign language vocabulary?

Practice . . . practice . . . practice. Simple note cards are your best investment. You can make them or buy boxes of them. The word is on one side and the meaning on the other. Start by looking at the meaning and recalling the word before you look at it. Then flip the cards and look at the word and try to recall the meaning. Use the word in a sentence. Scramble the order of the cards regularly (you do not want to remember them in sequence).

Practice retrieval often but in short pieces of time. This timing is called spaced practice and works well for permanent retrieval. Even though you may forget some of the words between practices, over time your retrieval will become reliable and automatic, necessary to move forward in foreign language study.

Should I use the same techniques for scientific/technical vocabulary as for foreign language vocabulary?

Not necessarily. When you first begin to study a discipline, the vocabulary seems foreign, and simple note cards sometimes help. Often you'll be expected to label the various parts of a diagram, chart, or picture. When you predict that sort of test question, it is important to practice the information in the same way in which you will be tested. So much of scientific/technical vocabulary requires sequential or associative memory performance that mnemonic devices (memory tricks) are helpful.

I've heard mnemonics are useful. What are they and how do I use them?

__Mnemonics__ are "memory 'tricks' . . . devices that facilitate the learning and recall of many . . . forms of difficult material" (Ormrod, 1999, p. 298). We use jingles, rhymes, acronyms (combine first letters to make a word), and acrostics (use first letters to represent words that, when combined, have meaning). Here are a few examples:

<u>C</u>ows <u>O</u>ften <u>S</u>it <u>D</u>own <u>C</u>arefully; <u>P</u>erhaps <u>T</u>heir <u>J</u>oints <u>C</u>reak? <u>P</u>ersistent <u>E</u>arly <u>O</u>iling <u>M</u>ight <u>P</u>revent <u>P</u>ermanent <u>R</u>heumatism—the first letter of each word is the first letter of the geological time periods in chronological order: Cambrian, Ordovician, Silurian . . . Triassic, Jurassic . . .

Making Mnemonics More Powerful and Accurate

- **Thoroughly learn and practice mnemonic devices in order to be effective.** If you remember a mnemonic device incorrectly, then chaos happens, and you will not be able to perform the information accurately.

- **Practice linking the mnemonic device to the information you are trying to retrieve.** This is crucial; remembering the device without remembering what it represents is useless.

- **Whenever possible, make meaningful connections.** The more information is linked and practiced by meaning, the more likely the information will be stored in neural networks based on meaning, and that type of memory is more permanent.

- **Practice items in sequence if the sequence is necessary for accurate content; scramble items for practice if there is no logical sequence.**

- **Use exaggerated visuals (size, color, humor, action) to strengthen the retrieval process.**

- **The mnemonics that we create are usually more powerful than those we get from other sources.** However, we found thousands of websites devoted to academic mnemonics, especially in the scientific/medical/health professions fields. In these fields, the need for mnemonic devices is so large that using other sources is time efficient. Here are just a few of our favorites:

www.medicalmnemonics.com

www.eudesign.com/mnems/_mnframe.htm

www.mnemonic-device.eu/mnemonics/

<u>C</u>an <u>I</u>ntelligent <u>K</u>aren <u>S</u>olve <u>S</u>ome <u>F</u>oreign <u>M</u>afia <u>O</u>perations?—the Krebs cycle in order: Citric acid, Isocitric, Ketoglutaric . . .

You can use mnemonic devices for any academic subject. Here are a few more examples:

FOIL—ordered steps for multiplying a binomial (First, Outer, Inner, Last)

HOMES—the Great Lakes (Huron, Ontario, Michigan, Erie, Superior)

i before e except after c . . . (spelling rule)

<u>N</u>ick <u>P</u>refers <u>L</u>ettuce <u>Y</u>ellow <u>T</u>omatoes <u>S</u>ardines and <u>H</u>am on <u>W</u>ednesday—the royal houses of England in order (Norman, Plantagenet, Lancaster, York, Tudor, Stuart, Hanover, and Windsor)

How can I remember . . .

Formulas or theorems?

Steps in a procedure, in economics and accounting courses?

The characteristics of a concept with the name of the concept?

Identifications and label them accurately?

College requires memorizing a lot of stuff that seems like busywork, but all those details are important and are going to show up on a test sometime—you can count on that. Our advice is to make a game out of it, preferably a portable game with note cards so you can carry them with you and practice at those in-between times.

We have already talked about using note cards for foreign language and some scientific/technical vocabulary. However, note cards are much more diverse. The next section includes examples of myriad other uses, and we are confident that you will discover many more. Remember that cards are also available in sizes other than three by five inches, and those bigger sizes can accommodate larger and more complex chunks of information.

Multiple Ways to Use Note Cards

Creating more complex note cards takes time, and students are frequently resistant to spending the time because they have not experienced the benefit of more sophisticated memory systems. However, memory theory explains that if we take the time to create the cards, we are selecting and storing the information in neural networks through multiple modalities (seeing, saying, writing), so the storage is much more powerful than simply looking at an item in the text or in notes. When we make such a strong connection through storage, then retrieval becomes much easier. Cornell notes and T-notes also are powerful retrieval practice systems, and one of the more difficult tasks for students is choosing what information to practice through their notes and what information to lift out and put on note cards.

The note card examples in Figure 6.1 are arranged from simple to complex, using the first four levels of learning. Your ability to accurately predict not only the content, but also the level of learning that you will be expected to perform, dictates the complexity and sophistication of the cards you produce. You can

FIGURE 6.1 Examples of Note Cards Ranging from Simple to Complex

Remember: Identification note card

Person, event, circumstance

Nelson R. Mandela

Data and their importance

Born: July 18, 1918; near Umtata
Aspired to become a lawyer
Joined African Nat'l Congress 1942
Formed ANC youth league 1944
Apartheid created 1948 when Nat'l Party
    won elections
ANC campaign—Defiance of Unjust Laws 1952
Nat'l Party outlawed ANC 1960
Sentenced to life in prison 1961
Freed from prison Feb. 11, 1990
Won Nobel Peace Prize 1993
Elected president of S. Africa on April 27, 1994

(Continued)

FIGURE 6.1 Examples of Note Cards (*Continued*)

Remember: Simple diagram note card

Name of diagram

Labeled diagram

Arthropod body plan

Segmented body plan,
exoskeleton jointed appendages

Remember: Formula note card

Name of formula/theorem

Formula and definition

Pythagorean theorem

$a^2 + b^2 = c^2$
The sum of the squares of the
sides (legs) of a right triangle
is equal to the square of the
hypotenuse.

Understand: Concept note card

Concept

Parts, components

Utilitarianism

- Theory of ethics—idea that the ultimate goal
  of any moral action is the achievement of
  the greatest good for the greatest number
- Should be the aim of all legislation
- Opposed to idea that one person's
  conscience determines good/evil since
  good/evil aren't determined by an individual
  alone
- Outlined by Wm. Paley <u>in Principles of moral
  and political philosophy</u> (1785) & by Jeremy
  Bentham in <u>Introduction to the principles of
  morals and legislation</u> (1789)

FIGURE 6.1 Examples of Note Cards (*Continued*)

**Understand: Example note card
(declarative knowledge)**

Data

Definition and example

Proportional
representation

Electoral system meant to produce a
legislative body where # of seats a party
holds is proportional to # of votes received
in most recent election
• 1st used in Denmark in 1855
• Used in early/mid 20th century in several
US cities (NY & Cincinnati) that hoped to
prevent machine politics & ensure minority
representation
• Now used in many European democracies

**Understand: Example note card
(procedural knowledge)**

Procedure

Steps of the procedure

Do Loop
(Process for advancing
numerical value)

1. Do While (condition is true)
2. (process statements)
3. Loop
Note: Avoid infinite loops
      Remember indents
- - - - - - - - - - - - - - - - - - -
Ex: Prints #'s 0–9
    Dim n as integer
    n = 0
    Do while n < 10
        picBox. Print n
        n = n + 1
    Loop

Application: Practicing problem note card

Problem

Solution

Completing the Square
Problem:
$x^2 + 4x + 3 = 0$

1. Subtract 3 from both sides.
   $x^2 + 4x = -3$
2. Divide the coefficient of x by 2
   and square, then add to both sides.
   $x^2 + 4x + \left(\frac{4}{2}\right)^2 = -3 + \left(\frac{4}{2}\right)^2$
3. Factor
   $(x + 2)^2 = 1$ A perfect square

(Continued)

FIGURE 6.1   Examples of Note Cards (*Continued*)

Analyze: Predict essay test question note card

Hypothesized essay question	Main points
What ways do American literature consist of a dialog between Puritanism and Transcendentalism?	1. The way they see the relationship between the individual and the community 2. How they relate to nature 3. The role and definition of religion in each school 4. The concept of America in each school 5. The difference between each school's concept of Fate

Analyze: Simple comparison/contrast note card

Name   2 x 2 or 2 x 3 matrix

The Ear

Anatomical divisions and functions

Anatomical division	Function
Outer ear (auricle & EAM)	Protection resonance transmission
Middle ear (drum & ossicles)	Impedance matching
Inner ear (vestibular system & cochlea)	Transduction of mechanical & hydrodynamic energy into neural impulses

choose to use color coding—that is, use a different color card or ink for different topics, and the like. Again, creating your own cards infuses this retrieval process with power.

ADVANCED STUDY TECHNIQUES

The simple techniques that we have suggested will help you learn concepts, formulas, steps in procedures, diagrams, and so forth, but successful performance on college tests usually requires more advanced techniques than you had to use in high school for several reasons. First, there is much more material, and teachers cover only part of it in class. Second, tests are less frequent, sometimes only twice a term. The first test usually occurs a month or later into the semester. Third, although some instructors give summary or study sheets, most do not. The combined effect of these differences results in placing the burden of study on students.

One advantage of using advanced techniques to organize and elaborate your own study material is that you are forced to select and process the information more deeply, thereby increasing the likelihood that you will understand and store the material by meaning. A second advantage is that the time you spend on these study techniques increases the likelihood that you will learn them deeply. A disadvantage is that organizing and elaborating take time and cannot be done at the last moment.

What follows are myriad examples of complex and powerful study strategies. Look carefully at the examples and determine which types could help you learn in your current courses.

Summarization Techniques

Lecture notes. If your instructor gives a review sheet, use it. If not, create a summary sheet of the major concepts and simultaneously create note cards and mnemonic devices for remembering important data. Do not include items you already know and retrieve well.

Text readings. Read the chapter summaries, then go through and look at your text markings. List the major concepts and data that you need to remember for the test, and create note cards for important data that you need to practice to be able to remember. Again, exclude items you already know and retrieve well. Read the chapter summary again.

Last-ditch effort summary. Create a one- to two-page summary or review sheet (or up to four, five-by-seven-inch cards) of the major concepts, theorems, formulas, and so on from all your sources. These are the items (words and structures) that you have now memorized as your retrieval clues for the content to be covered on the test. Practice retrieving the test content by looking at each item and explaining or describing it. Practice the last thing before going to sleep, the first thing the morning of the test, and again just before the test.

Visual or Graphic Organizers

Linear arrays. When information to be learned has an internal linear structure, either as steps in a procedure or as occurrences in time, using that structure as

FIGURE 6.2   Example of a Horizontal Array

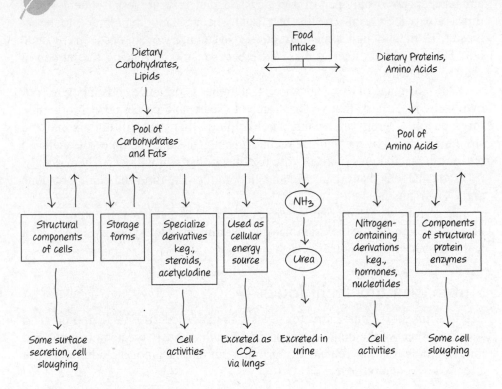

the retrieval device is especially powerful. Use either a horizontal or vertical line and mark the major parts of the process or the historical events (see Figures 6.2 and 6.3). Then add in as much detail as necessary, using different colors or shapes if that is helpful. A time line is a simple linear array, but time lines can be expanded to incorporate much more data if you wish. The linear structure is a helpful memory tool.

A more complicated linear array is a hierarchy or *tree structure*, a visual way of organizing or grouping information around class inclusion rules—that is, when items are a part of one group (Halpern, 1997) (see Figures 6.4 and 6.5). Biology, geology, and other fields contain much information that is best represented by hierarchies. Drawing the hierarchy and labeling it is an effective memory storage/retrieval practice. Using color or size to designate certain levels of the hierarchy helps you to remember the structure.

Yet another type of linear array is a flow chart, "a diagram showing the progress of work through a sequence of operations" (Guralnik, 1986, p. 537)

FIGURE 6.3   Example of a Vertical Array

American Revolution Time Line

1761 — Writs of Assistants
1763 — Navigation Acts
1764 — Sugar Act
1765 — Stamp Act
1765 — Quartering Act
1765 — Stamp Act Congress
1766 — Declaratory Act
1767 — Townsend Acts
1767 — Quartering Act
1770 — Boston Massacre
1772 — Gaspie Incident
1773 — Boston Tea Party
1774 — Intolerable Acts
1775 — Battle of Lexington & Concord
1775 — Battle of Bunker Hill
1776 — Ratification of Declaration of Independence
1776 — Battle of Trinton
1776 — Battle of Prinston
1777 — Battle of Saratoga
1780 — Battle of Yorktown
1783 — Treaty of Paris

(see Figure 6.6). It is usually shown as a series of steps or events in graphic shapes such as rectangles and triangles. This type of graphic organizer is useful for math, accounting, economics, computer science, and so forth. It is also useful to design the process necessary for completing a project or paper.

Matrices.   Often instructors expect students to demonstrate that they understand the differences and the similarities among complex sets of information. This level of performance is analysis, and a primary metacognitive strategy to master material at this level is the comparison/contrast matrix, a larger version of the note card

FIGURE 6.4 Example of a Hierarchy

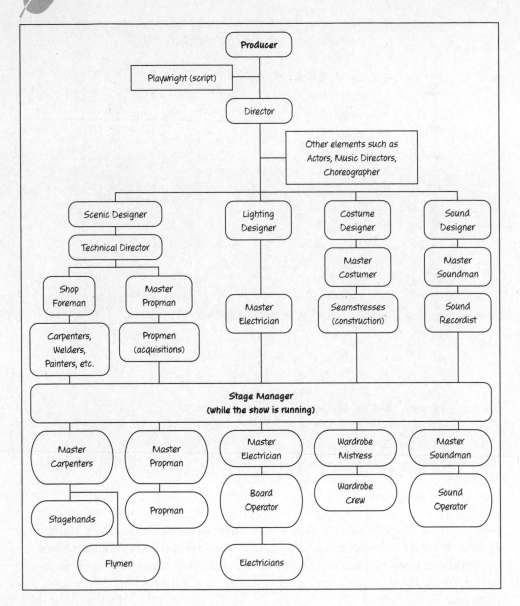

FIGURE 6.5   Example of a Tree Structure

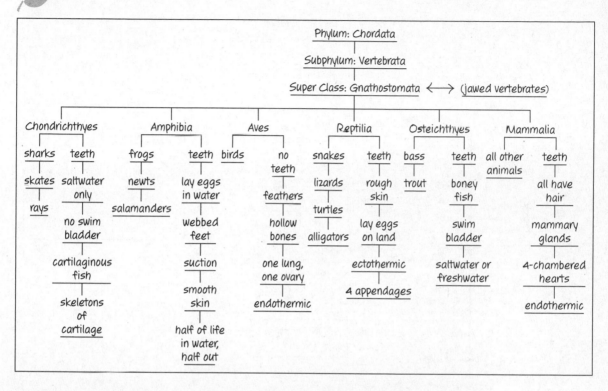

matrix introduced earlier in this chapter (see Figures 6.7 and 6.8). This type of matrix is a grid with several related topics along one side. The purpose of the matrix is to compare those topics across several dimensions (represented along the other side). Filling in the cells allows students to condense large amounts of information into one organizer. Empty cells indicate either that there is missing material that needs to be researched and added or that a relationship does not actually exist, in which case the cells remain blank. Creating a matrix is a powerful storage tool, and afterward it can be used for study practice. Again, color or exaggerated size helps emphasize certain points. A useful method of studying by a matrix is to ask questions (turn the dimensions into questions) and answer them.

Mapping.   Maps are visual attempts to represent the relationships among various concepts and data. They can be simple drawings created in a few minutes (e.g., types of geographical regions) or extraordinarily elaborate designs that take hours to create (e.g., drawing the relationships of the content of five medical chapters) (Hyerle, 2000). Effective maps often utilize color, drawings, size, and shapes that aid retrieval. Two frequently used types of maps are concept maps (or clusters) and networks.

FIGURE 6.6 Example of a Flow Chart

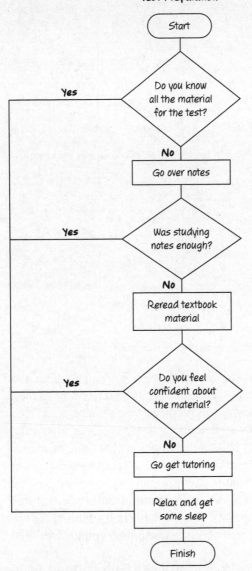

Test Preparation

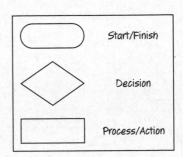

FIGURE 6.7   Example of a Matrix Comparing/Contrasting Authors

Authors	Major Themes of Work(s)	Influences on Works	Poem(s)/Story	Main Idea of Poem(s)/Story	Critics' Comments (of their time)
Sylvia Plath	• Horror • Death	• Father died of cancer when she was 10 • Pushed by mother to do well	1. "Daddy" 2. "Lady Lazarus"	1. Father died of cancer, guilt 2. Celebrating suicide attempts—ref. in both to Holocaust	Poems were "the longest suicide notes ever written"
Walt Whitman	• Sexuality • Ecstatic perception of man and nature	• Natural talent for journalism • Emerson, friend	1. "When I Heard the Learn'd Astronomer" 2. "The Dalliance of the Eagles"	1. Rejection of astronomer's perception of nature 2. Power of sexual drive, celebration of life force	"poetry of barbarism," "mixture of Yankee transcendentalism and NY rowdyism"
Emily Dickinson	• Calvinism = to look inwardly • Coldness of the world • Love, death, nature, immortality, beauty	• Emotional crisis brought on by lost love of a married man • Shakespeare, Keats, the Brownings	1. "I Heard a Fly Buzz—When I Died—" 2. "Because I Could Not Stop for Death—"	1. Disbelief in afterlife/immortality 2. Belief in immortality, death-gracious gentleman caller	"farrago of illiterate and uneducated sentiment"
Nathaniel Hawthorne	• Concern with American past • Human isolation and seclusion	• Life in Salem, Puritanism	"Young Goodman Brown"	Evil is the nature of every human being (abstract meaning)	Wrote with "all the fascination of a genius and all the charm of a highly polished style"
Edgar Allan Poe	• World of perversity, disorder • Fascinated by the bizarre	• Depression • Psychologically crippling childhood • Unsuccessful suicide	"Cask of Amontillado"	Conditions of revenge, death bed confession, obsessed with murder that he got away with	"demonic" "egotistic villain with scarcely any virtue"
Herman Melville	• Confrontation of innocence and evil • World filled with lost innocence and betrayed hope	• Sea life • Adventures while traveling	"Bartleby, the Scrivener"	Bartleby is a greater person than the narrator, who thinks otherwise	A man who could "neither believe nor be comfortable in his disbelief"

Concept maps allow you to group related information into two- or three-level drawings. You can use the bubble format or the spider format. Again, the use of color, size, and exaggeration helps make the map more memorable (see Figures 6.9 and 6.10).

Networks are the most complex and the most powerful types of maps. They require the most time to produce and should only be used when the content is especially complex and the expected performance level is analysis or above. Networks build on concept maps but have an extra step. All the links between the items are labeled: part, example, leads to, type, definition analogy, characteristic, evidence (Halpern, 2000) (see Figure 6.11). Because you have

FIGURE 6.8   Example of a Matrix Comparing/Contrasting Types of Music

	Medieval	Renaissance	Baroque	Classic	Romantic
Melody	Conjunct, stepwise, & smooth	Smooth, parts are melodic	Hymn tunes, overlapping	Refined, courtly short phrases	Folk–nature, patriotic
Harmony		Nonfunctional	Functional, tonic-dominant	Predictable, short phrases	Rich, thick, dramatic
Rhythm	Subtle, no downbeats or strong beats	Subtle	Bar lines & downbeats	Clear and concise, shows form	Folk–dance, irregular
Timbre	Single vocal line	Multiple vocal or instrumental lines	Orchestra, organ, and harpsichord	Vocal	Exotic colors, extremes, orchestra
Mood	Church chant	Meditative	Stately, courtly	Elegant, floppish	Emotionalism, dramatic, violent
Texture	(single voice) Monophony	Polyphony	Clear, refined	Extremes	Clear and unusual, dodecaphony
Composers	Associated with Pope Gregory	Palestrina, Des Pres	Bach, Handel	Mozart, Haydn	Chopin, Verdi, & Wagner

to determine the purpose of each link (and sometimes create labels to identify relationships), you must understand the deep structure of the content. Such deep processing creates powerful storage and retrieval of the information.

CASE STUDY

SUSAN, the woman we introduced earlier in this chapter, returned after the first round of exams to discuss her results. Her college mathematics grade of 79 was *"okay, not great, but okay."* Now that she knows what to expect, she's convinced she can do better. On the Political Science/Government exam, Susan stated, *"I predicted well, and I'm really glad I listened to the teaching assistant. That test was mostly at the remembering level, and I made an 84."* Her Physical

FIGURE 6.9   Example of a Concept Map Using the Bubble Format

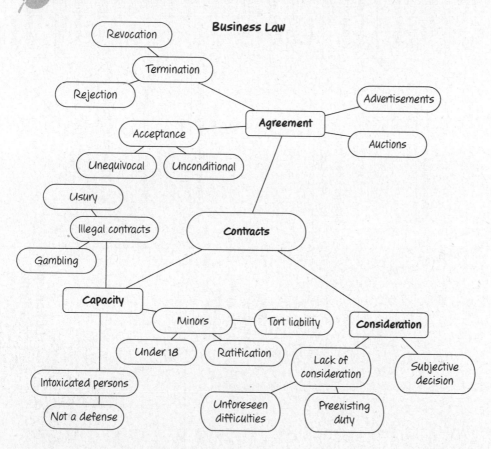

Geography grade, however, was a different story. This is how she described the situation: *"I am really scared about this course. I knew the material would be complex and technical, but I had no idea it would be so tough. I tried to find a study group, but without success, given my tight schedule. Even though I am reading the text before going to class and making note cards, I think I understand less than half of what I am reading. The lecture helps somewhat, but my teacher speaks very rapidly and will not allow questions. I made a 57 on the first test; I've never made a grade that low. This is already the fifth week in the term, and there* is no improvement!"

Case Study Question: In your opinion, are the learning modes (i.e., surface, deep, achievement) that Susan chose for each course still appropriate now that she has received her first exam grades? Why or why not?

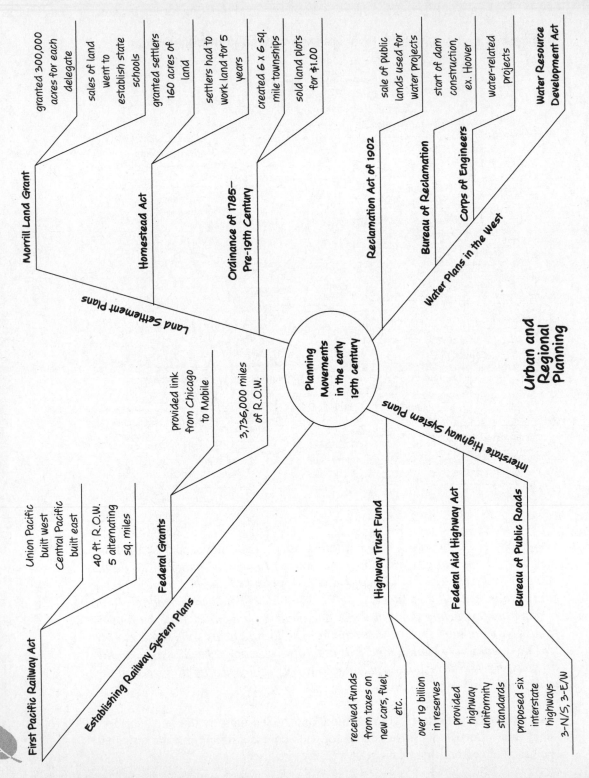

FIGURE 6.10 Example of a Concept Map Using the Spider Format

160

FIGURE 6.11　Example of a Process Network Detailing Meiosis

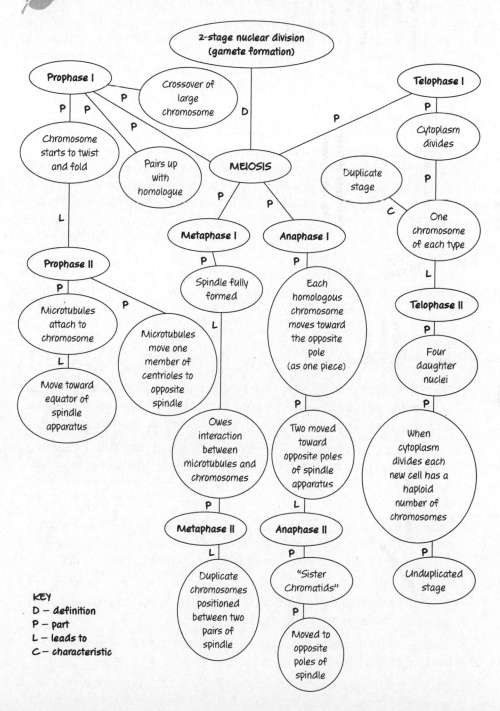

KEY
D – definition
P – part
L – leads to
C – characteristic

Case Study Question: What specific learning and memory strategies would you recommend Susan implement to earn Bs on her future college mathematics exams as well as her Political Science/Government exams? What specific immediate and long-term actions would you recommend Susan take to rescue her grade in Physical Geography? Keep in mind her goal is to earn a solid B in this course.

CONCLUSION

All your academic performances are merely rehearsals for your professional life. Tests and papers and projects matter, and the grades matter, but the ultimate purpose is to help you attain the thinking and performance skills expected of a college graduate. The material in this chapter, and the entire book, is intended for your use throughout your collegiate career. You will not use all these techniques in any one semester, but you might need them all before you complete college.

We believe that we learn best, and perform best, when we evaluate our own performance in relation to our goals and our values. The cycle is continuous, throughout school and life.

SUMMARY

- The intention of academic learning is for students to demonstrate their understanding and use of new information through a stylized set of performances such as quizzes, tests, papers, reports, projects, and presentations.

- Students need to determine the specific academic expectations of the instructor, what prior knowledge and skills they bring to the learning situation, and how they need to acquire the information and practice performing it.

- Outcomes of participation in college are knowledge in major and minor fields of study; the ability to learn independently, reason, problem solve, and think critically; a greater understanding of culture; and a system of personal ethics.

- A major responsibility of faculty members is to determine what the appropriate standards are for content fields.

- Commonly held standards for college grades generally differ from those held for high school grades.

- Predicting academic performance is based on appropriate responses to a set of questions that ask: What is the content? What is the level of learning needed?

- There are three different approaches to academic learning: surface learning, deep learning, and achievement learning.

- Simple techniques to aid memory include time lines, stories, note cards, and mnemonics.

- Mnemonics are memory tricks that facilitate learning and recall and include jingles, rhymes, acronyms, and acrostics.

- Mnemonics are more effective if they are thoroughly learned and practiced, solidly linked to the information to be retrieved, meaningfully connected, practiced in sequence, exaggerated visuals, and individually created.

- Note cards can be created for identification, diagrams, formulas, concepts, examples, possible essay questions, comparison and contrast, and practice problems.

- More advanced techniques for learning include creating summary sheets for lecture notes and text readings and creating visual or graphic organizers such as linear arrays, matrices, and maps.

KEY CONCEPTS

Academic performance

Achievement learning

Bloom's Taxonomy, Revised

Creating a story

Deep learning

Grades

Mnemonics (jingles, rhymes, acronyms, acrostics)

Note cards (formula, example, concept, test questions, identification, simple diagram, compare/contrast)

Predicting academic performance

Summarization techniques (lecture notes, text readings, last-ditch effort summary)

Surface learning

Time lines

Visual or graphic organizers (linear arrays, matrices, mapping)

GUIDED JOURNAL QUESTIONS

1. What does it take to make an A in a college course compared to making an A in a high school course? Which of your courses will be the most difficult to make at least a B in this term? Explain.

2. Describe an incident when you received a lower grade than you expected or felt you deserved (in high school or college). Did you talk to the instructor about the grade? What did you learn from the experience?

3. How fairly do exams evaluate your academic performance in various subjects? What other methods of evaluation do you prefer?

4. Typically, what type of performance is more difficult for you: an exam, an individual project, a group project, a paper, or a presentation/speech? Explain.

5. Think of a recent example when you simply wanted to learn by using a surface approach to learning. What methods did you use? What were the outcomes? Now describe a recent example when you engaged in a deep approach to learning. What methods did you use? What were the outcomes?

6. Can you think of a recent learning experience when you used or could have used mnemonics to aid your memory? Simple note cards? Complex note cards? Explain.

7. Can you think of a recent learning experience when you used or could have used summarization techniques? Visual or graphic organizers? Explain.

8. Of the many learning strategies discussed in this chapter, which methods appeal to you the most? Why? Which ones do not appeal to you? Which ones will you adopt this term and for which courses?

The Last Word

Of all the techniques in this chapter, visual and graphic organizers (especially matrices) are second nature to me now. I even use them at work—just ask my colleagues!

—*Carol Dochen*

Establishing Direction in Your Life

The promised land.

CHAPTER HIGHLIGHTS

- Fantasies, Dreams, and Goals

- Goals: The Foundation of Self-Regulation

- To Change or Not to Change?

I have a dream that my four little children will one day live in a nation where they will not be judged by the color of their skin but by the content of their character.
—*Martin Luther King, Jr.*

What are your dreams for your life? Now is the time to turn those dreams into reality. The insights you have achieved through the journal exercises and other assignments may have already engendered some changes in how you are living your life as a college student. The great traditions of psychology, education, spirituality, self-help, and theology stress that knowing ourselves well is the only feasible beginning to the construction of a healthy and productive life. You can begin to look at the specific strategies available as you contemplate how you wish to shape your collegiate experience.

Exercise 7.1

SELF-ASSESSMENT: Exploring Goals

With 5 being "Almost Always" and 1 being "Almost Never," assess your assumptions and feelings about your ability to set goals for your life. Rate each of the following statements honestly by circling the appropriate number. Completing this exercise will help you identify areas of concern you may have with goal-setting.

	Almost Always		Sometimes		Almost Never
1. I set goals for myself.	5	4	3	2	1
2. I base any goals I set on my core values and beliefs.	5	4	3	2	1
3. When I set goals, I choose ones that are achievable.	5	4	3	2	1
4. I am aware that different areas of my life (e.g., education, health, career, spiritual, financial) require different goals.	5	4	3	2	1
5. I can identify specific behaviors that I would like to either increase or decrease.	5	4	3	2	1
6. I have specific behaviors that I would like to maintain.	5	4	3	2	1
7. I can identify specific behaviors that I would like to either start or stop.	5	4	3	2	1
8. I prefer setting goals that can be accomplished within hours or days at the most.	5	4	3	2	1
9. I am comfortable setting goals that might take a year or more to accomplish.	5	4	3	2	1

10. I need help accomplishing   5   4   3   2   1
     goals once I've set them.

Add up the numbers you circled. Your total score will be between 10 and 50. The higher your score, the more likely you feel confident about your ability to set goals. For scores below 30, write or reflect on items for which you have concerns and consider talking with a trusted friend, a family member, a teacher, a counselor, or an advisor.

FANTASIES, DREAMS, AND GOALS

When we were children, other people managed our lives. As we grew, we practiced managing ourselves, from tying our own shoelaces to doing chores without being told. In the long transition between adolescence and adulthood, we increasingly take responsibility for how we live, and we begin to manage our own lives. Midlife, the other long transition period, often requires that we make major adaptations in how we manage our behaviors. Of all of life's tasks, managing our own behaviors seems to be the most difficult for many people. Beyond simplistic management of daily chores, living well or living toward our quality world means that we develop the flexibility to navigate the complexities of life. To do so, we must learn about *our effort to monitor and regulate our own behaviors, cognitions (thinking), and emotions so as to reach our goals*. That skill is called **self-regulation**. The essential foundation for self-regulation is competence in setting and reaching goals—goals that are congruent with our quality world (Baumeister & Vohs, 2004; Olsson, 2008). Thus, this chapter begins specific instruction about constructing achievable goals and then translating those goals into actions. In the following chapter, we present a simple model of self-regulation.

CASE STUDY

CHRISTINA is a second-semester student from a small rural community. Even though her parents did not complete high school, since the third grade she has dreamed of going to college. Those dreams started because her teacher knew that Christina liked to make clothes for her dolls and creative costumes for Halloween, and encouraged her to imagine herself as a clothing designer. This teacher challenged Christina to work hard in school and gave special attention to her academic achievements. Christina held on to the ideas of achievement throughout middle school, and her parents grew increasingly proud of her schoolwork. All the typical distractions erupted during high school—boys, clubs, the Internet—but Christina persisted on a college prep track, even though many of her friends succumbed to easier roads. Christina envisioned herself designing clothes for music performers. A few teachers encouraged her, and the high school counselor provided information about college scholarships. Christina and her parents drove to a nearby university for Visitors' Day. It seemed overwhelming, but also exciting, and she could envision herself being a student there. None of her older siblings shared her ambitions, but her family supported her desire to go to college. Her dream became a specific goal, and she worked nights and weekends during her senior year to save money.

The first college semester was tough for Christina. Even though she had enrolled in two art classes, she found her courses in sociology and communications far more interesting. Her goal to get to college had been met, but now what? What kind of life did she wish to make there? What should be her major? What type of professional life did she want? Christina found herself in a dilemma. After years of having such a clear-cut goal, she felt as if she were drifting, not really sure about what she wanted or how to get there. One strong habit she had already developed was to search for help if she felt confused.

Case Study Question: On your campus, where would Christina look for help in choosing a career path?

The difficult task, when we seriously look for the right direction in our lives, is differentiating among fantasies, dreams, and goals. **Fantasies** are *ideas that cannot happen;* they are fun to think about but they are not possible. Fantasies usually involve looking different or having talents we do not possess or acquiring fabulous riches. In our fantasies, we do not have to work for achievement. Everything magically appears.

On the other hand, **dreams** are *possible outcomes—sometimes probable and sometimes improbable—but they are possible.* When we begin to examine a dream or a wish, we begin to translate it into goals. A dream unexamined remains a dream forever. Christina had an early dream of going to college, and her teachers and parents helped her convert that wish into specific goals—good academic performance, college prep courses, college visits, scholarship applications. Christina came to believe in the feasibility of her wish; she believed her dream of attending college could happen. People around her helped her ask and answer the question: "Do I possess the necessary skills and talents, time, access to means, and opportunities?" (Gollwitzer, 1995, p. 289). Repeatedly she made decisions that moved her toward her goal. Along the way, she turned away from other roads, other possibilities. Each time she acted in a manner that supported her goal, she became more confident and believed in herself. Each time we keep our promises to ourselves, we become more trustworthy to ourselves (Branden, 1994, p. 26). Thus, Christina's belief in her own abilities increased because she did what she had set for herself to do; she trusted that she would act in ways congruent with her goals. As she progressed through high school, she made "a transition from wishes and desires to binding goals, . . . accompanied by a feeling of determination" (Gollwitzer, 1995, p. 289). This stage is called goal-directed action, and we will discuss it later in the chapter.

For a moment, however, reflect on the concept of the quality world introduced in Chapter 1. The visions we have of our perfect world fuel not only our fantasies but our dreams as well. If our quality world is ethical and based on our deepest core values, then the dreams that emerge can be translated into goals that will help our life resemble our quality world. Christina has accomplished her goal of attending college. Now she must discern what she wants to accomplish, why she wants those goals, and how to achieve them.

Case Study Question: What are the questions you believe Christina should ask and to whom should she ask them?

Case Study Question: From what you've read about Christina in this chapter, what do you know about her core values? How can she integrate her core values into her plans for choosing a major? A career path? Extracurricular activities?

Exercise 7.2

Dreams Do Come True

Your dreams are possible. The first step is to think about possible changes you hope to make in your life—especially possibilities connected to your quality world. This exercise will help you begin this process.

What are five dreams that you hope will come true for you? For each, tell why you hope to reach these dreams.

1. _____

2. _____

3. _____

4. _____

5. _____

GOALS: THE FOUNDATION OF SELF-REGULATION

As Christina has learned, goals set directions for our actions and our lives; they eliminate the aimless wandering through the days, not knowing what we want or why we are doing what we are doing. From our earliest days, we all have goals. Watch a baby intently reaching for an object or a toddler attempting to walk across a room or a young child struggling to read, and you will see determined effort to reach a specific goal.

Usually we have goals in many areas of our lives. Consider these areas as you begin the goal-setting process: education and training; career and job development; spiritual, religious, and character building; health and emotional development; physical and recreational; social, relationships, and family; financial; civic, service, and volunteerism. Here are sample goals for these areas:

- **Education/training:** *I will earn a master's degree in counseling education by my twenty-fifth birthday.*

- **Career/job development:** *I will be a school counselor by my twenty-sixth birthday.*

- **Spiritual/religious/character building:** *I will attend religious services once a week for the next three months.*

- **Health/emotional:** *I will lose 20 lbs. within the next six months.*

- **Physical/recreational:** *I will exercise by lifting weights and jogging at the student recreation center three days each week.*

- **Social/relationships/family:** *I will introduce myself to three new people each month during my first semester in college.*

- **Financial:** *I will save $25.00 a month for the next 12 months.*

- **Civic/service/volunteerism:** *I will volunteer at the humane society once a month for the next six months.*

Goals can be intermediate or final. Outcome goals are those goals that you set to achieve for a final product such as a final grade in a course or a certain GPA or graduation. Process goals are usually the strategies involved to reach an outcome goal, such as learning to use Cornell and T-notes. Often several process goals serve as reinforcements along the way to our reaching an outcome goal. Here are examples of outcome and process goals:

- **Outcome** (a final product such as a certain GPA): *I will earn a 3.5 GPA by the end of this semester.*

- **Process** (strategy to reach an outcome goal such as learning to use Cornell and T-notes): *I will go to the campus tutoring center to work on my statistics homework two days each week (for at least one hour each visit) for the entire semester.*

Setting goals that reflect our quality world and help us achieve the lives we want is an important skill that we can learn. In other words, we can study the principles of goal setting and apply those principles to our own lives. As you have reflected about your quality world, you have thought about the type of person you wish to become, the family and friends you wish to have, and the work you wish to do. Each of those is a lifetime desire. What are the long-term outcome goals that can lead to those desires? What constellation of process goals will lead you to that life you desire? Are your goals compatible with your ethics? These questions are not hypothetical, nor easily answered. They require careful scrutiny and thoughtful reflection.

Translating Goals into Behaviors

We recommend formulating your goals as actions (which are really behaviors). Behaviors are easily measured. You can measure an increase in the number of pages you read or a decrease in the amount of money you spend. We have found that decreasing or ending actions of obsessive behaviors such as smoking or overspending money is often a challenging goal to implement and obtain but also rewarding once it is met. Here are several ways that you can formulate your goals as behaviors:

- **Increase:** Increase specific actions such as exercising, eating healthy foods, studying, or making new friends on campus. Example: *I will meet and visit with at least one new person each week before or after class, on the bus, in the residence hall, and so on.*

- **Decrease:** Decrease specific actions such as procrastinating, spending time on the computer, watching TV, eating fast food instead of cooking, or displaying road rage. Example: *I will spend no more than one hour a day, Monday through Thursday, watching television or playing computer games for the rest of this semester so that I will have more time to study.*

- **Maintain:** Continue performance in some area at its current acceptable level such as attending class, persisting in community service involvement, exercising, or attending 12-step programs. Example: *I will continue to ride my bicycle three miles once a week in order to maintain my physical stamina.*

- **Start:** Depart from current routine or former habits and experiences such as beginning a new relationship, going to the library to study, taking exploratory courses in different disciplines, pursuing a leadership role in an organization, or joining an intramural sports team. Example: *I will take exploratory courses in two majors next term to search for a major.*

- **Stop:** Depart from current routine or former habits and experiences such as not speeding on the freeway, smoking, cussing around specific people, eating junk food, or gossiping. Example: *I will give up drinking carbonated soft drinks.*

- **Problem solve:** Institute action to resolve the difficulty *or* take preventive action so that the problem is unlikely to occur such as using mediation to resolve roommate disagreements, checking your account balance routinely, or keeping an updated calendar of assignments. Example: *I will review the status of my checking account online each week to prevent overdrafts.* Source: Adapted from W. Lee, W. (1978). *Formulating and Reaching Goals.* Champaign, IL: Research Press, pp. 21–26.

Not only do goals differ across areas of our lives, but they also differ in their immediacy or their distance. Some goals are immediate (today!), some are short term (1 year or less), some are intermediate (between 1 and 10 years), and others are long term (10 years or more). Here are examples of each of these types of goals:

- **Long term** (10 years or more): *I will have traveled to all 50 states by my fiftieth birthday.*

- **Intermediate** (between 1 and 10 years): *I will be promoted to vice president of finance at my job within the next five years.*

- **Short term** (1 year or less): *I will take the Graduate Record Exam (GRE) so that I can apply to graduate school within the next three months.*

- **Immediate** (within hours or days): *I will review my history notes for one hour by 4 P.M. today.*

We use smaller and more immediate goals as stepping stones to larger goals. It is helpful and motivating if we can see the connections between the immediate goals and our longer term goals. Reviewing those connections regularly strengthens our commitment to intermediate and long-term goals.

An assumption we must make in this text is that academic success in college is an appropriate goal for you, even though we realize that this may not be true for every reader. As you move through this chapter and the exercises, ruminate carefully about the purpose of attending college in your life. Can a college education help you reach your desires? Is this the right school? Is this the right time? Is this the right course of study?

Exercise 7.3

Turn Your Dreams into Goals

Now that you have listed your dreams, begin to reflect on how those dreams are connected to your values—those life beliefs you hold in the highest regard that are the foundation of your quality world. For example, if your dream is to receive a college degree in psychology, you probably value education. Think about your other values especially as they relate to your dreams. This exercise will help you explore your values and how they relate to your dreams.

List your top values that you hope will enhance your quality world and place them in order of importance, with 1 being the most important and 5 being the least important.

1. _____

2. _____

3. _____

4. _____

5. _____

Which values are connected to your list of dreams? Explain.

Now complete each of the following goal statements and answer the accompanying questions.

1. In 10 years I will . . .

Is this goal connected to a dream? ___ yes ___ no

Is this goal connected to one of your values? ___ yes ___ no

What area does this goal apply to (check all that apply)?

___ Education/Training	___ Career/Job Development
___ Spiritual/Religious/ Character Building	___ Health/Emotional
___ Physical/Recreational	___ Social/Relationships/Family
___ Financial	___ Civic/Service/Volunteerism

2. In 3 years I will . . .

Is this goal connected to a dream? ___ yes ___ no

Is this goal connected to one of your values? ___ yes ___ no

What area does this goal apply to (check all that apply)?

   ___ Education/Training   ___ Career/Job Development

   ___ Spiritual/Religious/   ___ Health/Emotional
         Character Building

   ___ Physical/Recreational   ___ Social/Relationships/Family

   ___ Financial   ___ Civic/Service/Volunteerism

3. In 6 months I will . . .

Is this goal connected to a dream? ___ yes ___ no

Is this goal connected to one of your values? ___ yes ___ no

What area does this goal apply to (check all that apply)?

   ___ Education/Training   ___ Career/Job Development

   ___ Spiritual/Religious/   ___ Health/Emotional
         Character Building

   ___ Physical/Recreational   ___ Social/Relationships/Family

   ___ Financial   ___ Civic/Service/Volunteerism

4. By next week I will . . .

Is this goal connected to a dream? ___ yes ___ no

Is this goal connected to one of your values? ___ yes ___ no

What area does this goal apply to (check all that apply)?

   ___ Education/Training   ___ Career/Job Development

   ___ Spiritual/Religious/   ___ Health/Emotional
         Character Building

   ___ Physical/Recreational   ___ Social/Relationships/Family

   ___ Financial   ___ Civic/Service/Volunteerism

Characteristics of Achievable Goals

We cannot stress strongly enough the crucial importance of discerning your goals through the lens of your quality world and your ethical system. Covey, Merrill, and Merrill (1994) tell a story of a man who spent years climbing the ladder of success only to find at midlife that the ladder was leaning against the wrong wall. We have witnessed students doggedly pursuing a major even when they do not like it only to be miserable after graduation, or students choosing social behaviors that conflict with their own values. We sometimes see students hurrying through school toward the earliest possible graduation date rather than taking enough time to explore a variety of options and experiences available in college.

Once you have discerned your goals, test them against four characteristics of **achievable goals**: *believable, realistic, desirable, measurable* (Nist & Holschuh, 2000, pp. 81–82). This strategy will help you determine whether you are conceptualizing your goals in ways that you can successfully accomplish.

Believable. The characteristic *believable* simply means that we are certain that we have the ability and the will to achieve the goal. We may draw upon our own beliefs that we can accomplish the goal (internal) or we may draw upon others' conviction that we have the necessary ability and will (external). Christina drew upon both sources to trust that she could achieve her goal of attending college.

Realistic. Once we believe we have the ability and will to achieve a goal, the next step is to ascertain whether the goal is *realistic*. External validation (reality check) is the means to assess whether a goal is realistic. Christina checked the realism of her goal by investigating and visiting colleges, talking with the high school counselor, maintaining her GPA, and attaining an acceptable score on the required standardized entrance exams.

Desirable. The third characteristic, *desirable,* is simple—how much do we want this goal? In crass terms, just how much are we willing to sacrifice? Christina sacrificed much of her social life and free time by working nights and weekends to save money for college to achieve her goal. Sometimes the price tag is high, sometimes not, but the degree of desirability is a great determiner of our motivation.

Measurable. The final characteristic, *measurable,* allows us to know when we have achieved a goal. *I want to be a good student* is not measurable; *I want to graduate with honors,* that is, a GPA > 3.5, is measurable. Christina's goal was measurable; she wanted to be accepted by and to attend a college.

Exercise 7.4

Which Goals Are Achievable?

Measure each of your goals stated in Exercise 7.3 against the four achievable criteria—believable, realistic, desirable, and measurable—by checking all that apply for each goal. Then rewrite any goals that do not meet all four criteria to make them achievable. Completing this exercise will reinforce the concept of learning to write achievable goal statements.

10-year goal: ___ believable ___ realistic ___ desirable ___ measurable

3-year goal: ___ believable ___ realistic ___ desirable ___ measurable

6-month goal: ___ believable ___ realistic ___ desirable ___ measurable

Next week goal: ___ believable ___ realistic ___ desirable ___ measurable

---

Translating Goals into an Action Plan

Creating the most appropriate goals for ourselves is no guarantee that we will reach them. The easiest example is the New Year's resolutions that often last less than a week. How can we translate goals into actions—actions that will help us accomplish the very goals that have spawned them? The answer comes from cognitive behavioral psychology, a branch of psychology that investigates how human behavior changes deliberately. The following is a commonplace example demonstrating how a student's goal of academic success in a freshman math class translates into the specific behaviors.

Tim is a geography major who wants to go to graduate school and earn a master's degree. He knows that he must make good grades to achieve that goal. This term he is taking a required class in college mathematics, and he is concerned because his high school math performance was weak. He knows he must make consistent, strategic efforts in studying for this class if he is to achieve the B he has determined as his goal. He believes he can accomplish his goal (*believable*). Although his prior math performance was weak, he did complete high school math and pass the mathematics portion of a college entrance exam (*realistic*). He wants this goal and is willing to sacrifice procrastination to achieve it (*desirable*); and he has set a specific result, a semester grade of B (*measurable*).

Action statement. The first step in translating a goal into an action is to specifically create an action statement. Tim writes,

> *I will work on my math homework at least one hour each day, five days a week.*

Tim has never before committed to study the same subject each day; thus, this behavior is a new or *innovative* action. It is important to note again that an action statement can *increase, decrease, maintain, start, stop, problem solve our* behaviors:

Let us return to Tim's action statement:

I will work on my math homework at least one hour each day, five days a week, beginning the first week of school.

In this example, working on math homework is the specific behavior. The unit of measurement or amount of behavior to be accomplished is one hour per day, five days a week.

Strategies and activities. The second step is to identify when, where, and how long the activity will take place.

I plan to work on math homework in the math lab from 12:00 to 1:00 P.M., Monday through Friday, so I can get help when I have trouble.

Gather materials. Step three is to gather the materials, supplies, and resources needed to accomplish the action statement. Examples relevant to Tim's action statement are the location and schedule of the math lab, a textbook and workbook, a calculator, the syllabus, class notes, pencils, and the names of other students in the class.

Price tag. Step four is called the price tag. Because every goal has a price, Tim must state what he must give up to obtain his goal. These sacrifices will likely include time, energy, money, and even the postponement of other goals. For example, *I'll have to eat lunch after math lab; otherwise I'll get too sleepy while trying to do my math. I'll record my favorite show while I'm gone.*

Rewards and punishments. Step five is identifying how to use rewards (including what you say to yourself) and punishments to help meet action statements. For example, Tim might make the following promises to himself: *Each day I work at the math lab, I can go home and eat a good lunch while I watch the recording of my favorite show. Each day I do not work at the math lab, I will not watch my show or go to the student recreation center.*

Set specific time lines. Step six is to evaluate the action by setting specific deadlines (time lines). Tim creates the following time line: *I will begin my actions the first week of school, and I will evaluate my progress after three weeks by averaging all my homework grades and talking with my math tutor. After the first exam, I will reevaluate whether I need to increase or*

Translating Goals into an Action Plan

1. Create an action statement.
2. Identify strategies and activities.
3. Gather materials, supplies, and other resources.
4. Determine the price tag.
5. Identify how to use rewards and punishments.
6. Evaluate by setting specific time lines.

decrease my study time in the math lab. Tim chooses to use his homework and test grades as the measure of his progress toward achieving his goal of a B in the course.

Exercise 7.5

Putting Your Goals into Action

Take the extra step by putting your goals into an action plan. The time it may take to rework your goals into an action plan will certainly pay off in the end. Use some of the goals you have already written or create five to seven new goals—especially goals you can complete during this semester. Try to have several outcome as well as process goals. Then address each of the following directives as you put each of your goals into an action plan.

1. Create an action statement.
2. Identify the strategies and activities.
3. List the supplies, materials, and resources you will need.
4. Determine the price tag.
5. Identify rewards and punishments.
6. Evaluate with specific time lines.

TO CHANGE OR NOT TO CHANGE?

Throughout this chapter, we have thoroughly examined goals—the essential foundation you need to regulate your behaviors, thoughts and emotions. We close by taking a look at the elements of change: why, what, and how.

Why Do I Need to Change?

Usually the first hint that we need to attend to a behavior, thought, or emotion is the nagging feeling that we are not accomplishing what we wish to accomplish. Sometimes it is a painful slap in the face by a low test score or a friend's hurt feelings. Whatever the initiating event, when we choose to look realistically at our goals and determine whether they are congruent with our ethical standards and then examine our behaviors, thoughts, and emotions, we are preparing to change.

What Do I Need to Change?

A clear understanding of the discrepancy between how we are acting, thinking, or feeling and how we should act, think, or feel points to the behavior, thought, or emotion that needs to change. When we select that target behavior, thought, or emotion and state it as a goal, we can apply to it the four characteristics of achievable goals (believable, realistic, desirable, measurable).

How Will I Change the Desired Behavior, Thought, or Emotion?

The key question is: *What can I do to increase the likelihood that I will exhibit the desired behavior, thought, or emotion?* There are numerous strategies that we can employ to help us reach our target goal: translating goals into actions, implementing or changing self-talk, examining irrational or unhelpful beliefs, monitoring triggering events, evaluating results of our actions, enlisting social support. If you are interested in detailed information on designing and implementing a self-change project, please see Chapter 10.

How Will I Monitor What Is Happening?

Once we have chosen the specific changes we intend to make, then our job is to focus on the new behaviors, thoughts, or emotions and persist in our efforts to reach them. Throughout this process we must regularly verify exactly what we are doing (reality check). To do this verification, we must be aware of what we are doing. In other words, we must be present to ourselves. This skill comes with practice and continual, gentle reminders to ourselves about what we are doing at any particular moment. Self-talk is especially helpful in learning this skill.

An important factor in self-regulation is our willingness to hold ourselves accountable for our new behaviors, thoughts, or emotions. The simplest way to assume this accountability is to verbally promise ourselves that we will exhibit a certain behavior, thought, or emotion by a certain time. However, we can increase the power of such a promise by writing it down and then checking it off when it is done. An even more powerful method is to announce to a roommate, a friend, a family member, or someone else with whom we feel comfortable that we are committed to making this change.

CONCLUSION

Formulating goals that are true to our values allow us to direct our time and attention so as to realize our dreams. Competence in setting and reaching our goals provides us with the essential foundation for regulating our behaviors, thoughts, and emotions. Regardless of whether we are traditional or nontraditional-age college students, selecting wise goals to pursue is especially important because these goals are destined to drive our efforts for many years.

SUMMARY

- The essential foundation for self-regulation is competence in setting and reaching goals. Self-regulation is our effort to monitor and regulate our own behaviors, cognitions, and emotions so as to reach our goals.

- Fantasies are ideas that cannot happen because we do not work to achieve them.

- Dreams are possible.

- Goals set the direction for our actions and our lives.

- Goal areas include education/training, career/job development; spiritual/religious/ character building; health/emotional; physical/recreational; social/relationships/ family; financial; and civic/service/volunteerism.

- Outcome goals are those goals that you set to achieve a final product such as a final grade in a course or a certain GPA. Process goals are the strategies involved to reach an outcome goal.

- Goal options include increasing, decreasing, maintaining, starting, stopping, or problem solving a behavior.

- Some goals are immediate (today!), some are short term (1 year or less), some are intermediate (between 1 and 10 years), and others are long term (10 years or more).

- To achieve a goal it should be believable, realistic, desirable, and measurable.

- To set a goal action plan, create an action statement, identify strategies and activities, gather materials, determine the price tag, identify how to use rewards and punishments, and evaluate by setting specific time lines.

- Changing behaviors, thoughts, or emotions involves specifically determining what and why to change, how to change, and how to monitor change.

KEY CONCEPTS

Academic self-regulation

Achievable goals: believable, realistic, desirable, measurable

Change

Dreams

Fantasies

Formulate goals as behaviors: increase, decrease, maintain, start, stop, problem-solve

Goal areas

Goal dimensions: outcome and process

Goal lengths: immediate, short term, intermediate, long term

Goals

Self-regulation

Translate goals into an action plan (six steps)

GUIDED JOURNAL QUESTIONS

1. Discuss the dreams that you had for yourself when you were very young. Now discuss your current dreams. How are they the same, and how have they changed?

2. Discuss three core values that guide your quality world. How have you come to hold these values? How have you incorporated these values into your life?

3. What goals have you previously set for yourself that have been achieved? What strategies did you implement for your success?

4. What goals have you set for yourself that you have not been able to achieve? Discuss the reasons why you have been unsuccessful.

5. When you set an achievable goal, you must make it believable. A believable goal means we have the ability and the will to achieve it. What does having "the will" to achieve a goal mean to you?

6. Every goal has a price tag (a sacrifice you must make to achieve a goal). Usually this means that you must give up something pleasurable to engage in something less pleasurable. What current price tags are you paying as you try to achieve several of your goals?

7. To use self-regulated learning, you need to set goals and monitor your progress in each class. Set an academic goal for each of your classes (either process or outcome). How will you monitor your progress?

The Last Word

My fantasy growing up was to be world famous. As I grow older, I dream of leaving this world a better place than I found it.

—*Russ Hodges*

Self-Regulation, Will, and Motivation

I know I can, I know I can.

8

CHAPTER HIGHLIGHTS

- Self-Regulation
- Will
- Academic Motivation
- Stages of Self-Regulatory Ability

If only I were motivated! Then. . .

Most of us long to feel eager about the tasks we have chosen. The energy and happiness seem automatic when we are eager to do something. It is so simple; all we need is an eagerness pill. If only it were that easy! In truth, the issue is that we must manage our own thoughts, behaviors, and feelings if we want to achieve our goals. Motivation is only part of the solution, but it does not just magically appear. Will, realistic goals, and persistence all contribute to our ability to manage ourselves. In this chapter, we will first investigate self-regulation and will. Then we delve into an extensive exploration of the factors of academic motivation. The chapter ends with a new model of the stages of self-regulation.

Exercise 8.1

SELF-ASSESSMENT: Self-Regulation, Will, and Motivation

With 5 being "Almost Always" and 1 being "Almost Never," assess your assumptions and feelings about your ability to take charge of your life. Rate each of the following statements honestly by circling the appropriate number. Completing this exercise will help you identify areas of concern you may have with self-regulation, will, and motivation.

	Almost Always		Sometimes		Almost Never
1. I am self-disciplined when it comes to attending class, reading, and studying.	5	4	3	2	1
2. I am able to delay having fun until after I finish with my schoolwork.	5	4	3	2	1
3. I can spread out work on a big assignment instead of waiting until the last minute to complete it.	5	4	3	2	1
4. I use positive self-talk to keep me focused and motivated.	5	4	3	2	1
5. I am aware of negative thoughts that can interfere with my success and actively try to change them.	5	4	3	2	1
6. I am aware of when my feelings (positive or negative) interfere with my actions.	5	4	3	2	1
7. I am a strong-willed person.	5	4	3	2	1
8. The more I value something, the more motivated I am to attain or achieve it.	5	4	3	2	1
9. The more I believe I need something, the more motivated I am to attain or achieve it.	5	4	3	2	1

10. I am motivated by my own   5   4   3   2   1
    expectations as well as the
    expectations of others.

Add up the numbers you circled. Your total score will be between 10 and 50. The higher your score, the more likely you feel confident about your ability to manage your life. For scores below 30, write or reflect on items for which you have concerns and consider talking with a trusted friend, a family member, a teacher, a counselor, or an advisor.

SELF-REGULATION

As humans, *our effort to monitor and regulate our own behaviors, cognitions (thinking), and emotions so as to reach our goals* is called **self-regulation**, that is, our ability to manipulate ourselves to reach specific goals. In psychology, such self-regulation is labeled internal locus (place) of control, as opposed to external locus of control, in which other people control or direct our behaviors. It is a normal desire to want to control our own behaviors; witness the three-year-old who insists on doing it (whatever it is) herself.

For the last 25 years, the needs and ambitions of individuals and organizations within our culture have created intense interest in self-regulation. Most individuals want to achieve, and most organizations feel pressure to achieve the highest results at the lowest cost. The result is that writers and researchers are discovering how we can improve our self-regulation (Baumeister & Vohs, 2004; Olsson, 2008). The remainder of this chapter and the following chapter give specific strategies to do so, especially in an academic setting.

Developing our self-regulation skills occurs throughout our lives. In our culture, most adolescents struggle with independence and responsibility, and they vacillate between dependence and independence in their academic lives as well as other areas for several years. The college environment is an especially difficult one for many students, for it presupposes a high degree of self-discipline or self-regulation. Some students can regulate their own behaviors appropriately, but many students struggle with the simple tasks of going to class, doing assignments in a timely manner, maintaining their finances, and even doing their laundry. Especially for students who rely heavily on their parents, the need for self-regulation can be intense.

Self-Regulated Learning

A good analogy for self-regulated learning is to think of a thermostat and how it monitors and regulates room temperature. The goal of the thermostat is the preset desired temperature.

Self-regulated learning is your ability to monitor and control your own behavior, thinking, and emotions as you acquire knowledge and skills during learning (Zimmerman, 1989).

Setting a goal is your preset desired attempt at change.

Academic Self-Regulation

We can deliberately increase our self-regulation by consciously using strategies developed by cognitive behavioral psychologists. Cognitive behavioral psychologists view every action through a triple lens: first, the observable behavior itself; second, the feelings of the person doing the behavior; and, third, the person's thoughts about the behavior. **Academic self-regulated learning** is *your ability to monitor and control your own behavior, thinking, and emotions as you acquire knowledge and skills during learning* (Zimmerman, 1989). In other words, we can actively control our behavior through access to resources such as time, study environment, peers, and teachers. We can control and change our motivational beliefs including self-efficacy, emotions, and affect (such as anxiety) to improve our learning. We can control cognitive strategies for learning, including what we say to ourselves, and we can use our self-understanding to recognize our own preferences and strategies.

Exercise 8.2

Self-Regulation

What are the behaviors, thoughts, and feelings that interfere with your academic success? Becoming aware of these behaviors, thoughts, and feelings is the first step in learning to use self-regulated learning strategies.

List five academic behaviors that interfere with your academic success.

Sample: *I watch too much television.*

1.

2.

3.

4.

5.

List five academic thoughts that interfere with your academic success.

Sample: *Before I take an exam, I always think I m going to fail.*

1.

2.

3.

4.

5.

List five emotions (feelings) that interfere with your academic success.

Sample: *I have continual fear of not succeeding when I am in a math course.*

1.

2.

3.

4.

5.

Self-regulation is a sprawling subject that encompasses many theoretical topics. Two critical topics are will and motivation, and we explore both in the following sections.

WILL

Motivation and talent are not enough to accomplish goals. All of us witness people who underachieve; for example, they are not motivated enough to do the work to attain a goal, even though they have the talents. No place is this more obvious than in school. Students know they have the talent they need to achieve the goal, their families and friends know they have the talent, but the students seem to lack the power to make themselves do what they want and intend to do. *The power of conscious and unconscious control that we have over our own actions or emotions* is the definition of **will** appropriate to our purposes in this text. At one time or another, all of us have wished to have a stronger will so that we could more easily reach a desired goal. Whether we wish to quit smoking or study more, we know that we have to use our will to control both our actions and emotions in order to reach our goals. Philosophers have pondered the obvious

differences among people for centuries. Interestingly, more than 2,500 years ago, Greek thinkers created the word *akrasia* to represent a deficiency of the will (Mischel, 1995).

Although most thinkers have agreed that there are individual differences in strength of will, a much more serious debate occurs when we investigate whether we can change the strength of our will. In other words, can we increase our will and thus control our actions, thoughts, and emotions in ways that help us reach goals that are important to us? Or are we limited to a predetermined level of will with which we were born?

All of us have witnessed individuals who seem to exert enormous will in a specific arena of their talents. Athletes, artists, scientists, writers—there are many public and historical examples of people who devote most of their energy and passion to excellence in one endeavor. They develop a specific talent to the highest degree possible through the dedication of their will.

Currently, we have yet to discover a comprehensive, modern theory of will, so we choose to use a pragmatic approach based on our experiences in helping students. As we have helped other students regulate their academic and personal behaviors, we have found that over time most students can increase the strength of their will. An important concept to understand is the difference between what we can directly will by our behaviors and what are our desired outcomes. We can will the first, but not the second. According to Kurtz and Ketcham (1992, p. 125),

We can directly will *knowledge* . . . but not *wisdom.*

We can directly will *pleasure* . . . but not *happiness.*

We can directly will *congratulations* . . . but not *admiration.*

We can directly will *reading/listening* . . . but not *understanding.*

We can directly will *going to bed* . . . but not *sleeping.*

We can directly will *meekness* . . . but not *humility.*

We can directly will *executing a play* . . . but not *winning a game.*

We can directly will *dryness* . . . but not *sobriety.*

Many people have secret doubts and fears that they do not have the will to maintain motivation and accomplish their goals. Our culture is an intensely achievement-based culture, and competition starts early. Children are taught that knowing the right answers, making the grade, winning the game matter.

Intense criticism at home or in the family can lead children to be afraid to try something, to take a risk. Academic self-confidence is fragile for most of us, even if we are talented. However, we know that students can increase the strength of both their will (Mischel, 1995; Smart & Wegner, 1996) and their academic motivation by using specific strategies.

Exercise 8.3

Your Will

Do you have conscious control over your own actions and emotions? This exercise will help you to seriously consider some questions as you strive for a deeper understanding of your will.

1. How often do you accomplish your intentions?

2. When you are confronted with a difficult task, do you persist or abandon it?

3. When you want something to occur, do you spend time dreaming about it or constructing strategies to achieve it?

4. How do you explain the differences in your levels of will in different areas of your life?

5. Describe any areas of your life that you feel are out of your control. What steps can you take to regain control?

6. How strong-willed are you?

ACADEMIC MOTIVATION

A working definition of **motivation** is *those thoughts and feelings that initiate, direct, and sustain action.* Obviously, there are many factors that affect academic motivation, both internal (intrinsic) and external (extrinsic), and we will consider the most important factors a little later in this chapter. We first want to look at five issues that researchers investigate in the motivation of college students (Woolfolk, 2004):

- **Choices.** What do we choose to do? Some students attend class regularly whereas others miss class to catch up on sleep, errands, and so forth.

- **Initiation.** How rapidly do we begin the behavior? Some students study before they go out with friends whereas others delay studying until the next day.

- **Intensity.** How hard do we try? Some students are actively engaged in the lecture/discussion in classes whereas others go through the motions of taking notes.

- **Persistence.** How long do we try? Some students are determined to understand study material and seek help when necessary whereas others give up when learning is difficult.

- **Thoughts/feelings.** What do we think and feel while we are engaged? Some students feel confident that they can successfully complete an assignment whereas others worry that they will fail.

CASE STUDY

As a sophomore, COLIN was a talented student who skated through high school, mastering the art of doing the least amount possible to get by. He had a dozen excuses for every result, and he had a high opinion of himself in high school because he was smart and popular. He cruised into college with those same behaviors and attitudes, but that cruising turned into a crash after his first round of exams. He was shocked and decided to try a little harder, but the seductions available on a college campus were stronger than his will. He made friends and enjoyed parties, but he continued to use the old, casual behaviors, such as not taking notes in class, skimming the readings instead of seriously studying them, and waiting until the night before to study. Inside Colin's mind, all his troubles occurred because of other people. It was all their fault! His roommate kept the TV on late at night so Colin overslept and missed his classes; his girlfriend expected him to spend time with her so he rarely opened his books; his classes seemed boring so he would daydream or sleep. His friends expected him to play hoops in the afternoon. There was never any time to study. Often he had good intentions, but distractions interfered.

Not surprisingly, his first semester ended with a pitiful GPA. For the first time in his life, Colin had publicly failed. His confidence was badly shaken, and he hated carrying the news home to his parents. They kept telling him how much they believed in him, but Colin had begun the dangerous slide downward into self-doubt. He felt more apprehension about his performance than he had ever felt before; in fact, sometimes he did not believe he was "college material." Maybe he should just leave and join the military or get a civilian job.

Case Study Questions: What were some of the choices Colin made that led to his poor academic performance? What behaviors can he initiate for the second semester? How can Colin help himself try harder in his new classes? What thoughts and feelings hurt Colin's academic motivation during the first semester? How can he change them?

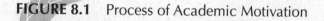

Research evidence and common sense tell us that these five factors are important in determining level of motivation. If we direct our attention to our own behaviors, thoughts, and feelings through the lens of these issues, we can determine our own motivation level, and we urge you to do just that. Take a few moments to reflect on your current level of academic motivation. Does it vary across courses? How much does procrastination impede your work? Are you a strong starter, a strong finisher, or consistent throughout the semester? Is your attitude about academics helpful to your efforts?

Psychological Elements that Impact Motivation

If we can understand and control the factors of choice, initiation, intensity, persistence, and thoughts/feelings, then we have a much greater opportunity to increase academic motivation. What influences these factors? Researchers have identified many psychological elements that seem to affect these factors. We have organized the most important into three groups: values, needs, and expectations. In Figure 8.1, the Process of Academic Motivation, you will notice that we have placed **opportunity** in the first position. In academic settings, opportunities abound; they occur with every assignment and every lecture. Each semester you begin with hundreds of academic opportunities. Attending an outside lecture, conducting research with a professor, engaging in serious conversation

FIGURE 8.1 Process of Academic Motivation

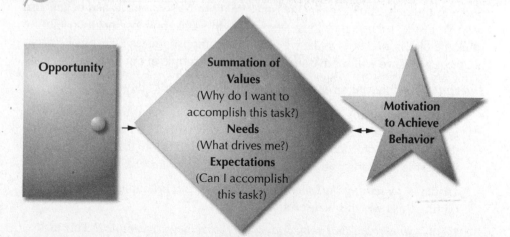

with fellow students, studying, seeking help from tutors, participating in test review sessions, writing, teaching a lab—all these and more are available.

When we consider an opportunity, we have three types of psychological elements that impact our level of motivation to reach the desired behavior or outcome.

Why do I want to accomplish this task? represents both internal and external values. Internal reasons include interest, utility, and goals. External reasons include incentives and expectations of others.

What drives me? is the key question for those elements of need that include our need for achievement, competence, self-worth, and creativity.

Can I accomplish this task? encompasses our expectations based on previous experience, observation of others' success, and feedback about our own performance.

Two other important expectations are the belief we hold about our ability to perform the particular behavior (self-efficacy) and how we explain our success or failure (attribution) (McMillan & Forsyth, 1991; VanderStoep & Pintrich, 2003). Both self-efficacy and attributions are explored later in this chapter.

When the psychological elements are added together, they impact our motivation to achieve the desired behavior. Each time we achieve the desired behavior, that success impacts certain psychological elements and our motivation usually increases. If we do not achieve the behavior, our motivation can decrease. However, sometimes an unexpected failure grabs our attention and shows us that our motivation and our behaviors need to change.

Values

Values are the reasons why we prize or disregard the completion of a task (VanderStoep & Pintrich, 2003). Internal reasons are those personal ideas and beliefs that we hold inside, such as how interested we are in a task, how personally useful we think the task is, and how much we want to accomplish the task. External reasons are the rewards we will receive and how important people in our lives will view us.

Internal.   The internal, or intrinsic, reasons include the following:

- **Interest**—*a feeling of curiosity or concern about something that makes the attention turn toward it.* Example: "I will/will not enjoy accomplishing this task solely for the experience of the activity" (note that sometimes interest is temporary and therefore termed *situational interest*).

- **Utility**—*something that serves a useful purpose.* Example: "I believe completing this task will be useful/useless to me."

- **Goal**—*something that somebody wants to achieve.* Example: "This task is/is not something I want to achieve."

External. The external, or extrinsic, reasons include the following:

- **Incentive**—*Something that encourages or motivates somebody to do something.* Example: "I will/will not be externally rewarded for completing this task."

- **Expectations of others**—*A standard of conduct or performance set by other people.* Example: "My [family, friends, boss, coach, and so on] expect/do not expect me to accomplish this task."

CASE STUDY

TAMARA is a sophomore taking her first course in communications. She is a traditional-age, first-generation student who entered college on a probationary contract. She knows that she must pass all her courses this term to remain in school, and she is determined to do well from the beginning of the semester.

Her assignment, the opportunity, is to create and deliver a persuasive speech, and she chooses the topic of free campus parking for students. All five value components will be positive for Tamara. She believes learning how to give a persuasive speech will be a useful skill in her chosen profession (utility); she will be rewarded with a grade (incentive); she will feel good about finishing the assignment (goal); she is interested in the parking issue because she had to pay more than $50 for a parking permit this term (situational interest); and her teacher expects her to complete this assignment (expectations of others).

Case Study Questions: Of the five value components Tamara listed above, which do you think motivated her the most and why? The least?

Needs

The second set of components for motivated behavior is needs (What drives me?). "Needs tend to motivate students to behave so as to attain satisfaction and rewards. They are innate feelings and beliefs that direct attention and energy toward determining priorities and goals" (McMillan & Forsyth, 1991, p. 42). The needs most relevant to academic motivation are achievement, competence, self-worth, and creativity:

- **Achievement**—*something that somebody has succeeded in doing, usually with effort.* Example: "I will risk to be successful/I am afraid of risk because I might fail" (Atkinson & Feather, 1966; McClelland, 1961).

- **Competence**—*the ability to do something well.* Example: "It is/is not important to me to accomplish my goals and control my surroundings" (Deci, 1975).

- **Self-worth**—*an individual's confidence in his/her personal value.*
  Example: "I want/do not want to have a positive opinion of my abilities"
  (Covington, 1984).

- **Creativity**—*the ability to use the imagination to develop new and original ideas or things.* Example: "I enjoy/do not enjoy thinking and expressing my own ideas."

TAMARA has many need elements that will enhance her motivation for her speech assignment. She sees herself as a good student (self-worth) who wants a collegiate education to further her skills and opportunities (competence). She is excited about researching the topic and creating her own arguments (creativity). Most importantly, she is willing to risk choosing an interesting topic because she believes it enhances her chance of success (achievement).

Case Study Questions: Which of Tamara's needs can you relate to the most and why? The least?

The achievement needs of college students are a rich field of study. "Depending on childhood environment (especially parenting) and other experiences, some people develop a strong need to achieve success, while others develop a need to avoid failure" (McMillan & Forsyth, 1991, p. 44). If we have a strong need for academic achievement, then we tend to work diligently at tasks and use feedback to improve. While we enjoy external rewards, internal rewards of feelings of pride and self-worth are highly motivating. If we fail at an academic task, we usually have the ability to use the feedback from that failure to improve our next attempt, even if we are temporarily embarrassed by our performance. If we perceive a task as realistically achievable, then we are motivated to attempt it.

The need to avoid failure is a serious danger to collegiate learning. If we are afraid to fail because we believe failure is shameful and humiliating, then we will avoid challenging tasks, opting for the easy way or the outrageously difficult way. In other words, our success is certain or impossible. We may also suffer from intense anxiety about academics and deliberately avoid attending class and studying. Occasionally, a student will exhibit this psychological characteristic of fear of failure in only one subject, such as math. If the academic anxiety is moderate, then the specific suggestions given in Chapter 13 for managing stress should help. If the academic anxiety is intense, then a counselor or tutor can provide a calmly structured environment with ample positive feedback. In that setting, students can overcome their fear of failure (McMillan & Forsyth, 1991).

Expectations

Can I accomplish this task? is the question that encompasses our judgment about our competence to achieve the task and our ability to control our behavior. The primary expectations relevant to academic tasks are as follows:

- **Previous experience**—*the total of the things that have happened to an individual and of his or her past thoughts and feelings.* Example: "In the past I have done well/poorly in similar situations."

- **Success of others**—*the achievements of peers.* Example: "I compare favorably/unfavorably with other people in this category."

- **Feedback**—*opinions and reactions to some actions.* Example: "I pay attention to evaluation according to how much I trust the source" (Deci, 1975).

- **Self-efficacy**—*the confidence that we can meet whatever performance standards the situation requires.* Example: "I feel/do not feel confident in my own ability to meet the challenge of. . . ." (Bandura, 1986; Branden, 1994).

- **Attribution**—*how we explain our academic success or failure.* Example: "I did well/poorly because. . . ." (Weiner, 1986).

TAMARA is confident that she can make a competent speech because she did well on the debate team in high school (previous experience, self-efficacy); however, college seems so much more competitive than high school, and she is surprised at the rigor of the professor's critiques (success of others). Therefore, she wants to rehearse her speech with the teaching assistant because she believes he can give her good information about improvement (feedback). She believes her past successes in high school speech have come from careful research and rehearsal, so she is using the same strategies for this speech (attribution). She wants to earn a B or better on this assignment because she considers that grade a reasonable goal given her experience, her preparation, and her practice. Through her needs, values, and expectations, Tamara has become highly motivated to achieve on this assignment (the opportunity).

Case Study Questions: Do you believe Tamara was more motivated by her internal expectations (i.e., previous experience, self-efficacy, attribution) or external expectations (i.e., success of others, feedback)? Why?

Our academic self-efficacy has a profound impact on our expectations. If we have high self-efficacy, then we are more likely to engage actively in learning, even if the tasks are difficult and complex, because we will persist (McMillan & Forsyth, 1991). Academic self-efficacy is a pivotal point in motivation. Many issues affect it—including previous experience, self-worth, competence—and it dramatically affects our choice of task, persistence, and so forth. Clearly, this characteristic is interwoven with our achievement needs. The combination of high academic self-efficacy and high academic achievement needs provides powerful motivation for academic behaviors. Conversely, low academic self-efficacy and low academic achievement needs can lead to a sense of helplessness and a lack of academic motivation.

Throughout our academic experiences, we explain our success or failure in many ways. Such explanation is termed attribution. Our beliefs about the causes of our academic success or failure influence our emotional reactions. LeFrançois (2000) says

> The cognitive view of motivation is based on the assumption that people continually evaluate their behaviors, look for reasons behind their successes and failures, anticipate the probable future outcomes of intended behaviors, and react emotionally to success and failure. It is not the attribution of behavior to one cause or the other that motivates behavior, says Weiner (1980); it is the emotions that occur as responses to specific attributions. The outcomes of attribution, he suggests, might be anger, guilt, gratefulness, or a variety of other emotions. (p. 303)

If we believe we are responsible for our own success, that our ability and effort help us become more competent, then our self-efficacy (confidence) improves. We believe we can control outcomes. Even if we fail at a particular task, we are willing to try again, changing strategies and increasing effort. We may take responsibility for not trying hard enough or even feel some guilt, but we believe we can be successful.

On the other hand, if we believe our success or failure is controlled by external factors, then we tend to attribute our performance results to luck, difficulty of the task, or outside circumstances. Even a successful outcome does not increase our confidence, because we do not believe we have caused the success. Sometimes, feelings of hopelessness occur if we believe we do not possess either the ability or the will to complete a task. Attributions, either positive or negative, are important factors in motivation, and the strategy for increasing academic motivation in the next section uses helpful attributions as well as other components of the model.

Figure 8.2 illustrates the combined components that affect academic motivation.

FIGURE 8.2   Three Psychological Elements Impacting Our Motivation

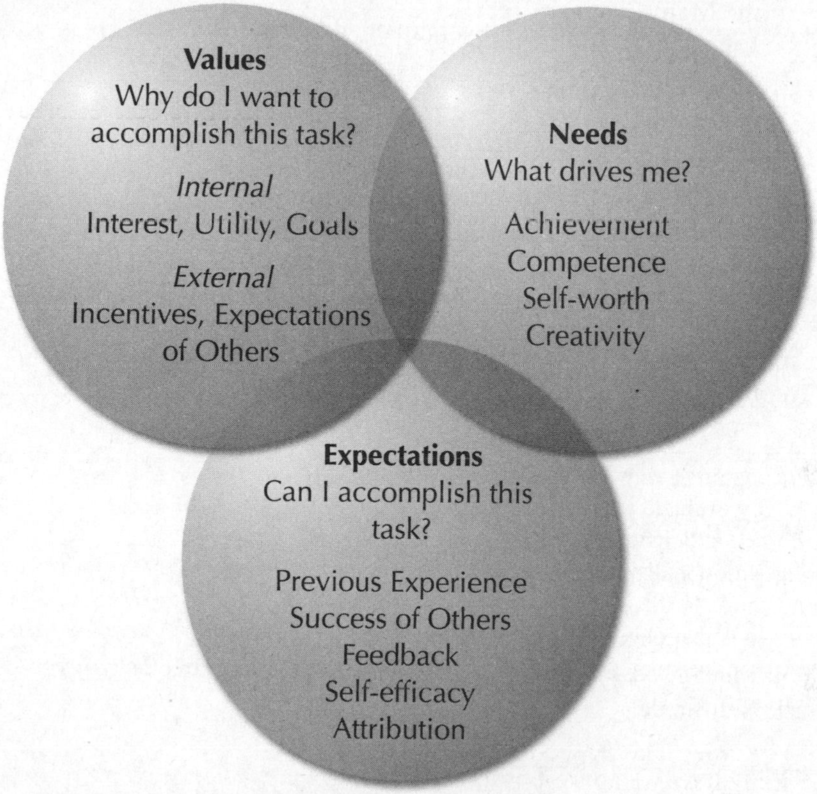

Values
Why do I want to
accomplish this task?

Internal
Interest, Utility, Goals

External
Incentives, Expectations
of Others

Needs
What drives me?

Achievement
Competence
Self-worth
Creativity

Expectations
Can I accomplish this
task?

Previous Experience
Success of Others
Feedback
Self-efficacy
Attribution

Exercise 8.4

Motivation for a Task

Select a major undertaking that you are about to begin. For example, list a possible major area of study that you are considering, or perhaps an upcoming major class assignment. Any important academic opportunity will suffice. Then answer each of the following questions. This exercise will help you assess your academic motivation for a task using the Process of Academic Motivation.

Describe in detail the academic opportunity you wish to accomplish.

VALUES: WHY DO I WISH TO ACCOMPLISH THIS TASK?

Internal Reasons

1. Do I have a genuine interest in this task?

_____ Yes _____ No _____ Unsure

2. Will completing this task be useful to me?

_____ Yes _____ No _____ Unsure

3. Have I set a realistic goal(s) to complete this task?

_____ Yes _____ No _____ Unsure

External Reasons

4. Will someone reward me when I complete this task?

_____ Yes _____ No _____ Unsure

5. Do others expect me to complete this task?

_____ Yes _____ No _____ Unsure

6. Are my expectations realistic?

_____ Yes _____ No _____ Unsure

NEEDS: WHAT DRIVES ME?

7. Is it important for me to gain competence in the task?

_____ Yes _____ No _____ Unsure

8. Will I feel good about myself as I try to accomplish this task—even if the task is difficult?

_____ Yes _____ No _____ Unsure

9. Can I express my own ideas and creativity as I complete this task?

_____ Yes _____ No _____ Unsure

EXPECTATIONS: CAN I ACCOMPLISH THIS TASK?

10. Have I had previous experience accomplishing this or a similar task?

_____ Yes _____ No _____ Unsure

11. Do I compare favorably with others who are also completing this task?

_____ Yes _____ No _____ Unsure

12. Will I use the feedback I receive from others while I am trying to accomplish this task?

_____ Yes _____ No _____ Unsure

13. Do I have a strong belief in my ability to accomplish this task?

_____ Yes _____ No _____ Unsure

14. Have I attributed my completion of a similar task to my own ability and effort?

_____ Yes _____ No _____ Unsure

Answering "No" or "Unsure" on at least two questions within each of the three categories (values, needs, expectations) may indicate a possible motivation deficit in that area.

We gradually develop self-regulatory ability from early childhood and we are heavily influenced by our families and our school experiences. The habits of academic self-regulation coalesce in elementary school, but puberty and adolescence strain those habits. By the time students arrive at college, their self-regulatory abilities are extremely varied. Some students easily slip into the demands of college life whereas others struggle.

The final section illuminates a descriptive model of self-regulation that we believe helps students try to increase their will and use appropriate behaviors, thoughts, and feelings in their academic lives.

STAGES OF SELF-REGULATORY ABILITY

From years of research, we now perceive the stages of self-regulatory ability to be chaos, stability, flexibility, and mastery. Progression through these stages is complicated, and it is possible, even likely, to live simultaneously in several stages in differing areas of our lives. For example, a student might have personal tasks such as budgeting and exercise under control through a rigid set of rules but she often delays writing papers or studying for tests.

Stage 1: Chaos

Most of us have experienced academic chaos at some time in our lives—those times when we lose track of assignments and due dates or we are so far behind that we cannot even decide where to begin. Occasionally, students even stop going to class without consulting their teacher or any campus office. Sometimes, such chaos is triggered by troubled personal relationships, anxiety, economic or family crises, depression, or major illness. Addictions of any kind also plunge a person into chaos. We know we are in chaos when our behaviors, thoughts, and feelings are routinely, even outrageously, inconsistent with our goals.

Climbing out of the pit of academic chaos is difficult, but possible. Usually a first step is to acknowledge that your life has become chaotic, and the second step is to seek help. A talk with a campus advisor or a teacher can outline the dimensions of the chaos. List the areas in which you have some control and those areas that are most frighteningly out of control. What information do you need and where can you find it? Set some specific tasks about finding that information in a timely way.

If the chaos is the result of personal or financial problems, then those problems must be ameliorated before academic order can be restored. Speaking with a campus counselor or your pastor is a sensible first step. Family emergencies or financial problems may necessarily supersede academics, and you may find it necessary to withdraw for the remainder of the term. Addictions are best helped by combining individual counseling and 12-step groups, such as Alcoholics Anonymous, Narcotics Anonymous, or Gamblers Anonymous.

If the chaos is solely academic, some obvious strategies are to find the syllabus for each course and reread all the requirements; then go to each professor during office hours to ascertain what your status in that course is. Discern whether each course is salvageable after your consultation with the professor. If it is not, then withdraw immediately. If it is salvageable, then make a clear and concise list of the priority tasks and set due dates for each one. Sometimes a professor is willing to negotiate your reentry into a course and even give you some extended due dates.

Stage 2: Stability

The logical path from chaos to stability is to consciously set and follow rules. To avoid the chaos that can engulf beginning freshmen, they often need to set the absolute rule of class attendance: to attend every class, without exception. Another example of an academic behavior that can move students out of chaos is to maintain a master calendar daily with all assignments and due dates written down. Setting aside a certain time and place for daily study, without exception, also helps students move toward stability. Fear is often a strong motivator in this process, because students in chaos are usually miserable and confused.

Helpful rules to stabilize your academic life include tracking daily tasks and making positive statements about what you are accomplishing. Ask family and friends for support and encouragement. If your friends are in chaos, see them only after you have done your daily tasks.

The power of such rules is comforting to many students and provides a structure lacking in the collegiate atmosphere. Once stability becomes our normal academic demeanor, we have school tasks under basic control. We know what is required in every course, we have set goals, our behaviors are sufficient to achieve our goals, and we begin to build confidence in our ability to follow the rules we have set.

Stage 3: Flexibility

As our confidence grows, we begin to trust that we have the self-control to implement the necessary behaviors, thoughts, and feelings to reach our academic goals. We realize that we can adjust to the circumstances and that we can still achieve our goals. In other words, we become more flexible. Part of the flexibility stage is the conscious experimentation with the rules from the earlier stage of stability. How absolute do the rules have to be? When can you break the rules or suspend them without damage to your achievements? For example, if you had set Tuesday evenings as a primary study time for history and one Monday your good friend calls and says he will be in your town on Tuesday and wants to take you to dinner, you will want to be with him. What happens to the study time? If you are at the flexibility stage, you will simply reschedule that time for earlier on Tuesday or later in the week and know that you will accomplish the necessary study in a timely way. Gradually, rules become principles, and we have the experience to judge each situation. In this stage, confidence fosters calm, and we tend to be less anxious. Our achievement of this stage is a powerful source of academic self-esteem.

Stage 4: Mastery

The last stage, mastery, occurs when the principles and the adjustments take place automatically, unconsciously. We have internalized useful habits. Managing our behaviors, thoughts, and feelings seems easy, and we can trust ourselves to manage the elements of our daily lives to foster the quality of our experiences. A good vision of a master student is an expert surfer who rides the waves with seeming ease. It takes effort and attention for that surfer to adapt to all the changes in the environment. A master student does the same. She accommodates the changes in work schedules, the demands of everyday problems, as well as the vicissitudes of life.

Possible Regression

An important realization about this concept of the stages of self-regulatory ability is that new and challenging environments can force us to regress to an earlier stage. For example, many high school students reach the flexibility stage when they are juniors and seniors. However, under the challenges of entering college, they may regress to chaos or the rigid rules of stability. The same sort of regression can happen to college graduates who enter their first professional job. We can usually regain our normal stage through the conscious adoption of earlier techniques.

Exercise 8.5

Your Self-Regulatory Ability

Your awareness of the different stages of self-regulatory ability and how they apply to your life is critical to your academic success as a college student. Answer each of the following questions. This exercise will help you analyze your current stage of self-regulatory ability and its impact on your life as a college student.

1. Which stage do you think best describes your current stage of academic self-regulatory ability?

   _____ Chaos _____ Stability _____ Flexibility _____ Mastery

2. Why did you choose this stage? Give three concrete examples to support your choice.

3. How does being in this stage help or hinder your academic success as a college student?

4. If you are currently in the stage of mastery, what three things can you do to ensure that you do not regress to a previous stage? If you are currently in the stage of chaos, stability, or flexibility, what three things can you do to reach the next level of self-regulatory ability?

CONCLUSION

In this chapter we have presented the primary definition of self-regulation, which is the ability to direct behaviors, thoughts, and feelings to reach goals. Two aspects of human nature, will and motivation, directly influence our ability to self-regulate. The stages of self-regulation—chaos, stability, flexibility, mastery—reflect the direction we want to achieve in reaching goals. In the next chapter, we will present primary proven strategies to strengthen academic self-regulation.

SUMMARY

- Self-regulation is our effort to monitor and regulate our own behaviors, cognitions, and emotions so as to reach our goals.

- Academic self-regulated learning is your ability to monitor and control your own behavior, thinking, and emotions as you acquire knowledge and skills during learning.

- Will is the conscious and unconscious control we have over our actions or emotions.

- Motivation can be defined as those thoughts and feelings that initiate, direct, and sustain action.

- Five factors determine our level of motivation: the choices we make, how rapidly we initiate the chosen behavior, the intensity of our efforts, our persistence, and our thoughts and feelings as we are engaged in the chosen behavior.

- The Process of Academic Motivation indicates that when we consider an opportunity to take an action, there are three types of psychological elements that impact our level of motivation to reach the desired behavior: values, needs, and expectations.

- The question, *Why do I want to accomplish this task?* represents values. *What drives me?* is the key question for the elements of need. *Can I accomplish this task?* encompasses our expectations.

- Values are the reasons we prize or disregard a task. They can be internal (intrinsic) and/or external (extrinsic). Internal reasons can be categorized as interest, utility, and goals. External reasons can be categorized as incentives and expectations of others.

- Needs are those factors that drive us to take on and sustain actions. The needs most relevant to academic motivation are achievement, competence, self-worth, and creativity.

- Expectations are the judgments we make regarding how competent we are to achieve a task and our ability to control our behavior. These judgments are based on the following factors: our previous experience in similar situations, how we compare with the success of others, feedback that we have received, our self-efficacy, and our attribution of our level of performance.

- Academic self-efficacy is our individual confidence in being able to meet the challenge being asked of us. The higher our level of self-efficacy is to meet the challenge, the more likely we are to be actively engaged in the learning experience.

- Attribution is how we explain our successes and failures. These explanations can be internal, our ability and efforts, or external, outside factors that control the outcomes.

- The stages of self-regulatory ability are chaos, stability, flexibility, and mastery. It is possible to live in more than one stage at the same time, and new and challenging environments can force us to regress to an earlier stage.

KEY CONCEPTS

Academic self-regulated learning

Expectations: previous experience, success of others, feedback, self-efficacy, attributions

Motivation

Needs: achievement, competence, self-worth, creativity

Process of Academic Motivation model: opportunity, values/needs/expectations, motivation to achieve behavior

Psychological elements that impact motivation: values, needs, expectations

Self-regulation

Stages of self-regulatory ability: chaos, stability, flexibility, mastery

Values: interest, utility, goals, incentives, expectations of others

Will

GUIDED JOURNAL QUESTIONS

1. How often and in what situations does your will (or lack of will) interfere with your learning and academic success? Explain.

2. Reflect back to a time in your life when you were highly motivated to accomplish a goal. What made you so successful? What thoughts and feelings do you remember? Were you mostly internally or externally motivated?

3. If you had to select only one, which would contribute more to your academic motivation—your values, needs, or expectations? Why?

4. How satisfied are you with your current academic motivation? Explain.

5. We believe "the need to avoid failure is a serious danger to collegiate learning. If we are afraid to fail because we believe failure is shameful and humiliating, then we will avoid challenging tasks, opting for the easy way or the outrageously difficult way. In other words, our success is certain or impossible." Do you agree or disagree with this statement? Why?

6. Self-efficacy is your confidence in your ability to complete a task. For which of your current classes do you have high self-efficacy? Why? For which do you have low self-efficacy? Why?

7. Remember Colin? Many of his friends left college after their first semester, but he managed to turn things around for himself. Why is it that some individuals make it in college and others drop out quickly? Can you think of several characteristics that successful students might share?

After having read this chapter, what questions can you ask or suggestions can you offer to a friend who says to you, "I am no longer motivated to attend my history class"?

The Last Word

When I'm truly motivated to complete a difficult task, the challenge is exhilarating. When I complete it successfully, my soul smiles to reward me.

—*Russ Hodges*

Strengthening Academic Self-Regulation

Pumping iron (will).

CHAPTER HIGHLIGHTS

- Flow
- Timeliness
- Strategies for Strengthening Academic Self-Regulation
- Using Self-Regulation to Improve Time Management
- The Killers

FLOW

Most of us can describe experiences in which our efforts were so engrossing and enjoyable that later we realized we were in as "positive a state as it is possible to feel" (Csikszentmihalyi, 1999, p. 825). At those times, we are so imbedded in the moment that we are not even aware we are happy; it is only after the fact that we have a sense of what has happened. Csikszentmihalyi (1999) labels such experiences as "flow" or "autotelic." He writes of a famous lyricist and former poet laureate of the United States who describes his flow experience, writing, in the following way:

> You lose your sense of time, you're completely enraptured, you are completely caught up in what you're doing, and you are sort of swayed by the possibilities you see in this work. . . . The idea is to be so, so saturated with it that there's no future or past, it's just an extended present in which you are . . . making meaning. (Csikszentmihalyi, 1996, p. 121)

Of course, we all want our work to allow "the full expression of what is best in us, something we experience as rewarding and enjoyable" (Gardner, Csikszentmihalyi, & Damon, 2001, p. 9). Goal setting, self-regulation, and learning strategies are the tools that can help us have more flow experiences in our lives and especially in our work.

We have chosen to share these ideas with you because we believe that study and learning is your work as a student and that you can experience these activities as flow experiences. For those of you who have found academics boring most of the time or only slightly bearable because of the potential rewards, our contention that study and learning can be deeply rewarding, both intellectually and emotionally, might seem silly. However, that is exactly what we contend, and we ask that you be willing to listen to the arguments with an open mind. After all, if we are right, then academics could become an entirely different experience for you. If we are wrong, then you have only lost a few minutes of reading.

In thousands of interviews, across age, culture, gender, and job, eight characteristics were mentioned repeatedly to describe such an enjoyable experience:

1. We have clear goals every step of the way.

2. We receive immediate feedback to our actions.

3. Our skills and the challenges we face are in good balance.

4. Our action and awareness are merged; we are not mentally separate from what we are doing.

5. We are totally focused on the task without distractions.

6. We are too involved to be concerned with failure (self-efficacy).

7. We are too involved to be self-conscious.

8. Our sense of the quantity of time passing is distorted.

If these conditions exist, then we enjoy the experience for its own sake—that is, the experience is autotelic (Csikszentmihalyi, 1996). "We feel 100 percent alive when we are so committed to the task at hand that we lose track of time, of our interests—even of our own existence" (Gardner et al., 2001, p. 5).

Clearly, flow is a desired state and far more possible than many cynics would allow. In this chapter and the next, we weave together some new ideas about self-regulation that, along with the beginning concepts we presented in Chapter 8, form an extraordinary set of tools you can use to manage your life well and, perhaps, increase your flow experiences.

Exercise 9.1

SELF-ASSESSMENT: How I Handle Time

You have heard it said before, "Attending college can be the very best time of your life." With 5 being "Almost Always" and 1 being "Almost Never," assess how you relate to and use time. Rate each of the following statements honestly by circling the appropriate number. Completing this exercise will help you identify areas of concern you may have about managing your time in college.

	Almost Always		Sometimes		Almost Never
1. I read, complete assignments, and prepare for exams without waiting until the last minute.	5	4	3	2	1
2. I successfully manage my academic procrastination.	5	4	3	2	1
3. I can accurately predict how much time it takes me to accomplish a task, reach a destination, and so on.	5	4	3	2	1
4. I am honest about and accept responsibility for how I spend my time.	5	4	3	2	1
5. I am aware of when I use time productively versus when I waste time.	5	4	3	2	1
6. I use self-talk to encourage myself to do things and/or to put things off.	5	4	3	2	1
7. With time, effort, and hard work, I believe I can develop my abilities and intelligence.	5	4	3	2	1
8. I make honest efforts to reach my academic goals by attending class, eating right, exercising, getting adequate sleep, and so forth.	5	4	3	2	1
9. I use some sort of planner or calendar (paper or electronic) to keep up with my coursework.	5	4	3	2	1
10. I use to-do lists, Post-It notes, and so on to keep track of daily or weekly tasks.	5	4	3	2	1

Add up the numbers circled. Your total score will be between 10 and 50. The higher your score, the more likely you feel confident about how you spend your time. For scores below 30, write or reflect on items for which you have concerns and consider talking with a trusted friend, a family member, a teacher, a counselor, or an advisor.

TIMELINESS

We all have tried to change our behaviors, thoughts, and feelings from time to time. Sometimes the beginning of a new semester motivates us to change how much we study, or we use New Year's Day as the reason for launching a diet. We use those magic words *willpower* and *discipline*. In other words, we have attempted self-regulation. We all want to be able to change what we do, feel, or think without effort or guilt, but creating positive change requires commitment, attention, and persistence.

Of all the ways in which college students want to change, one topic always tops the list. College students procrastinate, some more than others, but almost all do it. They do not do what they believe they need to do *when* they need to do it.

In 2007, estimates of procrastination in college students ran as high as 75 percent, with 50 percent of students reporting that they procrastinate consistently and consider it a problem. (Burka & Yuen, 2008, p. 6)

Whether it is studying for a psychology test, paying bills, beginning a research paper, or simply cleaning their room, they are experts at delaying, denying, rationalizing, avoiding. Some are perfectionists; others are afraid of success or failure. Some lack the academic skills necessary; some are bored or lazy. Some simply rebel at any authority figure, including professors. Most students want to *accomplish their goals in a timely manner, without guilt or self-punishment*. We have labeled that skill **timeliness**. *When we deliberately choose not to do the necessary action to reach a goal in a timely way* that is when we **procrastinate**. The push–pull between timeliness and procrastination dominates the lives of many people, increasing stress and anxiety. Self-regulation strategies help us move toward timeliness.

STRATEGIES FOR STRENGTHENING ACADEMIC SELF-REGULATION

The idea that we can change our thoughts and feelings, and thereby change our behaviors, may be a new concept to you, but many years of psychological research support that premise. In the remainder of this chapter and the ones following, we will examine numerous strategies. Some stress a cognitive/affective approach while others stress the behavioral, but all are powerful methods of putting you in control of your own academic life. As you read them, relate them to your own experiences as a student.

Ownership

Accepting full responsibility for our own thoughts and actions is the first step to strengthening academic self-regulation. Such ownership rests on the foundation of consciousness. We must be aware of the exact nature of our behaviors, thoughts, and feelings. One place to begin is to examine how we spend our time—exactly how we spend our time, not a romanticized notion of *I really studied for this history test* but, instead, the accuracy of *I studied for four hours for this test after I had finished all the assigned reading. During those four hours I reviewed all my class notes and my highlighting in the text. Then I outlined answers to possible essay questions.* We have to be aware and we have to be honest to accept full responsibility. Such dedication to the truth is central to our acceptance of responsibility.

Glasser (1998), Branden (1994) , and Peck (1978) are three dramatically innovative thinkers who created new ways for people to change their thoughts, feelings, and behaviors. Their combined theoretical work provides a strong foundation for academic self-regulation. All place ruthless and truthful acceptance of responsibility (ownership) at the core of their respective theories of personal freedom, self-esteem, and discipline. We agree that acceptance of responsibility is the essential first step to academic self-regulation; through it we take the power we need to create a purposeful life that is congruent with our quality world.

As we mentioned earlier, educational psychologists who have studied student motivation use the word **attribution** to *describe how students explain their academic successes and failures.* Students who believe that they can control the outcomes of their endeavors, that is, that they are responsible for their academic performance, are more motivated than students who attribute their performance to factors outside themselves—luck, teachers, events, and so forth (Weiner, 1986). If we believe that our

We Recommend

Choice Theory by William Glasser

The Six Pillars of Self-Esteem by Nathaniel Branden

The Road Less Traveled by Scott Peck

actions do not matter, then we become resigned and feel helpless. Claiming responsibility is a crucial first step in managing and increasing our motivation and academic self-regulation.

Although academic ability varies across students, most college students who are consistently motivated, and thus have consistent learning behaviors, can competently perform in most courses. An important corollary to claiming responsibility is having the courage, and perhaps some confidence, that you will act to reach your desires. That confidence is often called self-esteem.

Self-Esteem

From our earliest moments, we are aware of ourselves. Throughout the days and years that follow, we create a system of ideas, beliefs, and feelings about ourselves. Our parents, siblings, and friends can powerfully influence our thoughts and feelings about ourselves. That influence can be loving and positive, or it can be cruel and negative. When we have a distorted view of ourselves, when we believe we are bad or stupid or worthless or, conversely, when we believe we are wonderful, brilliant, or entitled, we do ourselves a great injustice. This topic is the subject of endless movies and books; many people seek counseling because their self-view or self-concept is distorted. Having an accurate self-view, grounded in a sense of our own worth, is an essential foundation for a good life.

How can we know if our view of ourselves is a healthy one? The primary indicator is something called self-esteem. *How we accept ourselves and the value and worth we place on ourselves* is called **self-esteem**. "Self-esteem is the reputation we acquire with ourselves" (Branden, 1994, p. 69). Branden is the primary authority in this field, and his works give specific directions on determining our level of self-esteem and, if necessary, moving it toward health. Our self-esteem is constructed from two sets of thoughts/feelings:

- **Self-efficacy:** *When we feel confident in our own abilities to meet whatever challenges life brings.*

- **Self-respect:** *When we feel confident that we deserve joy and happiness* (see Figure 9.1).

When we have both self-efficacy and self-respect, then we know that we have healthy self-esteem (Branden, 1994). Throughout Branden's writing, he emphasizes our responsibility to choose how we use our consciousness. He agrees with Glasser's (1998) contention that we are responsible for our choices.

Branden (1994) advocates six practices for creating and maintaining healthy self-esteem; in so doing, we are guaranteeing that our self-concept is

FIGURE 9.1   Constructing Self-Esteem

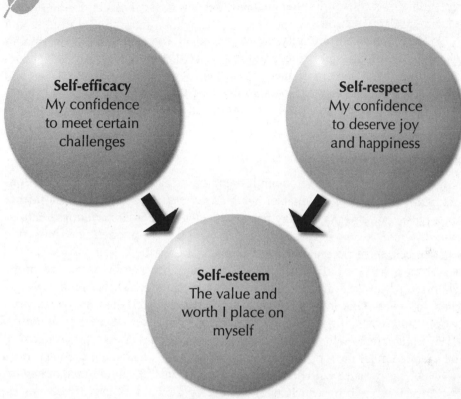

healthy as well. These six practices have a reciprocal relationship with the status and formation of self-esteem and self-concept and are how we create and maintain a healthy and vital self-esteem.

Intent

By our nature, we are purposeful, intentional, creatures—that is, we set goals and try to achieve them. When we are children, we have some goals of our own, but our families and our society push many goals on us. So an understandable reaction is resentment. Children and adolescents struggle with the resentment of imposed goals, even if they acknowledge the merit of them. As we move into adulthood, we have the opportunity to set our own goals—goals that are congruent with our quality world and with our values. Goal setting is a learned skill, and many college students have little practice in carefully creating an integrated set of realistic goals.

> ## Branden's Practices for Building Self-Esteem
>
> **To live consciously** means to attend to and understand what is really going on, both within ourselves and within our world. When we live consciously, we are in harmony with what we see and know.
>
> **To practice self-acceptance** is to be my own friend. It is to claim the totality of who I am and what I do.
>
> **To take responsibility** for myself means that I am responsible for my goals, my behaviors, my feelings, my happiness.
>
> **To practice self-assertiveness** means to speak for myself, to be who I am openly; to treat myself with respect.
>
> **To live purposefully** is to work to achieve my goals.
>
> **To have integrity** is to behave in ways true to my values.

In Chapter 7, we presented methods of setting effective and realistic goals. The composite picture of our combined academic, social, and personal goals becomes essential to the vision of our quality world. Realism and balance are critical to this picture thus our goals must be achievable. Effective and appropriate intentions expressed as goals are the foundation for academic self-regulation.

Initiation

In countless moments each day we choose actions that either lead us closer to our goals or farther away from them. *Those behaviors that will help us reach our goals* are **approach** or initiating **behaviors**. We all know these behaviors—it does not require a genius IQ: we attend class; we study; we exercise; we spend time with friends; we get enough sleep; we play; we tell the truth; we pay our bills; we honor our promises. It means we simply do what we know we should do to achieve a goal. If only it were as easy as it sounds, but each approach behavior has its underside, the **avoidance behavior**. Many of us develop the habit of avoidance—we do not balance our checkbook so that we do not have to face what we have spent; we "forget" an assignment; we spend time with people who do not fit our quality world. Many of us are continually pulled between approach and avoidance behaviors.

Sometimes college students exhibit extreme avoidance behaviors. They may spend much of their time socializing or working. They go through the motions of being a student by attending class sporadically, but they do not turn in papers on time and sometimes they do not even bother to take exams. Usually, they do not make the effort to withdraw or drop courses. Whatever they do, they avoid the reality of what they are doing. They pretend to themselves and their families that they are really trying. Such extreme behaviors can have a variety of causes, including rebellion, addiction, perfectionism, fear of success or failure, depression, and lack of goals. It is usually difficult, if not impossible, to rescue yourself from any of these extreme conditions without professional help. Luckily, most college campuses have counseling centers with professional staff expert in helping students recover. If you know someone (including yourself) who seems to fit this pattern, see a counselor soon and ask for help.

Mindset

Recent research by Stanford psychologist Carol Dweck reveals that people have two different mindsets: fixed or growth (Burka & Yuen, 2008). If we have a **fixed mindset**, we believe that *our talents and intelligence are unchanging and have to be proved again and again.* Academically, each assignment, each test, each project breeds anxiety. People with this mindset often procrastinate because their fear of failure is great.

The opposing mindset—a **growth mindset**—believes that *effort and hard work will develop abilities and intelligence.* People with this mindset seek challenges. If they fail, they are motivated to work harder. People with a growth mindset usually have lower anxiety, higher self-esteem, stronger approach behaviors, fewer avoidance behaviors, and better success. To change from a fixed to a growth mindset ask yourself Dweck's question: "Is success about learning or proving you're smart?" (Burka & Yuen, 2008, p. 29). Leaning into challenges as an opportunity to learn will serve you well.

Self-Talk

Self-talk is *our internal dialog,* and transforming it is a primary strategy of self-regulation of any behavior. Such transformation has the title *cognitive restructuring,* a type of psychological counseling called Rational Emotive Behavior Therapy, pioneered by Albert Ellis (Ellis & Harper, 1975). When we become aware of what we say to ourselves and thoughtfully analyze those statements, we have the ability to discern whether those statements are positive, logical, and reasonable. If they are not, then we can change them. Interestingly, our feelings often follow our thoughts, as well as generate them. Thus, transforming our self-talk can have long-term effects on our beliefs about our abilities and our worth.

If our thinking or belief structure is rational, then our self-talk is accurate, realistic, logical, and moderate. Rational thinking is desirable because it fosters approach behaviors and timeliness. The opposite, irrational thinking, promotes procrastination and anxiety, as well as shame and self-doubt (see Figure 9.2). We can become aware of the irrational thinking that fosters so much avoidance behavior and deliberately change our self-talk in order to slowly change our belief system into messages that will promote timeliness. Remember that it is imperative that we keep our promises to ourselves in order to trust ourselves.

An important causal relationship exists between beliefs and academic behaviors, which is evidenced by the resulting self-talk. A positive example is a student who has a healthy self-esteem, sets appropriate goals, uses positive rational self-talk, and completes assignments in a timely way. Conversely, a

FIGURE 9.2   An Analysis of Self-Talk

	Positive Statement	**Negative Statement**
Rational Statement	*This course material is tough, but I can learn it with help from a tutor, T.A., or the instructor.*	*I can't learn this material; it's too hard! I don't even know where to start.*
Irrational Statement	*If I go to class everyday and ask for extra credit assignments, maybe I'll pass.*	*I don't even care anymore because I can't learn this stuff. I'm sleeping in.*

negative example is a student who has a low sense of self-efficacy, uses irrational self-talk, and procrastinates on getting assignments done. The following list shows many of the common causes of procrastination and the corresponding irrational thoughts and self-talk.

- **Fear of Success**—*If I succeed then others will expect more and more of me.*
- **Fear of Failure**—*I failed before so I will fail again.*
- **Rebellion/Anger**—*This will hurt them more than it will hurt me.*
- **Lack of Self-Efficacy**—*I can't do it; I am not good enough.*
- **Unrealistic Goals**—*I can push myself to do more and more.*
- **Minimizing**—*I have plenty of time.*
- **Low Frustration Level**—*I am no good at this and will never succeed.*
- **Disorganization**—*I'll find it when I need it.*
- **Perfectionism**—*I have to make everything perfect.*
- **Lack of Rewards**—*I need others to motivate me.*
- **Inappropriate Commitments**—*I can do it all.*

Exercise 9.2

Procrastination Survey

We often procrastinate because of irrational thinking. However, once we become aware of those beliefs, we can begin to make positive changes toward timeliness. Completing this exercise will help you assess your tendency to procrastinate.

1. Review the list of common causes of procrastination and choose three causes of procrastination and the corresponding irrational thoughts and self-talk that you engage in frequently as a college student. Then use the continuum to rate the severity of each cause.

Cause of procrastination   Irrational thought/self-talk

_____   _____

Low (causes me   High (causes me
few academic problems) ⟵——————————⟶ severe academic problems)

Cause of procrastination   Irrational thought/self-talk

_____   _____

Low (causes me   High (causes me
few academic problems) ⟵——————————⟶ severe academic problems)

Cause of procrastination   Irrational thought/self-talk

_____   _____

Low (causes me   High (causes me
few academic problems) ⟵——————————⟶ severe academic problems)

2. Rewrite each irrational thought/self-talk statement in step 1 into a positive statement that will help you improve your timeliness and procrastinate less.

_____

_____

_____

CASE STUDY

LIZ is an extroverted, overinvolved sophomore who has a long history of procrastinating on academic projects. In high school, she was able to wait until the last minute, work frantically, and end up with a decent grade. The adrenaline rush was fun. Liz has continued this behavior in college but now finds that her grades are slipping dramatically. She has an important and complicated project in her marketing class due in three weeks, but luckily no exams or other major assignments. Besides attending weekly meetings of two student organizations, her parents' twenty-fifth wedding anniversary party is in ten days, and they live three hours away from her college.

Case Study Question: What cognitive/affective strategies would you recommend Liz use to accomplish work on this project in a timely manner so she can enjoy her parents' celebration without feeling anxious or guilty?

USING SELF-REGULATION TO IMPROVE TIME MANAGEMENT

Time is the great equalizer. You have the same 168 hours each week that everyone else has. How you spend that valuable commodity determines the quality of your life, just as surely as if you walked into a store and ordered it. You have probably already noticed that time passes more quickly for you than it once did. Those endless hours and days of childhood slip away by adolescence, and adulthood brings an ever-increasing acceleration. Whether you are 18 and just beginning college, or 26 and managing a full-time job while going to college, or 45 and returning to a campus after a long absence, you may fall prey to the conviction that you have enough time to do everything, enough time to forgo planning. This is a dangerous self-deception!

A hidden requirement for success in college and in the professional world is the desire and the ability to use time wisely. College graduates with professional jobs have learned to structure their own time and often the tasks as well. Such a skill is not instantly conferred on graduation, but it is slowly and painfully constructed throughout the college years. Time management is one of those phrases that many people respond to emotionally. Either it engenders guilt because we feel we never complete what we *should,* or it creates panic because we do not want to feel trapped in a prison of schedules. How to find the path to balance the place of reaching our goals in a way that is nurturing to our spirit is the subject of hundreds of books and seminars every year. Many topics already mentioned in this text can help you find that place of balance, and we hope the following information also will help you adopt a wise use of your time, a balance between structure and freedom.

Alignment of Subjective Time and Clock Time

Each of us has two senses of time: objective and subjective. **Objective time**, *measured in minutes and hours by clock and calendar, is the time sense we share with everyone else.* **Subjective time** *is our own unique sense of time passing.* The closer our subjective sense of time to clock time, the less we procrastinate. Many students, for whom procrastination is a serious problem, live in perpetual conflict between the reality of clock time (classes, assignments, work activities) and their emotional desire for the sense that they have an endless supply of time.

Several practical strategies can help you more closely align these two senses of time.

- Use a clock and calendar daily to plan and allocate your time.

- Compensate underestimation of time required for studying or other activities by adding extra time (i.e., if you believe you can read an assigned chapter in an hour, plan on one and half hours).

- Learn from experience how long various tasks take and use that experience.

Driving and Resisting Forces

In the battlefield of time usage, two forces repeatedly fight each other. **Driving forces** are those *ambitions that we want to achieve and to acquire.* These desires arise from deep within us. Some examples are our vision of our quality world, our identity of who we are and what we want to be, our purpose or where we want to go in life, our priorities, our integrity or honor, our accomplishments. Ideally, an important aspect of our driving forces is self-care (e.g., those activities such as exercise, rest, play, time with people we love, meditation, and prayer). Make no mistake—such activities help us renew ourselves so we can fulfill our vision of our quality world, a world of health and balance.

Standing opposed to the driving forces are **resisting forces**—an array of *impediments, circumstances, and mindsets that hamper, and sometimes stop, our efforts to achieve.* Roger Merrill (1987), a well-known time management expert, names some of these resisting forces: too many things to do, fatigue, conflicting wants/shoulds, not enough time or money, demands/expectations of others or lack of cooperation from others, lack of purpose and goals, unclear values, confused priorities, and lack of organization. To these we can add a distorted sense of subjective time, low self-esteem, and life crises. Good time use techniques diminish the effect of these resisting forces because they strengthen our drives and our coping abilities. Clarity about the circumstances that are our particular opponents helps us design the time plan that will enable us to reach our goals.

Productive versus Counterproductive Use of Time

How we spend our time determines the quality of our lives (Merrill, 1987). That expenditure of time can be roughly divided into two categories: productive and counterproductive. If we have considered what we want our lives to be as well as who we want to be, then our goals should flow from those considerations. When we *act in ways that support and further our goals,* whether they are academic, occupational, personal, social, spiritual, physical, or artistic, then we are **using time productively**. Because most of us are ambitious, we may have so many goals that we have to prioritize, and it becomes seductively easy to focus on those activities that seem time urgent or immediately rewarding, such as tests, social activities, and family needs. Thus, we may delay, or forgo, the activities that give us long-term benefit, such as rest, exercise, play, or those activities that maintain a balanced life, such as doing laundry, paying bills, and shopping for groceries. Productive renewal activities also include finding the academic major that truly fits us, building relationships, meaningful work, flow experiences, and meditation.

The concept of **counterproductive time** is only too familiar for most of us. Some obvious examples are working extra shifts during the semester and missing class or study time, taking a long weekend before several tests or finals, vegging out in front of the TV, overindulging in computer games, alcohol/drugs, and parties. Typically, we realize when we are using time counterproductively because we feel guilty. It may not be possible to completely eliminate counterproductive use of time; however, it is extremely important to limit it so it does not interfere with the quality of our lives. Self-regulation helps us maintain that limit through awareness, accountability, and action.

Crises interfere with our best intentions because they require an enormous amount of time. Preventable crises include bank overdrafts, bad hangovers, car breakdowns because of poor maintenance, sleeping through your alarm and missing a test, not saving your computer document before printing and then losing it all. Doing what needs to be done in a timely way is the best defense against preventable crises. Another type of crisis, however, is not preventable. Whether it is a serious illness, accident, divorce, death of a loved one—these and other catastrophic events can disrupt our lives and our academic work. As students, it is important to contact the campus dean of students office or the counseling center immediately for help in negotiating the best path for completing your academic work for that term.

Living well means that we strive to live productively as much as we can. Organizing and managing our time well means that we increase the amount of time spent productively. This task is difficult because the resisting forces mentioned earlier tend to push us toward wasting time. The uneasy feeling we get when we know we are not taking care of ourselves mentally, physically, emotionally, and spiritually is the clear indication we are not living in ways congruent with our goals.

Exercise 9.3

Monitoring Your Time

Monitoring your time can be a powerful tool to help you become more successful with self-regulation. This exercise will take you one full week to complete and it is in two parts. Completing this exercise will help you see trends in your time usage so that you can make appropriate adjustments.

PART I: TIME MONITOR

Keep track of how you spend your time for a week by completing the Weekly Time Monitor. At least three times a day, take a few minutes to update the time monitor to ensure accuracy in recording (it is all too easy to *overestimate* the amount of time you study and to *underestimate* how long you spend doing everything else!). A blank copy of this form is provided at the end of this chapter.

Weekly Time Monitor							
	Monday	Tuesday	Wednesday	Thursday	Friday	Saturday	Sunday
6:00–7:00							
7:00–8:00							
8:00–9:00							
9:00–10:00							
10:00–11:00							
11:00–12:00							
12:00–1:00							
1:00–2:00							
2:00–3:00							
3:00–4:00							
4:00–5:00							
5:00–6:00							
6:00–7:00							
7:00–8:00							
8:00–9:00							
9:00–10:00							
10:00–11:00							
11:00–12:00							
12:00–1:00							
1:00–2:00							
2:00–3:00							
3:00–4:00							
4:00–5:00							
5:00–6:00							

Once you have recorded how you spend your time for seven days, add up the number of hours you spent in each of the following categories (note: there are 168 hours in one week):

_____ Sleep	_____ Personal hygiene
_____ Class	_____ Meetings
_____ Study	_____ Spiritual
_____ Meals	_____ Television
_____ Family	_____ Computer/games
_____ Work	_____ Social
_____ Commute	_____ Other: _____
_____ Exercise	_____ Other: _____

PART II: USE OF TIME

Once you have analyzed your completed time monitor, place your week's activities into the three boxes below. Estimate how much of your time was spent in each of the three categories (how many hours). Then estimate the percentage of total time you spent in each category for the week (_____% of 168 hours).

Productive	Counterproductive	Crises

What changes, if any, would you like to accomplish in your use of time?

Underlying Assumptions for Effective Time Management

Many time management systems have appeared in the past 50 years. They range from spiral-bound day planners to computer programs to smart phones. However different they may appear on the surface, all share many of the same assumptions. Whatever format you choose, be aware of the following assumptions.

Assumption #1. Time management systems usually start with vision and goals. We have spoken in this text about our quality world and the goals that can emerge from our vision of how and who we want to be. Discerning our goals and checking them by the criteria of belief, realism, desire, and measurement allow us to build a strong foundation for effective time management.

Assumption #2. We are the owners, not the slaves, of our time. Although some of our time each day is fixed, such as work, class, and commuting time, we do control most of the rest of our time. We actively choose what we do and when we do it. Some simple examples are when we get up and when we go to bed; when and how long we eat; when we run errands or do household chores; when and how long we study, play, stare at the computer, and so on.

Assumption #3. A dramatic reality of our postmodern world is the amount of "stuff" we should handle each day. If we add up all of the incoming text messages, voice mail, assignments, social networking, and so forth, the sheer quantity of information we manage each day is enormous. David Allen (2001), a leading management consultant, brings a radical premise to the management of time and tasks. He believes that we must *handle all incoming data daily.* This control allows our minds to be clear and stress free, thereby increasing our productivity. Developing these abilities as a student is a direct investment in your life as a professional.

A simple adaptation of his process for students looks like this:

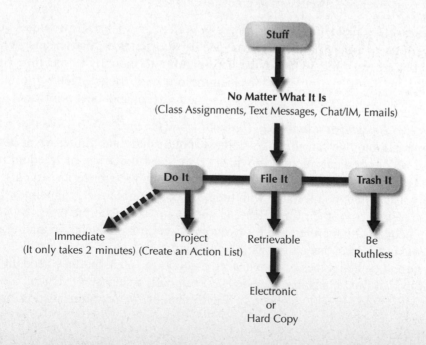

When "stuff" comes in, no matter what it is, do it, file it, or trash it so that all of your inboxes are cleared daily. Some "stuff" needs to be trashed. Be ruthless. Some of your "stuff" will need to be filed. Immediately discern whether an electronic or hard copy is necessary. File it where you can find it easily. If the task can be done within two minutes, do it then—don't postpone. If the task will require more than two minutes, then plan how you will accomplish it. Decide on your next action and put it in your planner or on a calendar if you need a reminder or a scheduled block of time. You may need project folders, white boards, and/or a place to store the task or project temporarily. File when complete.

Assumption #4. We ask ourselves: *What is the best use of my time right now?* (Lakein, 1973, p. 96). Holding this question in the back of our minds helps us realize when we are procrastinating, when we are overwhelmed, when we are confronted by a crisis that interrupts our time plan. Sometimes the best use of our time is to help a friend or to take a nap; sometimes it is to study the subject we like least because the test is tomorrow. *What is the best use of my time right now?* puts the question of priorities and flexibility forefront in your thinking.

Creating the Right Plan

"Planning is bringing the future into the present so that you can do something about it now" (Lakein, 1973, p. 25). However, our plan has to be the right plan for us or it will not work. To create the right plan, we have to answer the following questions:

What are my goals? The right plan encompasses the goals from all areas of our lives (see extensive discussion of goals in Chapter 7).

What are my priorities among those goals? Covey (1989) promotes first things first as a mantra for good time use. In simple terms, that means paying bills before watching TV, studying before going to the movie, spending time with your significant other before hanging out with friends, getting to work early, and so on. A good time or task plan helps us set and meet priorities.

How can I establish a time plan that will work for me? We believe that most people fall into two categories of feelings about using time. Either we need the sense of safety that structure provides *or* we need the sense of freedom that structure inhibits. In simplistic terms, people with a preference for structure or safety usually are comfortable with time-use planning. In fact, sometimes they spend too much of their time planning and do not complete the tasks. By contrast, people with a preference for freedom often fight the idea of planning, erroneously thinking that a time-use plan is a jail.

In reality, both types of people need a good time plan, but they need different types of time plans that include a list of goals, a semester calendar, a next action list, and a weekly planner. In The Essentials, we recommended using an academic planner to list all your academic commitments, and we provided several guidelines for its use. Now we are adding several more pieces to that original concept to give you a complete system. Such a system combines all the facets of your life in one place.

Next Action List

Allen (2001) suggests a **next action list** as a simple and highly effective daily strategy. You may write it in an electronic calendar, a daily planner, on a notepad, or on a Post-it note. It is *a list of the tasks that should be completed during the next day or week;* these tasks are separate from the normally scheduled times of class, work, meals, and sleep. A next action list is always changing as you check off those things you have completed and add new tasks. Sometimes you may have enough tasks that you will need to prioritize by marking some as As (top priority), some as Bs, and so forth.

Study Starts

If you have difficulty starting to study (but once you start, you keep going), then try a technique called study starts. A **study start** occurs when *we promise to do at least 10 minutes of study before a certain time of day.* For example, *I will start reading the assigned chapter in history by 5 P.M. this afternoon and spend at least 10 minutes on the task.* A study start breaks the impasse, the logjam, and once we have started, the likelihood is that we will continue. Some students contract with themselves to do a study start before 1 P.M. and another one by 5 P.M.

Additional Suggestions. If you have difficulty completing long projects, you can do at least one of the following:

- Set a specific date, time, and location to start. *(I will go to the library Wednesday after lunch.)*

- Talk yourself into starting by planning an immediate reward afterward. *(When I finish working in the library, I'll treat myself to an hour at the recreation center.)*

- Break the task into small, concrete parts. *(I'll list all the parts of a paper— potential topics, focused topic, thesis statement or idea, outline of points to cover, support for each point, and so on).*

- Choose one part and commit to working on it for 5–10 minutes only; then reassess whether to continue working or quit. *(I'll just brainstorm and write down ideas for my paper; then I'll decide whether to start my outline or come back tomorrow.)*

If you can start a project but have difficulty persisting to completion, then try these suggestions:

- Use self-talk to encourage or motivate yourself. *(I can finish this assignment on time if I stick to my schedule.)*

- Set interim due dates for each part with tentative rewards for each one. *(I'll put a calendar on my wall and list each due date. For each part I complete, I'll go to my favorite place to eat.)*

- Choose a partner who is working on the same or similar assignment and encourage each other to reach your goals. *(We'll meet at the library at 2 P.M. and find sources together.)*

- Maintain a system of rewards throughout the project. *(I've been making real progress, and I cannot quit now. So I'll be careful to keep giving myself rewards for each and every step.)*

Technology Aids

Smart phones, laptop computers, and netbooks are some of the hardware tools available now, and scheduling software is common on most desktop computers. All cost money and time in learning how to use and maintain them. As your life becomes more complex, especially if you are comfortable with technology, you may find that electronic scheduling is helpful. However, "even the best tool is no substitute for vision, judgment, creativity, character, or competence" (Covey, Merrill, & Merrill, 1994, p. 327).

CASE STUDY

MARCUS describes himself as a perfectionist; he prefers to do a job well, or not at all. As a junior computer major, he is an effective and able student in most of his computer courses, which tend to be highly structured. However, this semester he is taking world literature, a course that has little structure and few deadlines. His professor told the class to read the text deeply and with understanding and to think about what they have read from an analytical viewpoint. The midterm and final exams are primarily in essay format. The research paper is even more formidable because the professor expects each student to create a project. Marcus's response has been to procrastinate for the first month of the semester.

Case Study Question: How would you design a plan for Marcus that will help him study effectively for his exams and complete his research project in a timely manner?

THE KILLERS

There are three psychological conditions that can destroy academic performance: addiction, depression, and intense anxiety. All have the capacity to interrupt consistent academic behaviors.

Although alcohol and other drug use are obvious addictions, a new addiction has emerged. "More than 18 percent of college students are pathological Internet users, and 58 percent report that their excessive Internet use has disrupted their studying and classroom attendance and also lowered their grade point average" (Small & Vorgan, 2008, p. 51). It is the specific application—database searching, instant messaging (IM), online dating, shopping, gaming, porn—that is addictive, not the Internet itself. Compulsive spending is another addictive behavior college students often experience.

Clinical depression sometimes strikes college students because of the intense changes that are occurring in their lives. Common symptoms include feeling sad more days than not, sleeping more than ten hours a day or, conversely, not sleeping, weight gain or loss, irritability, and withdrawal from social contact.

Intense anxiety can take the form of a panic attack, blanking or freezing on a test, nervousness in or avoidance of new social situations, or episodes of unexplained fear.

If you believe you are experiencing any of these three circumstances, immediately contact a counselor or an advisor on your campus, as well as a trusted friend or family member. **Please do not delay**—help is available.

CONCLUSION

This book is entitled *Academic Transformation* because we passionately believe that students can recreate themselves academically—transforming themselves into the students they wish to be. The core of our ability to transform is self-regulation. This chapter has highlighted some of the effective cognitive, affective, and behavioral strategies that enhance self-regulation. We hope you are willing to adopt some of these strategies as you attempt the improvements you seek. Practice these strategies carefully and make them yours.

In this chapter we introduced the concept of flow, that magical feeling of completeness when we perfectly match our task. In the next chapter we write about balance; the two together form a union that can frame a satisfying life. We also write about the two most powerful and comprehensive strategies for self-regulation—key routines and self-change. Both utilize many of the strategies already presented.

SUMMARY

- A "flow" experience is one in which a person is so immersed in the moment that she is not even aware that she is happy. Goal setting, self-regulation, and learning strategies will all help create more "flow" experiences.

- Creating positive change requires commitment, attention, and persistence. The two competing foes in this battle are timeliness and procrastination.

- One strategy to help change our thoughts, feelings, and ultimately behavior is the concept of ownership, which is accepting full responsibility for our own actions and thoughts.

- Self-esteem is an accurate view of oneself, grounded in a sense of one's own worth. Key concepts to the strategy of self-esteem are self-efficacy and self-respect. Branden has compiled six strategies for improving self-esteem.

- Intent is the ability to set our own goals.

- The concept of initiation describes how we regularly choose actions that either lead us closer to, or further away from, our goals. The two competing interests in initiation are approach behaviors and avoidance behaviors.

- Mindset deals with how we perceive our own talents and intelligence. The two competing states in mindset are fixed mindset and growth mindset.

- Self-talk is our internal dialogue, and the goal is for that self-talk to be rational, accurate, realistic, logical, and moderate. It is possible to analyze and transform self-talk.

- There are three separate and distinct sets of competing interests when examining time management: objective time versus subjective time, driving forces versus resisting forces, and the use of time as productive versus counterproductive.

- There are four underlying assumptions for effective time management.

- There are some valuable tools for enhancing the ability to make wise decisions in managing time: creating the right plan, a "next action list," study starts, and technology aids.

- Addiction, depression, and intense anxiety will, when left unchecked, destroy students' academic performance.

KEY CONCEPTS

Alignment of subjective time
and clock time

Attribution

Branden's practices
for building self-esteem

Creating the right plan

Driving and resisting forces

Flow

Initiation: approach and
avoidance behaviors

Intent

Killers: addiction, depression
and intense anxiety

Mindset: fixed and growth

Next action list

Objective time

Ownership

Procrastinate

Productive vs. counterproductive
use of time

Self-efficacy

Self-esteem

Self-respect

Self-talk

Study start

Subjective time

Technology aids

Timeliness

Underlying assumptions for
effective time management

GUIDED JOURNAL QUESTIONS

1. Flow is described as a time when you are completely engrossed in what you are experiencing with no sense of time having passed. Describe an academic situation in which you experienced flow. If you have not experienced flow during an academic endeavor, then describe your experience of flow from a different perspective.

2. Intent is defined as your ability to set your own goals—especially goals that relate to your quality world. How easy or difficult is it for you to do this? Explain. List several self-set goals from your past that you have completed.

3. Describe a situation when guilt or self-punishment thwarted your ability to reach a past goal. Was this goal a self-set goal? Was it connected to your quality world? Explain.

4. Discuss a time when you made a bad choice or decision and took responsibility for it, even though you knew the consequences were going to be unpleasant. Have there been times when you have not been willing to take responsibility for such a decision? Explain.

5. Self-esteem is defined as the reputation we acquire with ourselves. Branden lists six practices for building one's self-esteem:

   - to live consciously

   - to practice self-acceptance

   - to take responsibility

   - to practice self-assertiveness

   - to live purposefully

   - to have integrity

   Select at least two of these practices that you will begin to fully develop for yourself. Explain why you selected those particular practices, and list some of the strategies you will use to start implementing them.

6. What methods do you currently use to manage your time? How well are these methods working? How many hours per week do you study? When do you complete the majority of your studying? When are your most efficient times to study (when you are learning at your peak)? Explain.

7. Academically, do you tend to have more of a fixed mindset or a growth mindset? Give several examples to support your choice.

The Last Word

Time—use it or lose it because you can't save it, you can't borrow it, and you certainly can't take it with you!

—Carol Dochen

Weekly Time Monitor

	Sunday	Monday	Tuesday	Wednesday	Thursday	Friday	Saturday
6:00							
7:00							
8:00							
9:00							
10:00							
11:00							
12:00							
1:00							
2:00							
3:00							
4:00							
5:00							
6:00							
7:00							
8:00							
9:00							
10:00							
11:00							
12:00							
1:00							
2:00							
3:00							
4:00							
5:00							

Making Behaviors
Work for You

Walking the academic tightrope.

CHAPTER HIGHLIGHTS

- Balancing Our Lives
- Key Routines
- Self-Change: A Holistic Approach to Changing Behaviors

The challenge of modern life, whether as a college student or a working professional, is to manage the time we have so that we reach our goal of a quality life—a quality life that incorporates what we want to achieve both personally and professionally. It is not an easy task to navigate the balance between doing what we *should* do for long-term goals (delayed gratification) and doing what we *want* to do right now (immediate gratification). Obviously, we benefit if we use vision rooted in our quality world, developing both long-term and short-term goals based on that vision, and managing our daily lives in a thoughtful manner.

In this chapter, we begin with specific examples of students who feel the unbalance in their lives and search for the path of balance. There are no simplistic answers to that search, but instead perceptive analyses grounded in the values of the individuals. The remainder of the chapter explores two powerful self-regulation strategies: key routines and self-change, a practical method of changing those behaviors that keep us from living a balanced life. Key routines harness habit to work for us; they can keep us out of chaos. If we need to change a specific behavior, especially an entrenched one, then self-change is the intensive technique that we recommend. The power of this technique lies in what we know from cognitive behavioral psychology, and with it we can change any behavior.

SELF-ASSESSMENT: Balancing My Life

The challenge of any college student is learning to balance academics, work, family, and personal and social interests. With 5 being "Almost Always" and 1 being "Almost Never," assess your ability to effectively balance your life while you are in college. Rate each of the following statements honestly by circling the appropriate number. Completing this exercise will help you identify areas of concern you may have about your ability to achieve and maintain balance in your life.

	Almost Always		Sometimes		Almost Never
1. I prioritize my daily tasks effectively.	5	4	3	2	1
2. I spend an appropriate amount of time organizing and planning.	5	4	3	2	1
3. Having flexibility in my daily schedule works well for me.	5	4	3	2	1
4. I resist the temptation "to play" when I have important work to complete.	5	4	3	2	1
5. When my life becomes too chaotic, I quickly build in structure to help myself	.5	4	3	2	1
6. I recognize important changes I need to make in my behavior.	5	4	3	2	1
7. I make important changes in my behavior when necessary.	5	4	3	2	1
8. I change my behavior without being forced by others.	5	4	3	2	1
9. I reward myself for a job well done.	5	4	3	2	1
10. I feel guilty when I break a commitment to myself.	5	4	3	2	1

Add up the numbers you circled. Your total score will be between 10 and 50. The higher your score, the more likely you feel confident about how you spend your time. For scores below 30, write or reflect on items for which you have concerns and consider talking with a trusted friend, a family member, a teacher, a counselor, or an advisor.

BALANCING OUR LIVES

"**B**alancing is the discipline that gives us flexibility. Extraordinary flexibility is required for successful living in all spheres of activity" (Peck, 1978, p. 64). Sometimes a good method for developing balance is to look at the characteristics of people who are our opposite in relation to the structure/freedom preference. What can we learn from those who are so different from us? If we prefer structure, we may need to learn to incorporate more play into our lives (but we are almost sure to schedule it!). If we prefer freedom, we may need to use a planner for schoolwork and personal tasks (even though it may be a struggle initially).

Let us now look at some specific examples of students needing to move toward greater balance in their lives and the steps they are taking:

Example: Preeta is an international student who has come to the United States to study computer science. She is so determined to succeed that she studies every moment that she is not working at her campus job. She has made few friends and seems anxious and worried.

Remedy: Preeta realizes that she will benefit from joining at least one campus organization and giving herself one hour a day to listen to music and relax.

Example: Jose is a single parent with an eight-year-old daughter. He works 25 hours a week and takes four courses. His day is nonstop from 6 A.M. to 9 P.M., as he juggles caring for his child, doing schoolwork, and working at his job. He feels exhausted and worries that he is on an endless treadmill.

Remedy: Jose begins to examine the resources in his extended family and the community for child care to allow him some time to himself, for both study and recreation.

Example: Kimberly is enjoying every aspect of college. She loves living on campus, and her room is always full of friends. The television is usually on as well as instant messaging on her computer. She has good intentions about exercising and study, but often finds herself at the end of the day with few tasks accomplished.

Remedy: Kimberly realizes that she cannot study in her room because it has far too many distractions. Her first priority becomes studying enough to maintain her scholarship, so she schedules study time at the library immediately after her afternoon classes. She finds a quiet study carrel, away from the elevators and walkways. She completes her studies before she goes back to the dorm. After a few weeks, she feels that her study behaviors are stable, so she schedules two workout sessions each week in the campus recreation center.

Example: Darius is a junior who lives off campus. He enrolls in at least 16 hours each term and is vice president of the student government association. He also participates in a professional organization for his major. He feels anxious most of the time because there are so many details to remember. Most importantly, he never feels that he is doing anything well.

Remedy: Darius begins to use a planner to help him remember the multitude of tasks. However, he also reevaluates his goals and makes some important changes. He turns down the offer of a leadership role in the professional organization, preferring just to participate as a member. He schedules time to play his guitar several times a week; it is an activity that he used to enjoy. He decides to take a break during the summer and work rather than take extra courses to graduate early.

Balance leads to inner harmony: "It is the selection of appropriate and realistic goals congruent with inner values. It is the resolution of wants and shoulds. It is the balance of work, family, community and personal priorities" (Merrill, 1987, p. 41).

Exercise 10.2

Balancing Your Life

Balancing your life is like learning to walk on a circus tightrope, high up in the air. It takes plenty of practice and patience. How well have you mastered your balancing act as a student? This exercise will help you focus on your ability to balance your life.

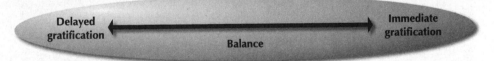

1. How well are you balancing doing what you should to reach long-term goals (delayed gratification) and doing what you want to right now (immediate gratification)?

   _____ Well _____ Somewhat _____ Poorly

2. If you answered "Well," explain what recent decisions and/or strategies have helped you delay gratification and improve or maintain balance.

3. If you answered "Poorly" or "Somewhat," explain three decisions or changes you could make to delay gratification and improve your balance.

KEY ROUTINES

Although our days are full of hundreds of behaviors, some conscious and some unconscious, just a handful of those behaviors have the capacity to influence all the others. Those few powerful behaviors are **key routines**. A primary method of strengthening our self-regulation is to identify and implement our key routines, *those five or six behaviors that keep us from chaos and move us toward mastery* (see Stages of Self-Regulatory Ability in Chapter 8). Key routines can be simple—getting enough sleep, balancing the checkbook—or complex—maintaining a detailed calendar, creating and maintaining healthy relationships. Interestingly, key routines vary from one person to another. What is powerful for you may not work well for your friend.

The variability of key routines is evident when we work with students. Two of our students come to mind: Todd, a second-semester freshman, and Cecilia, a single mother who has returned to college after a 15-year absence. Although both are full-time students and academically capable, neither one was prepared for the downward spiral into chaos that they had experienced the prior semester. Both started the spring term with good intentions, but they were worried, so they came to consult with us. Both already had discerned that they needed to change in order to be academically successful. Thus, they already had begun the process of improving their self-regulation.

CASE STUDY

TODD is a freshman—he lives on campus and belongs to several organizations. He works 15 hours each week in a campus office, takes five courses, has numerous friends, and dates regularly. He is a casual, laid-back guy who managed high school reasonably well. The changes inherent in living in a dorm and the freeform lifestyle available to freshmen caught him by surprise. He reports that he simply does not feel in control of anything, and he feels worried and guilty most of the time. Upon discussion, we discern that Todd was at the flexibility stage in high school, but he has regressed to a more chaotic stage now. He is still attending but barely passing most classes, and alcohol/drugs are not interfering with his life. He does not have any major financial, family, or emotional problems.

After discussion and reflection, Todd chooses to focus on four key routines: sleeping, attending class, scheduling, and exercising regularly. Like many freshmen living on campus, regular sleep is hard to accomplish. The dorm is active 24/7. Todd often delays studying until late in the evening, then goes online, and finally goes to sleep around 2 A.M. Even if he makes his nine o'clock class the next day, he is usually tired.

Case Study Question: What key routine does Todd need to put in place to get more sleep on a regular basis?

Attending every class is another key routine Todd chooses. Like many freshmen, Todd took most of his excused absences early in the term. Now, he realizes that he needs to go to every class. College teachers simply do not repeat what is in the book; they give new information in every lecture.

Case Study Question: What key routine does Todd need to implement to make sure he attends all of his classes for the rest of the term?

Of the four key routines Todd has chosen, scheduling is a new skill. College competency simply demands that students learn to schedule, plan, and keep a written or electronic record of activities and obligations. We spend several sessions with Todd to help him create the scheduling system that will function for him. He has to learn to implement it throughout each day, and that effort is intense. He learns that he prefers an academic calendar with space for each day's activities.

Case Study Question: What key routine can Todd implement to guarantee that his scheduling helps him meet his academic goals?

The fourth key routine Todd chooses is to exercise regularly. He already goes to the campus gym sporadically to work out. He decides that he will also run for 30 minutes three days a week before class and then come back to the dorm to get ready.

As an example, we asked Todd to check his key routine for exercise against the criteria we learned for setting achievable goals: believable, realistic, desirable, and measurable. He quickly sketches the following graph.

Todd's Key Routines

	Believable	Realistic	Desirable	Measurable
Exercising	√	X	√	√

After reviewing his plan, Todd realizes that he has scheduled his primary exercise early in the morning, a time with which he is already struggling. His choice is unrealistic. Reluctantly he goes back to his weekly schedule and chooses Tuesday, Thursday, and Saturday afternoons as the times he commits to exercise. He already knows that the best exercise for him is a 45-minute workout on machines followed by a 30-minute run at the track. He rightly expects that such exercise will quickly increase his energy and reduce his stress.

Todd works with us throughout the semester by regular appointments. We review his performance on his selected routines and then plan for the next several weeks. He struggles with the new routine of scheduling but gradually learns to rely on his academic calendar and his new habits. At spring break, he goes home and shows his mother what he is doing about scheduling. His mother, a corporate manager, laughs and pulls out her iPhone™, saying, "I couldn't do my work without this; it's a lifesaver. You are developing an important skill."

A student with a completely different set of balancing issues is CECILIA, a 32-year-old single parent with two children, ages eight and six. She works part-time and takes four courses at the downtown campus of a community college. Although she has some help with child care from her relatives, she carries the main responsibility for herself and her children. Cecilia is highly motivated to succeed in school; she wants to complete her degree, and she has a few credits from her time in college 15 years ago. This term she is experiencing the shock of the workload of parenting, working, and studying. She comes to the learning center for help in managing this new life. She reports that mornings are chaotic and she is exhausted and stressed by the time she arrives at class. Her children resist getting up and getting dressed. However, she is in control of her academic work.

After discussion, Cecilia realizes that although she is stable in her academic work, her family routines have become chaotic. Her goal is to have pleasant and less stressful mornings. She chooses several target behaviors that should ease the confusion and stress of the mornings. The night before a school day, Cecilia will supervise the children's packing of their backpacks; lay out their school clothes; and assemble any necessary notes, money, or supplies. She will pack their lunches and put them in the refrigerator. Then she will set the table for breakfast. The next morning she will arise 15 minutes early and dress before she wakes the children. Notice the specificity of these target behaviors. Each is designed to increase the efficiency and calm of school mornings, and each meets the criteria of believable, realistic, desirable, and measurable. Within just a week, Cecilia reports that this routine has become habitual, and she is able to concentrate much better in class.

Making Key Routines Automatic

A part of the mastery stage is the automatic execution of key routines—in other words, making our key routines habitual. When a behavior becomes a habit, we no longer consciously consider doing it or not doing it; we just do it. Whether it is going to class or paying the bills on time, doing habitual behaviors usually is not stressful. We do not have to make the same decision over and over again.

Moving from chaos to habitual key routines requires we accept responsibility for our actions. As we discussed in Chapter 9, accepting responsibility is the essential first step in academic transformation. Next comes the designing of several rigid rules about certain tasks, such as Todd has chosen for exercising. Keeping a written record of our performance of those tasks, plus reinforcing our accomplishment, helps us to hold ourselves accountable.

The movement from chaos to stability to flexibility and eventually to mastery takes time and practice. As you develop your ability to control (self-regulate) your behavior, you will realize which of your rules must be firm and which can be flexible. You will also learn to adapt your routines to your goals, because your goals may change in the process. For example, as you progress through college, your ambitions may become more specific. Thus, your goals will change, and your key routines as well. College is the training ground and the practice place for a well-managed life.

•

Exercise 10.3

Key Routines

Often you may find that life is controlling you as opposed to you controlling your life. How often do you feel out of control? This exercise will help you strengthen your self-regulation by establishing key routines to create stability out of chaos.

1. In which areas of your life are you experiencing chaos?

2. For what part of the chaos can you claim responsibility? In other words, what is your contribution to the chaos in your life?

3. What key routines can you immediately establish to help you stabilize your life?

4. What rules can you implement to support your key routines?

5. How honestly committed are you to these rules?

6. What positive reinforcements can you provide for yourself to support and maintain your key routines?

Implement two or three key routines and corresponding rules for a period of two weeks. Then write a one-page evaluation of your progress. If you are not experiencing success, rethink the project, consult with your instructor, make changes, and try again.

SELF-CHANGE: A HOLISTIC APPROACH TO CHANGING BEHAVIORS

We draw from the field of behavioral psychology in a deliberate attempt to help you change specific behaviors using the knowledge and techniques culled from years of psychological experiments. There are many ways to change behaviors, thoughts, and feelings; however, the most powerful method of self-regulation is a process called self-change. Self-change incorporates many of the strategies that we have presented in previous chapters, and it is the integration of these strategies that provides the power to make lasting changes.

Working to change a behavior first often leads to subsequent changes in thoughts and feelings. Although we can sometimes change behaviors because we are frightened or because there are powerful rewards involved, our good intentions can weaken over time, and our old behaviors creep back. Self-change increases our chances of reaching our behavioral goals because it is based on what we know about how people learn and change.

If you decide to try a self-change project, you must commit to a minimum period of three to four weeks. Although you may wish to focus on changing an academic behavior, we encourage you to think of other possibilities such as exercise, eating habits, smoking, money management, TV watching, computer use, and assertiveness. If you value yourself and wish to create a more desirable future, plan well, follow through thoroughly, and monitor your progress regularly so that you can achieve your goal. Remember, you have the power to make positive changes in your life. The following steps will assist you in completing a self-change program; blank forms are provided at the end of the chapter.

Step 1: Formulate a Target Behavior

Choosing a goal is the first step. Say, for example, your goal is to lose 15 pounds. Now translate your goal into a target behavior by identifying specific behaviors you can engage in order to reach your goal. To lose weight, your target behavior could be to restrict your caloric intake to 1,000 calories each day *or* to eliminate all snacks in-between meals *or* to run three miles a day *or* a combination of diet and exercise. If your goal is to increase your GPA, your target behavior could be to increase the amount of daily study time to two hours each day *or* to get tutoring in specific subjects three times a week *or* to complete all homework the day it is assigned. Your target behavior must be achievable (believable, realistic, desirable, and measurable), just like the action statements you created when you were learning to set goals in Chapter 7.

Step 2: Collect Baseline Data

Once you have selected a target behavior, you will conduct a seven-day observation period. Observe the behavior as it naturally occurs. Do not consciously try to change the behavior, although it may change slightly because of your increased awareness. We call this step collecting baseline data, and you will need to keep a record of how often, when, and where your behavior occurs as well as some of the thoughts and feelings you associate with the behavior.

FIGURE 10.1   Sample Behavior-Tracking Form

Date	Time	Count	Behavior	Feelings	Self-Talk	Consequences
2/16	4–5 P.M.	I hour	Completing homework; finished rough draft of English essay	Relaxed, motivated to finish	"If I get this done before dinner, I'll have time to read biology this evening."	Relieved, ready to turn rough draft in the next day for a completion grade
2/18	—	0 hours	Completing homework; was supposed to finish math but went to party instead	Had fun at the party but felt guilty all night for not doing math assignment	"I'll try to finish it when I get home or get up early."	Failed pop quiz in math the next morning

To lose those 15 pounds over the next month, count how many calories you consume each day *or* measure how much exercise you get *or* analyze the types of food you eat and when and where you eat them. What are you thinking and how are you feeling as you observe and engage in this behavior?

If your target behavior is to quit smoking, count the average number of cigarettes you smoke each day. Are there certain periods of time when you tend to smoke more often or less often? What types of activities cause you to crave a cigarette? How tense do you become between cigarettes? This information will be useful when you move to the third step, so record it in a daily journal or behavior-tracking log. (See Figure 10.1 for a sample behavior-tracking form. A blank one is provided at the end of the chapter.) We also encourage you to graph your behavioral observations; pictures often say more than words.

Another important part of collecting baseline data is to research your target behavior at your campus library. Find at least three good sources that can help you design your self-change project, and photocopy articles and relevant parts of book sources to keep as references.

Step 3: Design a Contract

The next step of the project is to design a self-change contract. (See Figure 10.2 for a sample self-change contract and Figure 10.3 for a sample four-week graph for a self-change project. A blank contract and graph are provided at the end of the chapter.)

FIGURE 10.2   Sample Self-Change Contract

Self-Change Contract

My overall goal for this self-change project is:
   To quit smoking cigarettes forever!

The target behavior I want to initiate, increase, maintain, decrease, or stop is:
   Stop smoking by the end of next month.

During the project, I will make the following *specific changes* (environmental, social, personal) to support my target behavior:
   I will leave my cigarettes in the car, carry gum/mints/toothpicks in my backpack, sit in nonsmoking sections of restaurants, and hang out with more of my nonsmoking friends.

During the project, I will replace negative self-talk about my behavior with positive self-talk such as the following:

Change   *I have to have a cigarette*   to   *I've made it all day without a
            after dinner.*   *cigarette, and I'm not going to
                                                                       give in now. I'll just chew another
                                                                       stick of gum.*

During the project, I will apply the following reinforcements and punishments to support my target behavior:

Each day I succeed in following the conditions of my contract, I will:
   Allow myself 30 minutes to listen to music or rent a video for the evening or take a walk with a friend.

Each day I fail to follow the conditions of my contract, I will:
   Wash and fold all of my laundry or lose one night of television/computer time or handwrite a letter to one of my relatives.

During the project, I will enlist the help of other people in the following ways to support my target behavior:
   I'll ask my friends not to smoke around me or let me bum cigarettes or to walk with me or to watch videos with me on the days I fulfill my contract.

Darvin Jones	**2/25/**
Student	Date
Beth Ruelos	*2/25/*
Project Partner(s)	Date
Russ Hodges	*2/25/*
Instructor	Date

FIGURE 10.3   Sample Four-Week Graph for a Self-Change Project

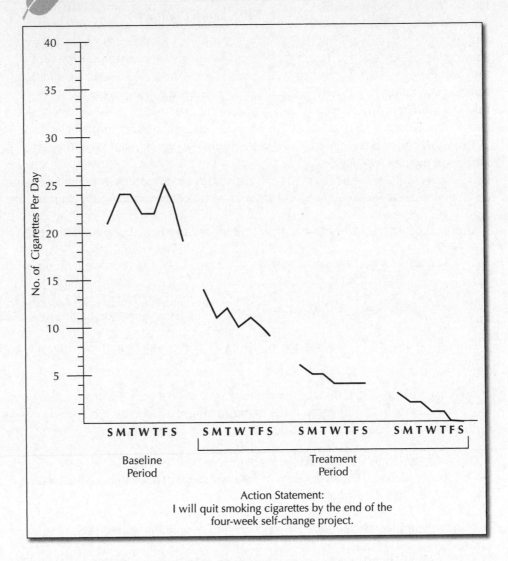

The contract is a detailed description of how you plan to achieve the target behavior. Because you will create a contract with yourself to change the target behavior, the most important part of the contract is your honor. You are promising to follow the terms of the contract—that is, impose the artificial consequences. The promise is to yourself, not your teacher, classmates, or family members (although their active support or sabotage can certainly affect your success). Honor lies at the heart of self-change. You may gradually shape your behavior by setting different levels of behavior for each of the weeks you attempt the contract.

Your contract will include self-imposed reinforcements (rewards) to administer as you experience success as well as a few self-imposed punishments when you are unsuccessful. Often natural consequences (positive and negative, immediate and delayed) that immediately follow behaviors do not reinforce the right things strongly or quickly enough. For example, smokers get immediate relief from nicotine cravings (positive natural consequences), but the serious health problems caused by smoking are usually delayed (negative natural consequences). Successful behavior change requires that you apply strong, immediate positive (or negative) consequences after you engage in (or fail to engage in) your target behavior.

Psychologists term these consequences reinforcements and punishments. **Reinforcement** is *a consequence that follows a behavior and increases the likelihood that the behavior will increase in frequency.* For example, the natural consequences of exercise are usually increased energy and better health (immediate and delayed), but regular exercise is one of the more difficult behaviors for people to maintain. An artificial consequence you can self-impose after each exercise session is listening to your favorite music or watching television for 30 minutes. Implementing **punishments**, which are *consequences that follow a behavior and decrease the frequency of the behavior from occurring,* is also effective in helping you achieve your target behavior. For example, the natural consequences of not studying are usually poor grades (immediate and/or delayed). An artificial consequence you can self-impose when you do not study is to deny yourself the use of your cell phone or computer for a day. Here are some examples of consequences (reinforcements and punishments) our students often use:

Reinforcements

Spending time with friends	Listening to music
Reading a magazine or book for fun	Spending time online
Going to the movies	Eating favorite foods
Engaging in favorite sports	Shopping
Taking an entire afternoon off for yourself	Playing video games

Punishments

Putting money in a jar and giving it all to a charity you dislike	Washing cars, clothes, or pets (your own or others')
Not allowing yourself daily pleasures (phone calls, getting online, TV shows, video games)	Taking the stairs instead of elevators or escalators
Doing household chores, especially those that are someone else's responsibility	Not allowing yourself dessert, snacks, soda, or pizza

A powerful part of this project is collaborating with a partner. Seek out the help of at least one other student in class who is supportive and willing to help you design your contract and provide you with consistent moral support during the treatment phase.

Step 4: Implement Treatment

The fourth step is your attempt to change your target behavior during the next two or three weeks, the treatment phase of the project. During treatment, you will follow the conditions outlined in your contract to try to change your target behavior and continue to update your daily journal or behavior-tracking log and self-change graph.

You may have to adjust your contract conditions because your target behavior is too challenging (e.g., studying four hours a day) or too easy (e.g., exercising 15 minutes a day). Ineffective reinforcements and punishments will also need to be changed. As noted earlier, an essential part of the treatment phase is your involvement with your self-change partner. You are expected to listen attentively and provide constructive feedback and encouragement to your partner; she or he is expected to do the same for you. If you find that you are not experiencing success in changing your target behavior within the first week, do not give up. Modify your contract conditions, reinforcements, and punishments, and seek additional social support from your friends, family, instructor, and self-change partner.

Step 5: Evaluate the Project

The final step is to evaluate the design and implementation of your entire project. Your evaluation should contain an analysis of your target behavior, baseline data collection results, contract design, and treatment-phase results. Focus on what worked and what did not work, and provide concrete reasons for the success or lack of success of your project. During the treatment phase, you may have achieved all, part, or none of your goal, so you should address the appropriateness of your target behavior goal and your future plans regarding further change. Do you plan to maintain the target behavior? Abandon it? Adjust it? Maintaining or continuing to change the target behavior will not happen by accident; it must be carefully planned. Continuing to monitor your behavior, especially when you begin to gradually withdraw the artificial consequences, is crucial to maintaining your behavior successfully.

As you study and struggle with the self-change project, you can gain mastery over one of the mysteries of being human—our ability to determine and direct our own lives. When we care enough about ourselves to believe that our own lives and efforts are important, then we care about managing our behaviors.

CASE STUDY

Saddened and disappointed by her grades on her first round of exams, SONDRA wondered what she had done wrong. She made a "B" in her Dance Class, a low "C" in her Psychology, History, and College Algebra classes, but made an "F" in Biology. She felt like a failure. Sondra felt as though she studied enough even though she was pledging a sorority. She also met a cute guy, Danny, in the dining hall and they had gone out a few times. Sondra was beginning to think she just was not meant for college.

In her psychology class, she decided to do a self-change project for extra credit. She chose study time as the target behavior and recorded baseline data for a week. The results surprised her. In seven days, Sondra had studied only five hours, but her sorority commitments had taken fifteen hours, and she had hung out with Danny over nine hours.

Case Study Questions: Sondra decides to study more. Help Sondra design a self-change contract. What should be her overall goal? Her target behavior? What specific changes does she need to make in her physical environment? Socially? Personally? How can she use positive self-talk to achieve her target behavior? What sorts of reinforcements do you think will help Sondra reach her goal? Punishments? Whom could Sondra depend upon to help her study more? List some ways in which Sondra can monitor her progress. What are some questions she can ask herself to evaluate the success of her project?

Exercise 10.4

Self-Change Project

Experience the gratitude of personal growth. Creating balance in your life means attempting to better yourself when possible, but this is not always easy. Attempting a self-change project is a big commitment, in both time (four weeks) and effort. You will identify a target behavior, spend one week collecting baseline data, and spend two to three weeks in a treatment phase. You will track and reflect on your progress, making changes along the way. Self-honesty and integrity are paramount. All of the forms you need to complete a self-change project are located at the end of this chapter. Successfully completing this project will provide you with a real sense of accomplishment as you make a positive change in your life.

STEP 1: FORMULATE A TARGET BEHAVIOR

To formulate a target behavior, address each of the following:

a. What are some changes I need to make for a more positive future?

b. Why do I want to make these changes?

c. What specific behavior do I wish to change?

d. How will I attempt to change this target behavior?

e. How will I monitor what is happening? In other words, what will I count or measure each day?

f. At what times or in which situations does my target behavior occur more frequently? Less frequently?

g. What self-talk am I using that causes this behavior to occur or not occur?

h. What specific behaviors can I identify that will help me reach my target behavior goal?

STEP 2: COLLECT BASELINE DATA

Keep track of your baseline data for a week on the behavior-tracking form and graph provided for you at the end of this chapter. Locate at least three library resources with information about changing your behavior.

Once you complete your baseline data collection, answer the following questions:

a. What were the results of my baseline data collection?

b. Did any of my observations surprise me? If so, which ones?

c. What were some of my recurring thoughts and feelings during this week?

d. What were some self-talk trends I noticed?

e. How did my library resources help me understand more about my behavior?

f. Now that the baseline period is over, has my target behavior goal changed? If so, explain.

STEP 3: DESIGN A CONTRACT

Using the contract form provided at the end of this chapter, design and complete a self-change project contract. Be sure that you, your partner, and your instructor each sign the contract. Be thoughtful of the reinforcements and punishments you implement, and make sure they are strong enough to support your efforts to change your target behavior.

Before you begin to fill out your contract, answer each of the following questions:

a. What things are likely to get in the way of my accomplishing this project?

b. How might I sabotage or resist the process of pursuing this project?

c. How committed am I to completing this project?

d. How will I demonstrate that commitment in my actions?

e. What are some abilities, strengths, and skills I already have that I can use?

f. Who are some people who would support me in pursuing this project?

g. What other resources (information, tools, techniques) can help me?

h. What types of reinforcements am I willing to work for? Examples include spending time with friends, going to the movies, shopping, and taking unscheduled free time.

i. What types of punishments would I implement for not honoring my contract conditions? Examples include putting money in a jar and giving it all to charity, riding the bus instead of driving, and not allowing time with friends on the weekend.

STEP 4: IMPLEMENT TREATMENT

During the weeks of treatment, you will follow and carefully monitor all aspects of the contract just like you did when you collected baseline data. Continue to update your behavior-tracking form and graph.

After each week of treatment, answer the following questions:

a. What was the outcome of my project during this week of treatment?

b. What were some of my recurring thoughts and feelings as I engaged in the target behavior?

c. What were some self-talk trends I noticed?

d. What things are likely to get in the way of my accomplishing this project?

e. How helpful was my social support (partner, friends, family, instructor)? How can I make better use of my social support?

f. How committed am I to completing this project?

g. Which reinforcements and punishments are working and why? Which reinforcements and punishments need to be changed and why?

h. What can I change immediately to make this project more successful?

STEP 5: EVALUATE YOUR PROGRAM

Using your graph, behavior-tracking form, and answers to the previous questions in this exercise, evaluate your success (or lack of success) with this project by answering the following questions:

    a. How well did I accomplish my target behavior, and how do I feel about my results?

    b. What did I do that was helpful, and how can I build on that strength?

    c. What did I do that was not helpful, and what did I learn?

    d. What happened that was surprising or unexpected?

    e. What did I learn most from my baseline data collection?

    f. What changes could I have made to the design of my contract?

    g. What changes could I have made to my reinforcements and punishments?

    h. How could I have better used my partner (social support)?

    i. Do I plan to maintain my target behavior? If so, how? If not, why?

CONCLUSION

Within this chapter, we have continued to explore the inner world of self-regulation using the concepts of flow, stages of self-regulatory abilities, key routines, effective use of time, balancing, and self-change. All are practical concepts, and all can help us strengthen our behaviors so that we are more likely to reach our goals.

SUMMARY

- Navigating the balance between doing what we should to achieve long-term goals (delayed gratification) and doing what we want to do right now (immediate gratification) is a continuous challenge for students and professional workers alike.

- According to Peck, "Balancing is the discipline that gives us flexibility. Extraordinary flexibility is required for successful living in all spheres of activity."

- There are a handful of behaviors that have the capacity to influence all the others, and they are termed *key routines*. It is the turning of key routines into habitual behaviors that is important to one's movement from chaos to mastery.

- We can improve our self-regulation by realizing that we need to change, targeting the specific behavior to change, strategizing how we can change it, paying attention to the new behavior, and being responsible for our actions.

- The five steps in implementing a self-change project are formulating a target behavior, collecting baseline data, designing a contract, implementing treatment, and evaluating the project.

- Creating and carrying out a self-change project requires commitment, attention, and persistence.

KEY CONCEPTS

Balancing

Key routines

Reinforcement

Punishment

Self-change (target behavior, baseline data, contract, treatment, evaluation of project, reinforcement, punishment)

GUIDED JOURNAL QUESTIONS

1. Analyze your self-discipline for college by answering the following: How difficult or easy is it for you to delay gratification? Accept responsibility? Balance between immediate and delayed gratification? Explain and use examples for each.

2. What other key routines (besides the ones mentioned in the text) could you suggest for Todd to help him out of chaos? What key routines do you need to implement for yourself and why?

3. What is the one thing you would like to change most about your life? Explain. What stands in your way of making this change? What benefits will you experience? When would you like to begin making this change?

4. How well are you able to use reinforcements to shape or change your behaviors? In what situations have you used them successfully? How well are you able to punish yourself? What punishments have you tried and how successful were they?

The Last Word

*Deciding to change is the first step, but knowing **how** makes changing even the most difficult behaviors possible.*

—Carol Dochen

Behavior-Tracking Form

Date	Time	Count	Behavior	Feelings	Self-Talk	Consequences

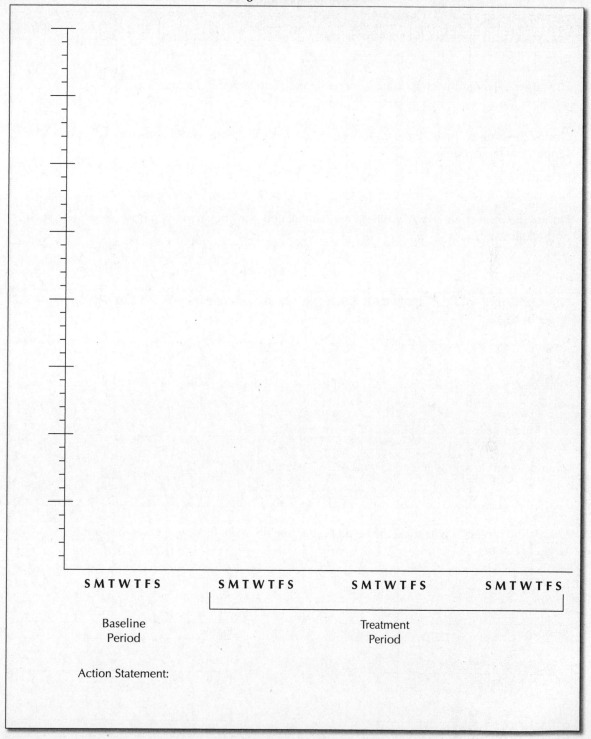

SMTWTFS   SMTWTFS   SMTWTFS   SMTWTFS

Baseline   Treatment
Period   Period

Action Statement:

Self-Change Contract

My overall goal for this self-change project is:

The target behavior I want to initiate, increase, maintain, decrease, or stop is:

During the project, I will make the following *specific changes* (environmental, social, personal) to support my target behavior:

During the project, I will replace negative self-talk about my behavior with positive self-talk such as the following:

During the project, I will apply the following reinforcements and punishments to support my target behavior:

Each day I succeed in following the conditions of my contract, I will:

Each day I fail to follow the conditions of my contract, I will:

During the project, I will enlist the help of other people in the following ways to support my target behavior:

_____   _____
Student   Date

_____   _____
Project Partner(s)   Date

_____   _____
Instructor   Date

Patterns in Human Development

All these people are like me?

. . . the development [of humans] resembles what used to be called an adventure of the spirit.

—*William Perry*

Almost always, we see ourselves through three lenses. I am an individual, unique in this world, a product of all I was born with and all I have experienced. I am a member of a group (or groups) of humans with whom I share some idea or circumstance (my family, my friends, my country). I am human, like all other humans—I was born in this world and will die in this world. I laugh, love, think, work, play, worship. Each of these lenses has a name: the individual, the group (culture), the universal. We can deepen our self-awareness by examining ourselves through each of these three lenses.

In this chapter, we look carefully at a primary concept called *developmentalism*. It is the story of how we are alike as all humans (universal) and how we are like some humans (culture). In the next chapter, we look at several personality theories that describe how our uniqueness arises from the interaction of our personality and the specific circumstances of our lives. By combining both worldviews, we can come to a rich understanding of ourselves and how to live our lives well and wisely.

255

SELF-ASSESSMENT: My Independence

Striving for personal independence is a major goal of many college students. With independence comes a move toward making your own decisions and working for your own approval. With 5 being "Almost Always" and 1 being "Almost Never," assess your level of independence. Rate each of the following statements honestly by circling the appropriate number. Completing this assessment will allow you to begin to examine your movement toward a new stage of psychological development.

	Almost Always		Sometimes		Almost Never
1. I manage my time, money, and academic obligations responsibly.	5	4	3	2	1
2. I tend to closely examine many alternatives before I make a major commitment.	5	4	3	2	1
3. I take full responsibility for the decisions and choices I make, no matter what the outcome.	5	4	3	2	1
4. I see making mistakes as a learning opportunity and not as personal failure.	5	4	3	2	1
5. I am becoming psychologically less dependent on my parents, spouse/partner, and/or children for emotional support.	5	4	3	2	1
6. I am not afraid to voice my own opinions to others— even to my parents, teachers, spouse/partner, or children.	5	4	3	2	1
7. I feel comfortable respectfully challenging someone's beliefs or opinions when I disagree with their views.	5	4	3	2	1

8. I rely more on myself than   5   4   3   2   1
   on others to find or create
   my own happiness.

9. I am okay with being viewed   5   4   3   2   1
   as different or having dif-
   ferent beliefs from my peers.

10. I am beginning to seek out   5   4   3   2   1
    the meaning and purpose
    of my own life.

Add up the numbers you circled. Your total score will be between 10 and 50. The higher your score, the more likely you are to be moving into independence and autonomy. For a score below 30, write or reflect on items for which you have concerns and consider talking with a trusted friend, a family member, a teacher, a counselor, or an advisor.

THE UNIVERSAL: STAGES AND TRANSITIONS OF LIFE

From conception to death, the one constant in human life is change. The amount and the rate of change may vary over our life span, but its relentless roll occurs, whether we welcome it or shrink from it. Across every dimension of life—physical, mental, emotional, spiritual—we change in predictable patterns and timing. These commonalities are some of the universal dimension of humanity. Augsberger (1986) says,

> Five dimensions are universally present among humans: *biologically* we are a common species; *socially* we have common relational prerequisites; *ecologically* we must adjust to a common atmosphere and a limited number of climates; *spiritually* we invariably seek to touch the numinous, the transcendent, the meaning of our existence; and *psychologically* we have an intraspecies sameness of processes. (p. 52)

In addition, Augsberger (1986) refers to the human psychological processes as "the psychic unity of humankind" (p. 55), which includes the cognitive abilities to perceive, memorize, and reason; the ability to feel (emotion); and the ability to exercise free will or volition.

The arc of life begins with the helpless dependence of infancy, throws off limitations as adulthood brings independence, rises to interdependence in maturity, and subsides again to dependence in later years. Our movement through the life span occurs in alternating *periods of rapid, irreversible change* (**transitions**) and *periods of stability* (**stages**). Although writers from earlier times and places have described these life stages, Erikson (1963, 1982) was the one who conceptualized the Western worldview in his famous Eight Stages of Psychosocial Development. Each stage has a conflict that must be resolved for the individual to move forward in a healthy manner. Recently, other scholars have elaborated on Erikson's work by adding other stages (Newman & Newman, 1995).

For our purposes in this book, we present the Stages and Transitions of Life, an adaptation of stage theory that emphasizes six crucial transition periods, each with its subsequent stable stage. The length of the stages varies enormously. The first stage is prenatal and the transition from prenatal to childhood is birth. Childhood is a relatively long stage, which ends abruptly with the onset of puberty, a transition. Youth usually begins around age 15; the transition to independence from family begins between 17 and 20 years of age and lasts from seven to ten years. During this transition to independence, people explore numerous options by pursuing education, jobs, and relationships. As they make serious, long-lasting commitments to relationships, careers, and ideas, they are ending the transition to independence and moving into the stage of adulthood. During this stage people develop their families, their personal lives, their professional careers—in other words, their role and place in society. Sometime in their forties a new transition emerges, called midlife. Like the independence transition, it typically lasts from seven to ten years. Several important things happen in midlife. People tend to question the commitments they have made and lived by for 20 or so years, they search for a deeper meaning or purpose in life, and they begin the long journey toward maturity. Increasingly in Western culture, they make powerful decisions about changing their lives. With good health, the stage of maturity can last into the seventies. The next transition—withdrawal—occurs when people appear to lose interest with the external world and move to a quieter pace of life marked by the stage of old age. When we place the stages and transitions in sequential order, the pattern in Figure 11.1 emerges.

Exercise 11.2

Identifying the Stages and Transitions of Life

Developmental psychologists believe that major transitions take place throughout our lifetime and that we move from one developmental stage to the next during these transition periods. Answer the following questions to determine where you and those closest to you are.

1. What stage or transition do you believe most characterizes your life right now? How congruent is your developmental age with your chronological age?

2. Where in the list of stages and transitions would you place the people closest to you, such as your parents, spouse/partner, children, and good friends?

FIGURE 11.1   Life Stages and Transitions

LIFE STAGES AND TRANSITIONS			
Stage of Life	Transitions to	Life Stage Age	Length of Transition from One Life Stage to Another
Prenatal		0	
	Birth		10 months
Childhood		0–12 years	
	Puberty		18 months
Youth		13–27 years	
	Independence		7–10 years
Adulthood		27–50 years	
	Midlife		7–10 years
Maturity		50–75 years	
	Withdrawal		10–15 years
Old Age		75+	
	Death		Years/Months/Days

INDEPENDENCE

The transition time between youth and adulthood has greatly expanded for much of Western society during the past century as higher education has become more available. That time, called independence, is the gradual movement from the security and protection of our families to the acceptance of responsibility for our own lives—psychologically, financially, and emotionally. For many people, especially college students, it is a time of fits and starts, a time of striving for independence and rushing back to the security of family. The entire transition usually takes seven to ten years, and sometimes even longer. There is awkwardness in the transition to independence for most people; it is rarely graceful or smooth. Parents and older siblings sometimes interfere by giving unwanted advice. A large part of this transition time is the trying on of ideas, roles, language, and beliefs different from those of our families. Becoming independent is a crucial step toward becoming a healthy adult.

During independence, college students *develop across seven dimensions* called **vectors** by Arthur Chickering, an expert in understanding college students' lives (Chickering, n.d.).

These seven vectors are as follows:

- *Developing competence—intellectual and interpersonal.*   Intellectual competence involves more than mastering content. It is the building of mental skills of comprehension, analysis, and evaluation. Ideally, the ability to create new ideas or applications increases. Interpersonal competence is the ability to work with both individuals and groups in both personal and professional relationships.

Where would you place your intellectual competence?

Needs improvement ‹————————————————————————› Strong

Where would you place your interpersonal competence?

Needs improvement ‹————————————————————————› Strong

- *Managing emotions.*   The task of managing emotions is to be aware of them, acknowledge them, and express them appropriately.
Where would you place your ability to manage emotions?

Needs improvement ‹————————————————————————› Strong

- *Moving into autonomy.*   The characteristics of this vector are learning to function with relative self-sufficiency, taking responsibility for pursuing goals, and becoming less constrained by others' opinions.

Where would you place your current level of autonomy?

Needs improvement ‹————————————————————————› Strong

- *Developing mature interpersonal relationships.*   This involves the tolerance and appreciation of others' differences, a greater capacity for intimacy, and an increased ability to choose healthy relationships and make lasting commitments.

Where would you place your ability to develop mature interpersonal relationships?

Needs improvement ‹————————————————————————› Strong

- *Establishing identity.*   A solid sense of self emerges through the "(1) comfort with body and appearance, (2) comfort with gender and sexual orientation, (3) sense of self in a social, historical, and cultural context, (4) clarification of self-concept through roles and life-style, (5) sense of self in response to feedback from valued others, (6) self-acceptance and self-esteem, and (7) personal stability and integration" (Chickering, n.d.).

How well established is your sense of self?

Needs improvement ←——————————————————————→ Strong

- *Developing purpose*.   This involves a growing ability to unify one's many different goals within the scope of a larger, more meaningful purpose, and to exercise intentionality on a daily basis.

How well developed is your sense of purpose?

Needs improvement ←——————————————————————→ Strong

- *Developing integrity*.   The increasing ability to act based on one's values and beliefs.

How well developed is your integrity?

Needs improvement ←——————————————————————→ Strong

Source: Adapted from Chickering, A. (n.d.). *The Seven Vectors: An Overview*. Retrieved from http://www.cabrini.edu/communications/ProfDev/cardevChickering.html)

Chickering's seven vectors state the ideal development of an individual through the transition of independence; however, certain circumstances can interfere or delay the acquisition of these seven vectors. Recent research indicates that heavy use of multiple electronic devices can delay the development of an adolescent's frontal lobe of the brain. That part of the brain does not complete development until the early twenties, and it is that part of the brain from which judgment, generosity, and empathy come (Small & Vorgan, 2008). If you believe your use of computers, cell phones, games, or other electronic devices borders on addiction, then we urge you to seek professional help, starting with your campus counseling center.

CASE STUDY

JASON, a 20-year-old junior business major, feels he is finally finding his way through college and into adult life. A popular and athletic teenager, he entered college as an engineering major and quickly found that he was bored in his classes and unmotivated to study. His grades were marginal; his attention wandered in class and when he tried to read. Jason watched his friends make decisions about majors and life paths, but he held back. His twentieth birthday was not a happy time because he felt frightened that he was directionless. He felt like he was wandering without any goals. His parents voiced increasing dismay, and he thought about leaving college altogether. Two long weeks after that birthday, he made an appointment at the campus career center and began a series of discussions with a counselor. After completing several assessments, Jason gradually came to understand that his talents lay in oral communication and persuasion. He interviewed several successful marketing graduates of the college and, for the first time, could see himself developing a career in professional marketing. Everything began to fall into place.

How can simply finding the right career path make everything fall into place? Well, Jason is in the midst of the transition period called *independence,* and this career decision is the result of many factors; however, it is only a first step in a long process. In the space of just a few years, his life has changed across three major dimensions: how he thinks (cognitive), how he feels (affective), and what he does (behavioral). **Independence** is *that time in which we are initiated into the adult world;* in just a few years, we become an equal of people we had heretofore seen as impossibly older.

Independence means that our living arrangements change; we usually move away from our families, both physically and psychologically. Finances change too, as we contribute more to our own support and are responsible for monitoring the business of life. Our lifestyle also changes in this period. Jason's life reflects all these changes since he has come to college. He is working a part-time job to help with expenses because his sister is entering college. He has moved out of the dormitory into his own apartment with two new friends, and he has become serious about cycling. He even has joined the cycling club on campus and rides long distances regularly in the surrounding countryside.

The radical difference in Jason's life is that his relationships have changed. His parents now give support and express concern but no longer make decisions for him. They are willing to listen but offer fewer suggestions. All but one of his high school friends have drifted away, and his college friends are different in their values and behaviors. His college roommates and friends are ambitious and directed, and most are in long-term romantic relationships. Jason still goes out with his group of friends, but he has had few serious relationships. He feels ready for such a relationship and has spent significant time contemplating the characteristics he wants in that person.

Case Study Questions: What characteristics do you believe Jason now is looking for in a person he can establish a serious relationship with? Using Chickering's seven vectors, give a brief analysis of Jason's development for each vector.

Exercise 11.3

Your Self-Perceptions

Your views about yourself can influence your quality of life. Answer each of the following questions, then write at least two specific examples to support each of your answers. This exercise will help you identify some of your current self-perceptions and gain insight into areas that you can work toward as you make transitions from one stage in your life to the next.

1. Do you see yourself as having the potential to succeed in life?

    _____ Yes _____ No _____ Sometimes

    Examples:

2. Do you see yourself as trustworthy?

    _____ Yes _____ No _____ Sometimes

    Examples:

3. Do you see yourself as an independent person?

    _____ Yes _____ No _____ Sometimes

    Examples:

4. Do you see yourself as loveable?

    _____ Yes _____ No _____ Sometimes

    Examples:

5. Do you see yourself as a loving person?

    _____ Yes _____ No _____ Sometimes

    Examples:

6. Do you see yourself as confident?

    _____ Yes _____ No _____ Sometimes

    Examples:

7. Do you see yourself as caring and accepting?

    _____ Yes _____ No _____ Sometimes

    Examples:

8. Do you see yourself as a happy, positive person?

    _____ Yes _____ No _____ Sometimes

    Examples:

9. Do you see yourself as making a positive contribution to society?

_____ Yes _____ No _____ Sometimes

Examples:

10. Do you see yourself successfully making a transition from one stage of your life to the next?

_____ Yes _____ No _____ Sometimes

Examples:

Exercise 11.4

How Others See You

Do you have misperceptions about how others view you? Do your friends really know your strengths and weaknesses? Could you learn anything about yourself from their perceptions? To learn the answers to these questions, ask two close friends whom you rely on and trust to give you honest feedback. Ask them to write a list of your top five strengths or best attributes and give specific examples of each. Then ask them to list five attributes they would like to see you improve and to provide specific examples of each. Remember to use the feedback for personal growth and insight and be sure to thank them for their help.

PERRY'S THEORY OF COGNITIVE AND MORAL DEVELOPMENT

Our cognitive development makes a huge journey during the transition of independence. Although many theorists and researchers have attempted to explain how our minds develop during this period, no one has better captured the flow of that change than William Perry (1970). Perry posited a journey of intellectual and moral development in the independence period through nine stages that can be grouped into four categories. For the purposes of this text, we look only at the categories, although you may wish to investigate the full theory in the classic text *Forms of Intellectual and Ethical Development in the College Years* (Perry, 1970). See Figure 11.2 for a student's perspective of Perry's stages of cognitive development.

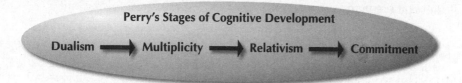

Perry's Stages of Cognitive Development

Dualism ➡ Multiplicity ➡ Relativism ➡ Commitment

Category 1—Dualism

People in the dualism stage believe there is a correct answer to every question. They view knowledge in terms of absolutes and try to conform all their knowledge into being either right or wrong or good or bad. They depend on authorities (such as their college professors) for such truths, and they resist thinking independently or making their own value decisions. As students, they believe teachers should deliver knowledge to them. They view learning in terms of simply memorizing information and then selecting the correct answer for an exam. Difficulties arise for them when they witness authorities in disagreement.

When Jason was 16, he believed that there was a right and a wrong answer to everything, and his job was to find the authority that knew the right answer and learn it. Sometimes the authority was a peer, sometimes a teacher, sometimes his parents. He felt comfortable with questions that asked him to remember and understand, but he had two classes that required more considered opinion. He was uncomfortable in those classes primarily because he did not know what the teacher really wanted. Facts were his friends and ambiguities were stressful. He rarely questioned the dominant views of his peer group.

Category 2—Multiplicity

The movement to multiplicity means that students, for the first time, begin to view knowledge as being based more on opinion rather than certainty. They become more accepting when authorities disagree with each other or when an authority, at least temporarily, is in search of an answer. As students, they begin to view their opinions as being equal to others', and they sometimes fault their authorities (teachers) for not seeing the value in their answers.

By the time Jason entered college, he understood that there are conflicting answers to many serious questions. Although he still believed that there were *right* answers (such thinking often took the form that there was one perfect major for him or one perfect mate), he acknowledged that some problems seem not to have solutions and thus everyone has a right to his or her opinion. Jason still looked to authorities for the final answer, and he remained impatient with professors who resisted giving simplistic answers. He often expressed his opinion that they were just incompetent because they did not know the answers.

FIGURE 11.2   A Student's Perspective of Perry's Stages of Cognitive Development

	Dualism	Multiplicity	Relativism	Commitment
Knowledge perspective	I believe knowledge is either right or wrong, good or bad. Answers exist somewhere for every problem and authorities know them. Knowledge is quantitative.	When authorities do not know the answer, everyone has a right to their own opinion; none can be called wrong. Authorities are still searching for the answers.	I view knowledge in relation to context—everything is valid, but not always equal. Point of view is relevant. I evaluate knowledge based on evidence and logic. Knowledge is qualitative.	I make a commitment, an affirmation, or a decision. Major commitments include choosing a career, choosing religious and political affiliations, and choosing a mate.
Instructor	She is responsible for teaching me. She is the ultimate source of my learning.	He is the authority on the topic; he will provide the answers to difficult questions.	She provides guidance and many sources of learning. She facilitates discussion. She challenges me to create new questions.	He is interested in my commitment affirmation, or decision. He allows me to form my own opinion.
Goal of learning	Learning is mastered by memorizing. I memorize facts, dates, places, and events.	I comprehend the material. I do not just memorize it. I begin to see the importance of ideas.	I apply and analyze what I am learning. I consider differing points of view and grapple with difficult issues.	I synthesize and evaluate the information. I form an opinion and seek personal relevance.
Expectations	Please tell me what to learn. Stick to the syllabus. Will this information be on the test?	Help me understand how different pieces of information relate. You want me to search for the answers, but eventually you will tell me what is correct.	Do not give me answers; let me struggle to solve problems. There may be many correct answers.	My answer is correct as long as I can support it with evidence. I need to find personal relevance with what I am learning.
Method of testing	I prefer objective tests—true/false, multiple choice, matching.	I prefer objective and some subjective tests—short-answer and fill-in-the-blank questions.	I prefer subjective tests where I can support my answers through logic and evidence.	I prefer subjective tests that ask me to make some kind of commitment to a choice or an option.
Grades	If I get all the correct answers, then I will earn an A.	I hope my teacher allows for effort, especially if I understand the process of getting the correct answers.	My grades should reflect my ability to support my answers with sound reasoning, logic, and evidence.	I understand grades are important, but I learn for the sake of learning and expanding my knowledge.

Multiple opportunities crowded Jason's life. In college, he was confronted with a myriad of choices about politics, religion, lifestyle, and ethics. Many of his professors did not seem interested in ritualized answers; instead, they promoted inquiry and asked questions. He had to write essays and his grade was based on the quality of his argument. Like most freshmen, Jason struggled, thinking that the professors cared more about how much he could write rather than thoughtfully constructed responses to questions. By his sophomore year, Jason had made real progress in cognitive development. He was enjoying the freedom of exploring new ideas and positions. His religious beliefs came under scrutiny, as did his political views. He heard speakers and read authors who challenged the philosophy of his family, and gradually he began to relinquish his search for outside authority.

Category 3—Relativism

Students at the relativism level of cognitive development begin to question everything. The initial reaction of most students as they enter relativism is that all opinions are equal; however, many college assignments help students recognize that their opinions are evaluated by the quality of the supporting evidence they provide. Authorities are not asking for the one right answer but for students to have the ability to support an opinion (answer) with data and solid reasoning. Students begin to see knowledge as relative, depending on the context or circumstance. They begin to enjoy the art of debating both sides of an issue, seeking personal relevance for each. Students search out their own truths.

Jason's twentieth birthday was a turning point. Although he had begun accepting responsibility for his behaviors several years prior, he now realized that his life was in his hands. He knew that the responsibility for choosing a major and a career was his, so while he investigated the options carefully, he took control of the process. He realized that his choice to major in marketing was just one step in a complex series of choices.

Relativism is the freedom to ask and attempt to answer any question. It is a delightful, exciting time for many and a terrifying time for others. For those who find it exhilarating, they relish trying on new ideas (as well as companions, hairstyles, and language). Relativism can be a playful time intellectually, but it is not intended as a permanent place. Rather, it is a time of exploration and daring, a time in which we challenge any and all assumptions.

Perry (1970) noted that cognitive growth to relativistic thinking is not always possible for every person. He presented three deflections to growth: retreat, escape, and temporizing.

Retreat

Retreat is a *regression to earlier stages*. It is fair to say that not everyone is en-amored with relativism. For some people, the loss of absolutes, even temporar-ily, is unbearable. They run away in one of two ways. First, they may retreat back to the safety of dualism, sometimes even moving back home and trying to re-create a safer time with old friends and ideas. Second, they may choose an extreme version of retreating. Such extremes include joining groups that es-pouse rigid belief systems, whether military, political, or religious. Cults are the epitome of dualism in which one figure is the absolute authority.

Escape

In **escape** the student *avoids commitment by settling in at the relativistic stage and rejects further movement*. Typical of this stage is alienation and abandon-ment of responsibility by not making a commitment. Another common word that describes escape is *drifting*. Students caught in escape often passively dele-gate responsibility to fate. They drift into majors or weak relationships. They often drift out of college because nothing seizes their interest.

Temporizing

Perry (1970) defined **temporizing** as a *postponement of movement for a full academic year*. Sometimes people temporize—that is, they stay in relativism, treading water and refusing to move forward. They do not seriously explore career choices but, instead, take a variety of entertaining courses. Although they may work, they rarely seek jobs or internships that could give them use-ful experience in a journey toward a career. In other words, they stay in rela-tivism but they do not use the opportunities that relativism provides for further growth.

An important characteristic of both escape and temporizing is avoidance. Avoidance is simple in our society; alcohol and other drugs provide an easy path, as do social or family over-involvement. Some students work all the time, thereby avoiding the important questions that relativism initiates. Others over-use campus organizations and stay so busy that they cannot thoughtfully ex-plore the questions that relativism raises.

Jason's twentieth birthday galvanized him into action. In many ways he had been drifting. Now he felt compelled to explore his many choices. He took the time and made the effort to understand himself and his deepest long-ings, his talents and abilities, his values and goals. These months were intense and full of powerful insights. He shared pieces of his journey with those peo-ple he trusted, and for the first time, he really listened to their responses and encouragement. He was almost ready for the fourth category of Perry's model—commitment.

Deflections to Cognitive Growth

Complete the following statements to determine which deflections you may have experienced with regard to making commitments:

I have retreated from making a commitment when I . . .

I have escaped from making a commitment when I . . .

I have temporized a commitment when I . . .

Category 4—Commitment

Relativism allows students to exercise reason as they look to alternatives; it allows them to examine themselves and their lives. However, reason alone does not move them to commitment. When they are ready to decide how and why they want to live their lives, then they are poised to commit to particular beliefs, values, relationships, principles, and work. According to Perry (1970),

> The word 'Commitments,' then, refers to affirmations: in all the plurality of the relativistic world—truths, relationships, purposes, activities, and cares, in all their contexts—one affirms what is one's own. As ongoing creative activities, Commitments require the courage of responsibility, and presuppose an acceptance of human limits, including the limits of reason. (p. 135)

Note that Perry (1970) uses a capital C when he talks about category 4. By this he means that Commitments (choices) made after relativism are choices made after all the alternatives are examined. We can make commitments (lowercase c) at any time in our lives, but only the ones in category 4 follow the use of reason with numerous options. A powerful example is the startling difference between two 17-year-olds getting pregnant unintentionally and a couple in their thirties deliberately choosing parenthood. The two adolescents may make a thoughtful choice to become committed parents, but they have not had the time or the opportunity to explore what directions their lives might have taken without the pregnancy. They have a limited knowledge and experience base. No matter what action they choose, their lives are changed forever. Perry differentiates between a commitment and a Commitment. Although both are honorable and important, only the latter is a truly free choice.

Jason stands at the beginning of Commitment. The first stage of his professional life is his Commitment to the world of business. Marketing will require initiative, it will probably be more autonomous than collaborative, and there will be continual pressure to meet external goals. His reflections have led him to the conviction that he has the talent and interest to enjoy such a working life. Advanced courses and internships can help him narrow options and focus on a specific type of marketing. As he begins to take his business courses, an ethics course catches his attention.

Jason's father is a quiet and reserved man, unlike Jason's uncle, who is loud and aggressive. As Jason studies the principles of business ethics, he realizes that his father's business practices are built on solid ethical practices and have gained the respect of peers and customers. On the other hand, his uncle always has a new scheme, a new company, but he never stays anywhere long and has become an uncomfortable presence in the family. His uncle rarely follows through with promises, and Jason remembers many disappointments. Jason's father, Mike, owns a small accounting business, and Jason worked for him during high school. Many times, Mike's clients would tell Jason how much they trusted his father and that Mike always looked after them. Sometimes a new client would push Mike to bend the rules about a tax report, but Mike always held to his convictions, even if the client went to another company. Jason really took his father's behavior for granted; he always knew he could count on his father's word. In the ethics class, he begins to see that his father had made deliberate choices about how he wanted to be as an accountant, and Jason determines that he wants to live and work by the same ethical standards. By committing to a set of ethical business standards, Jason is making an important step toward the higher levels of moral reasoning, those that include abstract concepts of justice. Jason's relationships with authorities have also changed dramatically. Now he consults with people who have expertise and knowledge in a specific area and he pays close attention to what they offer him. However, he realizes that they do not have final answers or complete knowledge but that they are also grappling with relativistic knowledge. They may be more expert than he, but he no longer accepts their conclusions unconditionally. Jason is realizing that he is becoming his own authority—that is, he must determine his own beliefs, opinions, and actions.

Another realization for Jason is his Commitment to maintain the friendships he has. He has joined a campus business fraternity. Although he knows that most college friendships end, he is willing to work hard to maintain relationships with his four closest college friends. Close, trusted friends have a high value for Jason, and he is determined to maintain such relationships.

Jason also knows that someday he wants a Committed relationship, but he has not yet found his partner. He dates and has had a few short romantic relationships, but he realizes that he feels no urgency. Partnership is a long-term goal, one that will come eventually.

Exercise 11.6

Matching Your Cognitive Level to a College Course

Your current developmental level of cognitive growth and the way a class is taught can sometimes be a challenge. Select a challenging course for which you are currently enrolled, then answer the questions that follow. This exercise will help you assess the level of this challenging course in which you are currently enrolled.

1. What cognitive level of development does your teacher exhibit? Using Perry's stages of cognitive development, analyze your teacher's cognitive level of development according to the following criteria:

   a. attitudes and behaviors toward students (e.g., absolute authority, facilitator, colleague, friend)

   b. instructional methods used (e.g., lectures, class discussions, group work, presentations, research)

   c. types of assignments and activities (e.g., independent, collaborative, papers, case studies, group projects, simulations, laboratories)

   d. types of examinations (e.g., multiple choice, true/false, matching, short answer, essay, case studies, in-class exams, out-of-class exams)

   e. course policies (e.g., mandatory class attendance, allowance for some excused absences, no taking of attendance, penalty for turning in late assignments, allowance for make-up tests)

   f. teaching styles (e.g., teaches in absolutes, allows for opinions, encourages problem solving, allows for creativity)

2. What is your cognitive level of development for this class? Analyze your cognitive level according to the following criteria:

   a. attitude toward how your teacher interacts with you and the class

   b. comfort level with your teacher's instructional methods

   c. amount of extra readings and assignments you complete

   d. ability to successfully perform well on assignments

   e. ability to successfully complete and pass examinations

   f. comfort level with the course policies

3. If there is congruence between you and your teacher, how can this be useful for your learning the material and completing the course? If there is incongruence, how can this hinder your learning?

MIDLIFE

At the beginning of this chapter, we said that the two longest transition times were independence and midlife and that they are, in many ways, parallel experiences. Ideally, by the time people are in their midtwenties, they are making Commitments to work, family, friends, faith, and society. The next years in adulthood usually involve hard work in building families and careers, but they tend to be stable stages. Sometimes when people are in their late thirties or forties, another transition begins. This time, the beginning is usually not tied to a specific chronological event such as going off to college. Instead, an increasing dissatisfaction and unease emerges. What was a complete life just the week before now seems limited or pale. Most people do not welcome this change; they tend to put more effort into the tasks of their lives. However, the dissatisfaction increases, and the old ways of thinking and being begin to disintegrate. This transition time is called **midlife**, and many writers follow the conviction of Carl Jung, an influential Swiss psychiatrist in the early 1900s, that midlife is *the beginning of the second half of life, a time of exploration into the inner life, a journey toward integration and wholeness* (Brewi & Brennan, 1999).

What causes tension in many families is that as daughters and sons move into the independence transition, their parents are moving into midlife. Jason's parents are no exception.

CASE STUDY: Jason's Parents

MIKE's business is stable and he enjoys it, but his wife, SARAH, is increasingly worried about her job. She finished three semesters of college 20 years ago, then secured a job as a teller in a large bank. Although she has had a few small promotions and raises over the years, she is frustrated because she has been routinely bypassed for management positions. She has watched as banking has changed dramatically over the last 10 years; there have been many buyouts and layoffs and no one feels secure. She and Mike have had long conversations; they need her income with two children in college and one in high school. Additionally, Sarah's mother has recently fallen and broken a hip, so she has moved in with them. What if the bank is sold and Sarah is laid off? Because she has had to invest so much time in parenting, she has been willing to work at a repetitive, low-level job, but lately she has become restless and dissatisfied.

Sarah is moving into the midlife transition with pressure from both internal and external forces. She is ready to have a more demanding and interesting work life, even though her parenting responsibilities are not over. However, she can see the end of active parenting; her youngest child, Justin, is 15. She is also concerned about the changing nature of banking because technology is replacing so many jobs. With trepidation, Sarah visits the local community college and inquires about enrolling in its night program. To her relief, she finds that many students at that college are older and the advisor seems unsurprised that she is considering finishing a degree.

During the Christmas holidays, she sits with her children and tells them that she is planning to take two courses during spring term. Jason and his sister, Meredith, are excited at the news of her plans, but their younger brother, Justin, becomes angry. He responds, "What about me? Who's going to watch after Grandma, since the caretaker leaves at five? Dad always works late, so who's going to cook dinner? It's not going to be me! That's not fair!"

With Mike's support, Sarah has made the decision to reenter college. Her restlessness and unease are signaling that she is beginning again the cycle that Perry described. She has spent 25 years honoring the commitments she made as a young woman; she will continue to honor those, but now she is ready to chart a new professional path for herself. In some important ways, she is reentering the cycle at the point of multiplicity. Her initial choice is to major in accounting, but she feels unsure about what she really wants to study and what type of professional job she wants. Two courses are a cautious beginning.

Sarah is adopting a gradual move into midlife, but many people do not have the opportunity to change gradually. Divorce, widowhood, empty nest, disability, layoffs, military retirement—all of these and more propel midlifers into rapid and unexpected changes. Sometimes depression or boredom motivates the change; sometimes the search for knowledge and self-fulfillment is the impetus. Whatever the cause, the result is almost always a second journey through multiplicity, relativism, and Commitment.

This journey is often as puzzling to a midlifer as it is to someone in the independence transition. Many older students return to college with the expectation that they will learn new things, but they usually do not expect to experience dramatic internal changes in their beliefs, thoughts, and goals. Then they find themselves examining and discarding long-held convictions, adopting new visions, and becoming invigorated by a wealth of possibilities. Although many of these changes are exciting, they can also threaten the stability of relationships with family and friends. The student is changing, but those around her may resent the change.

Case Study Questions: If you are in midlife, how are you changing in terms of Perry's model?

If you are a traditional-age student, using the lens of Perry's model, describe a person you know who is in midlife and some of the challenges and changes that person is facing.

By her second semester, Sarah is surprising herself. First, she often contributes to class discussion whereas in the past she was shy and quiet. Her behavior at home has also become more assertive, and both Mike and Justin have taken more responsibility for the household and Grandma. Sarah's grades are also excellent; she made the dean's honor roll her first semester. Although she gets tired juggling all the facets of her life, she is excited about what she is learning and how she is changing. More and more, she trusts her own judgment. Her hesitancy in many areas, including work, is falling away. Sarah's increasing ability to discern her own voice—that certainty of self based on conviction and experience—is a characteristic of relativism, especially of midlifers who are moving through it for the second time.

Autonomy

Autonomy is *psychological emancipation.* Corey & Corey (1993) give an expanded definition of an autonomous person as one who can "function without constant approval and reassurance, is sensitive to the needs of others, can effectively meet the demands of daily living, is willing to ask for help when it is needed, and can provide support to others" (p. 34).

In this chapter we have focused on two transition periods—independence and midlife—because they are the two most relevant periods for college students. In each, the process of cognitive and moral development posited by Perry (1970) leads to autonomy, that confident sense of self-determination, self-sufficiency, and self-reliance. Now we can see how many of the concepts we have presented in these chapters describe an individual's journey to autonomy. In Chapter 8 we discussed attribution theory, how we explain our successes and failures. Taking responsibility is the first step we make to claim control over our lives. An essential psychological task of the independence period is *to shift our perception of who or what controls us from outside of ourselves to within.* The classic term for that concept is **locus of control** (place of control). Do we believe that we control our behaviors or do others control them? If we have the generalized mindset that we are in control and we are responsible, then that mindset permeates every aspect of our lives.

The period of independence moves us to autonomy, which is the normal status of adulthood. The midlife transition, however, moves us to another sense of autonomy. In midlife, we have to explore carefully the limitations of autonomy. We begin to discover that we are not totally free, although sometimes we wish to be released from all our Commitments and obligations. Our actions can impact others in important ways, and we begin to realize that we have obligations to ourselves, our families, our local community, and the larger community of humankind. Sarah, Jason's mother, is just beginning that journey. She has much to discover about her values and beliefs, and she will be astonished by the power and ferocity of the midlife transition. She believes that she has made the decision to return to school only for economic purposes. Although that may be made the decision to return to school only for economic purposes. Although that may be the initial reason, she soon finds that many of her comfortable ideas are being challenged at every turn. These challenges are often unexpected and disconcerting, and Sarah will find herself questioning many things. As she changes, and she almost surely will, her family may or may not be encouraging. The college experience tends to accelerate the cognitive and moral process, whether for traditional college-age students or midlifers, but the outcomes for each will differ.

Jason is developing a strong sense of autonomy as he moves through the independence period. That self-direction will serve him well as he develops his professional and personal life in adulthood. Sarah has embarked on a path that should lead her to question many things she has heretofore simply accepted. She may question what role work and career will play in the next part of her life; she may explore the desire for more power in the workplace; she may begin a serious study of her spiritual beliefs; she may discover intense interests in other places and peoples; she may commit to new actions or beliefs.

You will notice that this discussion of autonomy is congruent with the expanded definitions of autonomous learning that form the foundation of this text. Learning to be successful in college can foster your growth toward autonomy, your psychological emancipation.

Exercise 11.7

The Interview

This chapter has focused on major transitions and current developmental stages of growth. Now take the time to learn from someone who has gone through similar experiences by interviewing a person in a different developmental stage from yours (preferably someone in a more advanced stage of development) and answering the following questions. Completing this exercise will help you look to another person for guidance and to learn from his or her life experiences.

1. What is it about this person that you most admire?

2. How has this person handled major transitions in his or her life?

3. What would this person do over again if he or she could?

4. What is this person most proud of accomplishing?

5. What advice does this person have for you about making your next developmental transition?

CONCLUSION

The developmental stages and transitions of life provide us with an intellectual model to help us understand our own and others' thoughts, behaviors, and feelings. These changes erupt in us regardless of our own desires; it is as if we have time-release capsules inside us. Living each stage and each transition well frees us to lean into the next part of life with excitement and anticipation, rather than fear and dread.

SUMMARY

- One constant in human life is change.

- There are five dimensions present among humans: biological, social, ecological, spiritual, and psychological.

- Our movement through life occurs in alternating periods of change (transitions) and stability (stages).

- The six stages in the life are prenatal, childhood, youth, adulthood, maturity, and old age.

- Movement through these different stages affects how we think (cognitive), how we feel (affective), and what we do (behavioral).

- The six transition periods in life are birth, puberty, independence, midlife, withdrawal, and death.

- The transition of independence is moving from youth to adulthood, and the transition of midlife is moving from adulthood to maturity.

- According to Arthur Chickering, college students develop across seven dimensions or vectors during independence.

- According to William Perry (1970), dualism, multiplicity, relativism, and Commitment are the four categories of intellectual and moral development that adults experience as they move through the transition period of independence.

- Students in the dualistic stage see the world in terms of no uncertainty: knowledge is right or wrong, good or bad. They depend on authority figures to tell them how to think.

- Students in the multiplicity stage begin to view knowledge as being based more on opinion than certainty. Lack of answers is viewed as temporary.

- Students in the multiplicity stage begin to view knowledge as being based more on opinion than certainty. Lack of answers is viewed as temporary.

- Students in the relativism stage evaluate knowledge based on the quality of evidence supporting it. They see knowledge from a contextual point of view, derived through one's experiences and values.

- Retreat is a deflection from making a commitment by regressing to an earlier stage.

- Escape is a deflection from making a commitment by settling in at the relativistic stage and rejecting further movement.

- Temporizing is a deflection from making a commitment by postponing it.

- Commitment is a major affirmation or choice made after several alternatives are examined.

- Perry uses a capital *C* when one makes a Commitment in relativism. Commitments made before relativism are distinguished by a lowercase *c*.

- The midlife transition begins during the second half of life and is a time of exploration into the meaning of one's life.

- Moving through developmental stages leads to autonomy or a confident sense of self-determination, self-sufficiency, and self-reliance.

- Autonomy is psychological emancipation.

- Locus of control is the perception of whether we are controlled by external forces or internal forces.

KEY CONCEPTS

Autonomy

Chickering's seven vectors of student development: developing competence, managing emotions, moving through autonomy toward interdependence, developing mature interpersonal relationships, establishing identity, developing purpose, developing integrity.

Deflections: retreat, escape, temporizing

Independence

Locus of control

Midlife

Perry's theory of cognitive development: dualism, multiplicity, relativism, Commitment

Stages

Transitions

The universal (stages and transitions of life)

Vectors

GUIDED JOURNAL QUESTIONS

1. If you are a traditional-age college student, describe what it is like moving from the stage of *youth* to *adulthood* through the transition time of *independence*. Discuss two major turning points associated with this transition period. What struggles or major conflicts have you had to overcome as you move from one stage to the next? What struggles are yet unresolved?

    or

    If you are a nontraditional-age college student, describe what it is like moving from the stage of *adulthood* to *maturity* through the transition time of *midlife*. Discuss two major turning points associated with this transition. What struggles or major conflicts have you had to overcome while moving from one stage to the next? What struggles are yet unresolved?

2. Who has been most instrumental in your life in helping you make major transitions? Give specific examples of what that person did that was helpful to you.

3. What do you miss most about being in the stages of childhood and youth? What do you miss least about those stages of your life?

4. Do you wish to become more independent in your life? If so, how do you plan on accomplishing this goal? Do you have fears related to more independence? If you do not wish to become more independent, why not?

5. To what degree do you believe you can live by your own set of values and standards and still be sensitive to the needs of other important people in your life?

6. How frustrated do you feel when there is no apparent answer to a question? How comfortable do you feel with "it depends"?

7. Which of the following statements best represent your current thinking? Support your answer by referencing Perry's theory of cognitive development.

    a. I want my college instructors to tell me the answers to my questions.

    b. I want my college instructors to guide me in finding answers to my questions.

    c. I want to find my own answers to my questions.

8. According to Perry's theory of cognitive development, what do you estimate your developmental stage to be? Use at least three examples

of decisions that you have made or values you have chosen that would support your analysis.

9. Can you be in more than one of Perry's stage at a time? For instance, reflect on your current stage in relation to your parents, your college teachers, your spouse/significant other, and so on.

The Last Word

Since my parents encouraged me to be independent at an early age, it's much easier for me to follow their lead and support the independence my children are striving to achieve.

—*Carol Dochen*

Exploring the Diversity of Individuality

I've just gotta be me.

CHAPTER HIGHLIGHTS

- Individuality
- Talents
- Preferences
- Myers-Briggs Type Indicator®
- Temperaments

One gift of human awareness is the awakening realization that each of us is a unique being. Yes, we share much with others of our species and our culture, but the uniqueness of "I" comes from the interaction of the qualities and abilities with which we were born, the circumstances of our lives, and the unique path we have taken through each developmental stage.

In Chapter 11, we examined some aspects of theories related to the universal and the cultures that help us understand ourselves. In this chapter, we study concepts and theories that aid us in grasping how each of us is different from others. From the outset, however, it is important to note that a crucial difference about the value of the individual versus the group exists between the Anglo cultures of Western Europe and the United States and the cultures of the rest of the world as well as specific subcultures within the United States.

SELF-ASSESSMENT: How I Am Different

A healthy sense of self is a trait of a secure and confident individual in mainstream Western culture. With 5 being "Almost Always" and 1 being "Almost Never," assess the ways you express your individuality. Rate each of the following statements honestly by circling the appropriate number. Completing this exercise will provide you with the opportunity to reflect on some of the characteristics that make you unique.

	Almost Always		Sometimes		Almost Never
1. I express who I am by the clothes, body art, jewelry, and/or hairstyles I wear.	5	4	3	2	1
2. Some of the music I listen to is different than what my friends would expect me to like.	5	4	3	2	1
3. I have a hobby or sport (e.g., photography, cooking, wake boarding, soccer, knitting, gardening) that I am good at.	5	4	3	2	1
4. I have a special talent or ability (e.g., fluent in two languages, a whiz at computers, play/sing/ create music).	5	4	3	2	1
5. I have some different beliefs about politics, religion, drugs and/or alcohol than some of my friends.	5	4	3	2	1
6. I am an adventurous eater in that I like to try foods from a variety of cultures and regions.	5	4	3	2	1
7. My cultural background is different than that of some of my friends.	5	4	3	2	1

8. My major/minor and other academic interests are an important part of my identity.

   5   4   3   2   1

9. I am actively involved in at least one organization or activity about which I feel passionate.

   5   4   3   2   1

10. I have my own dreams and goals that I would like to accomplish someday.

    5   4   3   2   1

Add up the numbers you circled. Your total score will be between 10 and 50. The higher your score, the more likely you feel confident about being your own person. For scores below 30, write or reflect on items for which you have concerns and consider talking with a trusted friend, a family member, a teacher, a counselor, or an advisor.

INDIVIDUALITY

Two terms—individuality and individualism—sound similar yet mean dramatically different ways of being. Let us look first at **individualism** because it is the more common term. "Individualism refers to one's self-concept, to the image of oneself as an individual unit whose motivations and behavior are aimed at individual goals, as opposed, for instance, to a member of a group whose behavior is directed toward smooth harmonious interpersonal relations" (Augsberger, 1986, p. 86). Many of the world's cultures do not support individualism; rather, they support the value of the group over the individual. Many American families from Latin, Asian, Native American, and Middle Eastern subcultures, as well as religious groups, value group centeredness over individualism.

Individualism ←——————————→ Group centeredness

American college students represent the entire range of beliefs about individualism versus group centeredness. An initial step in understanding ourselves is the realization of our position on the spectrum. Have we been raised to choose and pursue our own individual goals? Or have we been raised to satisfy our desires within the context deemed best for the group (family) to which we belong? Or are we somewhere in between? How much do we agree or disagree with the values of our family/group?

As educators we have witnessed many of our students struggle with conflicts between their goals and the goals of their families:

> *My parents have always dreamed that I would become a doctor, but I am interested in psychology.*
>
> *I have three exams next week, but my grandfather is ill. Do I go home or stay at school to study?*
>
> *Should I take over the family business or pursue a different career path?*
>
> *I have started attending my roommate's church, and my family makes fun of me.*
>
> *I might want to work in America for a few years before I return to my home country, but I'm not sure if I would be allowed to.*
>
> *My children complain that I don't have time for them anymore because all I ever do is study.*
>
> *I am dating a person from another cultural group, and my family is really angry.*

American community colleges and universities generally model the value of individualism by creating a competitive environment in which our success is determined by our ability to set and achieve our own goals. Even though specific courses may require collaborative work through group projects, the ultimate purpose of the institution is the education of the individual. Our transcripts belong only to us.

Individuality is the term we use in this text to describe "the development of differences within the personality" (Augsberger, 1986, p. 86). We believe this term is much more appropriate for students who are learning how to be successful in college because individuality occurs across the complete range of individualism/group centeredness. Thus, we are all capable of developing as individuals. Besides the obvious physical differences among us, we differ markedly in both cognitive and emotional attributes. Although there are numerous methods by which people explore their own individuality, we have chosen to focus on two specific characteristics that we hope will give you a clear self-portrait. Each is a way of reflecting on ourselves, and we have labeled these characteristics *talents* and *preferences*.

These two characteristics—talent and preferences—combine to create our own learning style. **Learning style** is most often used as "a metaphor for thinking about individual differences" (Jonassen & Grabowski, 1993, p. 234). In the past few decades, many educators attempted to help students understand their own ways of learning. Self-report instruments, such as Kolb's *Learning Style Inventory*

(1999) and Dunn, Dunn, and Price's *Learning Style Inventory* (1984), rely on student reflections. All try to measure a student's holistic approach to learning, but they have differing premises and use different measurements. We believe that you will be able to ascertain your unique learning style through reflections on your talents and your preferences.

TALENTS

Talents are *those abilities that come as a result of the interaction of our genes, our environment, our experience, and our effort.* We are all born with an astounding array of gifts, and we spend our lives enhancing those gifts or ignoring them. For many decades, our society has used the term *intelligence* to denote a specific set of two talents, linguistic and logical–mathematical (Gardner, 1995). These talents are useful in an academic environment, and educational achievement tests examine both areas. However, these two talents are only two of eight intelligences that educational psychologists use to categorize talents that are relevant to an academic setting (Gardner, 1983; Gardner, 2000). Our understanding of our talents across these eight dimensions of intelligence help us gain accurate self-knowledge, which can then help us understand ourselves as learners. A clear view of our own talents helps us make good decisions about work and how we can better lead our lives.

Exercise 12.2

Animal School

We are unique individuals with our own special talents and gifts. To understand more about how we differ from each other, read the following fable and answer the accompanying questions:

THE ANIMAL SCHOOL: A FABLE
George Reavis

Once upon a time the animals decided they must do something heroic to meet the problems of a "new world" so they organized a school. They adopted an activity curriculum consisting of running, climbing, swimming, and flying. To make it easier to administer the curriculum, all the animals took all the subjects.

The duck was excellent in swimming—in fact, better than his instructor. But he made only passing grades in flying and was very poor in running. Since he was slow in running, he had to stay after school and also drop swimming in order to practice running. This was kept up until his webbed feet were badly worn and he was only average in swimming. But average was acceptable in school so nobody worried about that, except the duck.

The rabbit started at the top of the class in running but had a nervous breakdown because of so much make-up work in swimming.

The squirrel was excellent in climbing until he developed frustration in the flying class where his teacher made him start from the ground up instead of the treetop down. He also developed a charley horse from overexertion and then got a C in climbing and D in running.

The eagle was a problem child and was disciplined severely. In the climbing class, he beat all the others to the top of the tree but insisted on using his own way to get there.

At the end of the year, an abnormal eel that could swim exceeding well, and also run, climb, and fly a little, had the highest average, and was valedictorian.

The prairie dogs stayed out of school and fought the tax levy because the administration would not add digging and burrowing to the curriculum. They apprenticed their children to a badger and later joined the groundhogs and gophers to start a successful private school.

Does this fable have a moral?

Source: Reavis, G. H. (n.d.).

1. What lessons can you infer from this fable?

2. As a student, which animal can you most identify with? Explain.

Multiple Intelligences

Educational psychologists now use the term *multiple intelligences* from a theory by Howard Gardner to differentiate human talents into eight categories. Gardner first introduced his theory of seven multiple intelligences in 1983, when he wrote *Frames of Mind: The Theory of Multiple Intelligences.* His theory expands and challenges the more traditional view of intelligence, especially the use of standardized Intelligence Quotient (IQ) tests. IQ assessments typically measure a person's linguistic and mathematical aptitude and assign a number that represents the person's intelligence. Gardner felt that an individual's intelligence should not be measured in such a limited realm.

Gardner (1995) defines **intelligence** as *"a biological and psychological potential that . . . [is] a consequence of the experiential, cultural, and motivational factors that affect a person"* (p. 202, italics added). In other words, he believes intelligence emerges from both a biological and cultural basis. The biology of intelligence, for example, may be understood by the connections formed between brain cells as learning occurs. Most educational psychologists would agree that intelligence is biologically based. However, Gardner adds a new perspective by including culture as an influence. He believes all societies value different types of intelligences. The cultural value placed on a person's ability to acquire certain skills and perform certain tasks is the motivational factor that affects a person to gain mastery in certain skills.

> **Gardner's Eight Multiple Intelligences**
>
> Logical–mathematical
> Linguistic
> Musical
> Spatial
> Bodily–kinesthetic
> Interpersonal
> Intrapersonal
> Naturalist

Gardner believes that a person's intelligence will grow and change over time and that the different intelligences rarely operate independently; rather, they complement each other as a person develops skills and solves problems. The seven original intelligences are logical–mathematical, linguistic, musical, spatial, bodily–kinesthetic, interpersonal, and intrapersonal. In 1996, Gardner added an eighth intelligence that he named naturalist (Gardner, 2000). Let us now examine each of these eight intelligences in detail.

1. **Logical–mathematical intelligence** is *the ability to calculate, quantify, consider propositions and hypotheses, and carry out complex mathematical operations.* It enables us to perceive relationships and connections and to use abstract, symbolic thought; sequential reasoning skills; and inductive and deductive thinking patterns. Logical intelligence is usually well developed in mathematicians, scientists, and detectives. Examples include solving mathematical problems as well as creating hypotheses based on observation and testing those hypotheses.

2. **Linguistic intelligence** is *the ability to think in words and to use language to express and appreciate complex meanings.* Linguistic intelligence allows us to understand the order and meaning of words and to apply metalinguistic skills to reflect on our use of language. Linguistic intelligence is the most widely shared human competence and is evident in poets, novelists, journalists, and effective public speakers. Examples include easily understanding subtle and complex verbal arguments as well as writing clear and persuasive prose.

3. **Musical intelligence** is *the capacity to discern pitch, rhythm, timbre, and tone.* This intelligence enables us to recognize, create, reproduce, and reflect on music, as demonstrated by composers, conductors, musicians, vocalists, and sensitive listeners. Interestingly, there is often an affective connection between music and the emotions. Mathematical and musical intelligences may share common thinking practices. Examples include performing instrumentally or vocally, creating musical compositions, and accurately critiquing musical works.

4. **Spatial intelligence** is *the ability to think in three dimensions*. Core capacities include mental imagery, spatial reasoning, image manipulation, graphic and artistic skills, and an active imagination. Sailors, pilots, sculptors, painters, and architects all exhibit spatial intelligence. Examples include imagining a picture and creating three-dimensional models.

5. **Bodily–kinesthetic intelligence** is *the capacity to manipulate objects and use a variety of physical skills*. This intelligence also involves a sense of timing and the perfection of skills through mind–body union. Athletes, dancers, surgeons, and craftspeople exhibit well-developed bodily–kinesthetic intelligence. Examples include excelling in a sport as well as engaging in needlework/arts and crafts.

6. **Interpersonal intelligence** is *the ability to understand and interact effectively with others*. It involves effective verbal and nonverbal communication, the ability to note distinctions among others, sensitivity to the moods and temperaments of others, and the ability to entertain multiple perspectives. Teachers, social workers, actors, and politicians exhibit interpersonal intelligence. Examples include maintaining healthy friendships and effectively interpreting nonverbal cues.

7. **Intrapersonal intelligence** is *the capacity to understand oneself and one's thoughts and feelings and to use such knowledge in planning and directing one's life*. Intrapersonal intelligence involves not only an appreciation of the self, but also of the human condition. It is evident in psychologists, spiritual leaders, and philosophers. Examples include understanding reasons for your own behavior as well as creating goals that reflect your desires and values.

8. **Naturalistic intelligence** is *the ability to recognize, identify, and classify patterns in nature such as plants and animals*. Individuals with this intelligence are keen observers of their environments. They are particularly interested in the balance and relationship between humans and nature. Farmers, hunters, ecologists, landscapers, meteorologists, biologists, and holistic healers share these traits. Examples include identifying flora and fauna that are edible as well as being aware of the subtle changes of stars during various seasons.

In 2003, Gardner addressed common questions about his multiple intelligences theory at a professional conference. His comments reflect the organic, evolutionary nature of psychological theories—they are a work in process, never completely finalized. In his words,

> To begin with, there will be efforts to propose new intelligences. In recent years, in addition to the explosion of interest in emotional intelligences, there have also been serious efforts to describe a spiritual intelligence and a sexual intelligence. My colleague Antonio Battro has proposed the existence of a digital intelligence and has indicated how it may fulfill the criteria that I have set forth. And at this conference, Michael Posner has challenged me to consider "attention" as a kind of intelligence. I have always conceded that, in the end,

the decision about what counts as an intelligence is a judgment call and not an algorithmic conclusion (Gardner, 2003, p. 10).

To learn how you can enhance each of your multiple intelligences, see Figure 12.1.

FIGURE 12.1 Enhancing Each of Your Multiple Intelligences

Intelligence	Activities to enhance each intelligence
Logical–mathematical Intelligence	Learn to use the scientific method. Ask more questions when learning. Learn deductive logic strategies (syllogisms, Venn diagrams). Learn to use inductive logic strategies (analogies). Think mathematically by creating more graphs and placing knowledge into common patterns. Work with numbers (averages, percentages, calculations, probability, formulas). Overpractice each type of math problem you are learning. Use T-notes and write out procedures used to solve problems—not just examples. Think of real-life examples when learning mathematical concepts.
Linguistic Intelligence	Learn to focus listening and concentration skills during lectures and classroom discussions. Practice public speaking at every opportunity (oral reports, answer questions, engage in classroom discussions). Build your vocabulary by learning Greek and Latin roots and reading often for pleasure. Improve your writing skills by taking classes that require research papers, essays, poetry, and essay exams. Use outlines to study lectures and textbook chapters.
Musical Intelligence	Listen and create various sounds, rhythms, and lyrics. Create rhythms and songs for the material you are learning. Learn to play a musical instrument. Learn to read musical notation. Learn music associated with periods of history.
Spatial Intelligence	Be attentive to nonverbal communication. Practice drawing. Organize information graphically (flow charts, outlines, matrices, concept maps). Highlight materials with color. Visualize material by using imagery (pictures in your mind). Draw pictures when taking notes to illustrate concepts. Learn by watching films, videos, and slide shows.
Bodily–kinesthetic Intelligence	Learn by using drama (role plays, simulations). Manipulate objects to learn (board games, puzzles, scientific equipment). Engage in physical activity while learning such as move from group to group or different locations while learning. Use computers (video games, touch screens, eye–hand coordination activities).

(Continued)

FIGURE 12.1   Enhancing Each of Your Multiple Intelligences (*Continued*)

Intelligence	Activities to enhance each intelligence
Interpersonal Intelligence	Work with others in class (collaborative learning activities, team projects). Attend study groups outside of class (supplemental instruction, peer tutoring, review sessions). Learn from service projects. Engage in multicultural experiences (interview others from different cultures, role-play events from diverse perspectives). Teach others after you learn the material. Debate others over class material.
Intrapersonal Intelligence	Acknowledge and express feelings as you learn. Learn more about yourself through self-assessment inventories. Understand your own ability to learn (use metacognitive strategy). Reflect and think about class material. Journal (write reflective answers to questions). Study by yourself in a quiet area. Meditate.
Naturalist Intelligence	Observe nature. Identify groups or species, recognizing flora and fauna. Interact with your physical surroundings. Work with plants and animals. Learn outdoors through field observations. Relate material you are learning to the environment when possible. Select research topics that relate to nature.

Source: Adapted from Campbell, L., Campbell B., & Dickinson, D. (1999). *Teaching and Learning Through Multiple Intelligences*. Boston: Allyn & Bacon.

Exercise 12.3

Your Multiple Intelligences

Determining how you learn best is one way to assess your unique talents or multiple intelligences. Check only the statements that are most often true for you. Completing this exercise will help you identify areas of strengths (talents) and areas for future growth. The assessment is based on Howard Gardner's multiple intelligences theory.

I learn best when I

_____ 1.   move around my physical surroundings.

_____ 2.   am with another person or groups of people.

_____ 3.   use three-dimensional thinking, visualizing, or conceptualizing.

_____ 4.   use my physical skills and stay active.

_____ 5. use my artistic skills and imagination.

_____ 6. reflect and think about how what I am learning affects me.

_____ 7. incorporate sounds, rhythms, pitch, and tone.

_____ 8. use mathematical concepts or logical reasoning.

_____ 9. use my musical skills.

_____10. explore nature and the environment.

_____11. express myself using words.

_____12. assess my own feelings about the material.

_____13. verbalize the material to myself or others.

_____14. teach others and am sensitive to their needs.

_____15. recognize patterns and create classifications.

_____16. work with plants and animals.

Statements 8 and 15 correspond to logical–mathematical intelligence.

Statements 11 and 13 correspond to linguistic intelligence.

Statements 7 and 9 correspond to musical intelligence.

Statements 3 and 5 correspond to spatial intelligence.

Statements 1 and 4 correspond to bodily–kinesthetic intelligence.

Statements 2 and 14 correspond to interpersonal intelligence.

Statements 6 and 12 correspond to intrapersonal intelligence.

Statements 10 and 16 correspond to naturalist intelligence.

a. Based on the statements you checked, which multiple intelligences best describe you?

b. How do they affect your range of choices of majors and careers?

c. Are there any weaknesses you wish to strengthen? If so, how do you plan to strengthen them?

CASE STUDY

SARAH and JASON, the mother and son you met in Chapter 11, are good examples of two people from the same family who differ across the eight dimensions of intelligence. Whereas Jason is competent in logical–mathematical abilities and below average in spatial abilities, he excels in interpersonal abilities. His move from engineering to business marketing as a major makes good sense because he was able to discern a better match for his talents. His good bodily–kinesthetic abilities fuel his love for intramural sports, but he decides to enroll in a golf class to acquire a lifelong individual sport to enhance his future business career.

His mother, Sarah, has excellent logical–mathematical and good linguistic abilities, as evidenced by her competent work history and her first semester's grades. She plans to improve her linguistic abilities by taking advanced and technical writing courses. Although she enjoyed performing as a singer during high school and her early college years, she abandoned that interest when she had a family. In spite of juggling a demanding schedule of work, classes, and family, she decides to join the church choir, a hidden desire she has had for many years.

Case Study Questions: Jason and his mother, Sarah, share which one of Gardner's multiple intelligences? Do you think these intelligences are inherited? Why or why not?

Discerning your talents across all the dimensions of intelligence helps you make wise decisions in educational, vocational, and leisure activities as well as relationships. Thoughtful self-reflection may include data from school and test performances, but it should also include many other memories and opinions. It is important to remember that you can improve your abilities through study and practice. Ask yourself these questions:

What are my talents?

How do they affect my range of choices?

Are there any weaknesses I wish to strengthen?

If so, how do I plan to strengthen them?

PREFERENCES

A second reflective strategy to further our self-understanding is the use of a personality classification system. There have been many systems postulated over the centuries, from the Chinese ideas of yin/yang and personality traits attributed to our birth year to the Hindu ideas of spiritual personality types (reflective, emotional, active, experimental) to the Greek ideas of four humors (earth, air, fire, water) to Carl Jung's system of eight personality types to more recent versions (Jung, 1923; Jung, 1971). We say that men are from Mars, women from Venus; that we are Coke or Pepsi people; that our personalities are shaped by our birth date (astrology). In educational psychology, we categorize learners by their learning styles, a metaphor for thinking about individual differences (Jonassen & Grabowski, 1993).

All of the aforementioned examples represent just some of the myriad ways humans have tried to understand themselves and others close to them. As teachers, we have tried to help our students make sense of these systems and choose one or two as tools to help them ascertain their inclinations, their values, and their strengths. All of these systems share a common concept—**cognitive** (*thinking*) and **affective** (*feeling*) **preferences**, defined as *the way we prefer to use our minds and hearts.* In simple terms, these theories all postulate that much of the seeming variation in human behavior

is not due to chance; it is in fact the logical result of a few basic, observable differences in mental functioning.

These basic differences concern the way people *prefer* to use their minds, specifically, the way they perceive and the way they make judgments. *Perceiving* is here understood to include the processes of becoming aware of things, people, occurrences, and ideas. Judging includes the processes of coming to conclusions about what has been perceived. Together, perception and judgment, which make up a large portion of people's total mental activity, govern much of their outer behavior, because perception—by definition—determines what people see in a situation, and their judgment determines what they decide to do about it. Thus, it is reasonable that basic differences in perception or judgment should result in corresponding differences in behavior (Myers & Myers, 1980, p. 1).

Preferences form much of what we term *personality,* and careful reflection about our own preferences can help us set meaningful goals, discern the best circumstances of study and work, and create better relationships. There are thousands of books and hundreds of Internet sites devoted to preferences. Many educational psychologists create theories about the ways we learn by studying preferences of students.

In this section, we look at the primary theory of personality preferences, the *Myers-Briggs Type Indicator*® (MBTI®), which is based on the work of the Swiss psychiatrist Carl Jung. Next we examine the concept of temperament as explicated by David Keirsey, an internationally renowned psychologist. Throughout this tour we pay special attention to those concepts that can help college students move toward academic and personal success.

Exercise 12.4

Learning About Preferences

You have probably developed the viewpoint that certain learning strategies work better for you than others. To illustrate the concept of preference, follow the directions below.

a. Sign your name as you normally do on the line below:

_____

b. Now sign your name using your opposite hand:

_____

Although you were probably able to use both hands to sign your name, your less preferred hand took more effort, time, and concentration. Learning preferences can be viewed the same way. You have come to depend on a few preferences to take in and process information.

c. Under what circumstances might you need to use your opposite hand to sign your name or even to write?

d. Under what circumstances might you need to more fully develop additional ways to take in and learn information and not simply rely on your preferred methods of learning?

Source: Idea for signature exercise from DiTiberio, J. K., & Hammer, A. L. *Introduction to Type in College.* © 1993 by Consulting Psychologists Press.

Exercise 12.5

SELF-ASSESSMENT: Your Learning Preference

Assessing the way you learn best can be helpful information for a successful college experience. The following exercise may be useful as a beginning point in exploring your preferences.

Directions:
Read the two preferences in each row. In a **learning situation**—that is, when you are *listening* to a lecture, *reading* a book, *concentrating* on homework,

writing a paper, or *preparing* for a test—which **one** of the two characteristics describes you **most of the time?** Put a "✓" in that circle.

SCALE I

Extraversion	*OR*	**Introversion**

○ I prefer action and variety.

○ I prefer talking to people when doing mental work.

○ I often act quickly, sometimes with little reflection.

○ I prefer to see how others do a task and to see results.

○ I want to know what other people expect of me.

Total number of ✓'s for E_____

○ I prefer quiet and time to consider things.

○ I prefer to do mental work privately before talking.

○ I prefer to understand something *before* trying it.

○ I prefer to understand the *idea* of a task and to work alone or with just a few people.

○ I prefer setting my own standards.

Total number of ✓'s for I_____

SCALE II

Sensing	*OR*	**Intuition**

○ I usually pay most attention to *experience* and what something *is*.

○ I prefer to use my *senses*—see, hear, say, touch, smell—to find out what is happening.

○ I dislike new problems *unless* I've had prior experiences regarding how to solve them.

○ I enjoy *using skills already learned* more than learning new skills.

○ I am *patient with details,* but impatient when the details become complicated.

Total number of ✓'s for S_____

○ I usually pay most attention to the *meanings* of facts and how they *fit together.*

○ I prefer to use my *imagination* to come up with different ways and possibilities to do things.

○ I like solving *new* problems. I dislike doing the same thing over and over.

○ I enjoy *learning new skills* more than practicing old skills.

○ I am *impatient with details* and don't mind complicated situations.

Total number of ✓'s for N_____

SCALE III

Thinking	*OR*	**Feeling**

○ I prefer to use *logic* when making decisions.

○ I expect to be treated with *justice and fairness.*

○ I may neglect and hurt other people's feelings *without realizing it.*

○ I can get along with *little or no harmony* among people.

○ I tend to give more attention to *ideas or things,* rather than to human relationships.

Total number of ✓'s for T_____

○ I prefer to use *personal feelings and values* when making decisions.

○ I expect praise and like to *please other people,* even in small matters.

○ I am usually very aware of *other people's feelings.*

○ I feel unsettled by arguments and conflicts; I prefer *harmony* among people.

○ I often can predict how others will *feel.*

Total number of ✓'s for F_____

SCALE IV

Judging	*OR*	**Perceiving**

○ I prefer to make a *plan* and to have things settled and decided ahead of time.

○ I prefer to make things come out the way they *ought to be.*

○ I prefer to *finish* one project before starting another.

○ I usually have my *mind made up* and may decide things too quickly.

○ I live by *standards and schedules* that are not easily changed.

Total number of ✓'s for J_____

○ I prefer to stay *flexible* and avoid fixed plans.

○ I deal easily with *unplanned and unexpected* happenings.

○ I prefer to start many projects, although I may have *trouble completing* all of them.

○ I usually am seeking *new information* and may decide things too slowly.

○ I live by *making changes* to deal with problems as they come along.

Total number of ✓'s for P_____

Scoring: For Scales I–IV, total the number of "✓'s" in each column. Write the totals next to each preference.

Preferences

Scale I: _____ Extraversion (E)   *or*   _____ Introversion (I)

Scale II: _____ Sensing (S)   *or*   _____ Intuition (N)

Scale III: _____ Thinking (T)   *or*   _____ Feeling (F)

Scale IV: _____ Judging (J)   *or*   _____ Perceiving (P)

   Your dominant, clearer preference is the higher of the two numbers for each scale. Circle the term with the higher number for Scales I–IV, then write the four letters representing your "type" (for example, "ESFP" or "ISFJ"): _____

Consider these factors when using your four-letter type (Lipsky, 2004, p. 7):

1. The higher the number, the more dominant or clearer is the preference.

2. If the difference between the two numbers is slight—that is, only 1 point—then this measure is showing no clear-cut dominant type for you on that scale.

3. By completing this informal exercise, you are receiving an *approximate* measure of your learning preference.

Source: *People Types and Tiger Stripes,* 3rd edition, by Gordon D. Lawrence, Center for Applications of Psychological Type, Gainesville, Florida. Used with permission. This exercise is *NOT* a type indicator, nor does it replicate the Myer-Briggs Type Indicator®, which is a validated instrument.

MYERS-BRIGGS TYPE INDICATOR®

The MBTI® is a questionnaire that helps people understand their personalities through cataloging their preferences. It is widely used in American and international business as well as on American college campuses. Created by Isabel Myers and her mother, Kathryn Briggs, the MBTI® is a set of forced-choice questions—that is, each question has two opposing answers. Several forms of this questionnaire exist, but it must be administered by a psychologist or someone especially trained in the field. Most college counseling centers administer this instrument, and your instructor may require or suggest that you take it. We strongly concur that the MBTI® is a useful tool and believe that the rest of the information in this chapter will be more useful if you can receive your specific results. The forced-choice structure of the questionnaire works well because the MBTI® is based on the Jungian premise that ways of perceiving and judging occur in opposing pairs.

Acquiring Information

As Jung (1923) points out in *Psychological Types,* humankind is equipped with two distinct and sharply contrasting ways of perceiving. One means of perception is the familiar process of sensing, by which we become aware of things directly through our five senses. The other is the process of intuition, which is indirect perception by way of the unconscious, incorporating ideas or associations that the unconscious tacks on to perceptions coming from outside (Myers & Myers, 1980, p. 2).

All of us have both ways of perceiving, but all of us also developed early in life a preference for one way over the other. That preference is easy to observe in small children, and the preference grows in competence as a child will enjoy and use the preferred way over the nonpreferred way. Again, it is important to remember that we have both abilities; however, repetitive practice allows the preferences to develop more fully.

Sensing. People who develop their preference of **sensing (S)** tend to pay attention to what they hear, see, feel, taste, and smell. Their senses tell them what is real, and this preference keeps them in the present moment. They trust their own experience, not the experience of others. Students who have this preference often read well for detail and can memorize facts that they can confirm by experience. They prefer clear, unambiguous assignments and instructions. They value practicality and rarely question the validity of the presented material. They strongly prefer material that is presented in sequential order. The sensing way of perceiving is especially useful in learning that requires an orderly memorization of specific information.

Intuition. People who develop their preference of **intuition (N)** tend to focus on ideas implied by the information; in other words, they like to go beyond the data and look at the relationships among ideas and the possibilities. They tend to disregard the present moment and feel comfortable thinking about the future. As students, they read for the ideas and often miss the specific facts; memorization is difficult because they are interested in the large view. The order or sequence of presentation is usually irrelevant to them. They value originality and usually create their own interpretations of material. Therefore, they want teachers to value and support their independent thinking. The intuitive way of perceiving is necessary in learning that is primarily conceptual and analytical.

Both ways of perceiving or gathering information are necessary for competency in college learning. Whichever is our preference, we must quickly learn to develop our nonpreference. If we have always relied on our senses to learn, then subjects and teachers whose focus is abstract and conceptual will challenge us. We will have to stretch.

CASE STUDY

JASON is a good example of someone with a preference for sensing. He lives and thinks in the present; he enjoys practical, concrete activities. Remember that he originally majored in engineering; even his final choice of a major, marketing, is a practical, specific activity. He is wisely choosing a work life that is congruent with his preference. However, to be successful in college and in his professional life, he is developing his intuitive capabilities in order to function well in business and marketing. He must understand trends and the nuances of the market and be able to analyze his customers' needs.

Now that Jason has discerned the major course of study most appropriate for him, he brings his sensing strengths to his work as a student. He can read for details easily and creates note cards that help him memorize factual information. His class notes reflect the concrete information the instructor is presenting, but he has trouble attending to the larger themes in the material. To compensate for this undeveloped preference for intuition, Jason uses three specific study strategies. First, as he reads the texts, he uses a pre-reading technique that helps him see the larger ideas in a text chapter before he reads for the details. Second, he has a study partner in each class that stresses ideas and concepts. He deliberately chooses partners who are strong in intuitive learning, so he can help them with the specifics and they can help him learn the concepts. Third, he uses a mapping technique that focuses on the ideas of larger sections of material, such as an entire chapter or several weeks of lecture notes.

Case Study Question: What additional strategies can you recommend to Jason to help him more fully develop his *intuition* preference?

Making Decisions

As humans have two ways of perceiving, so too do we have "two distinct and sharply contrasting ways of coming to conclusions. One way is by the use of *thinking,* that is, by a logical process, aimed at an impersonal finding. The other is by *feeling,* that is, by appreciation—equally reasonable in its fashion—bestowing on things a personal, subjective value" (Myers & Myers, 1980, p. 3).

Thinking. Obviously, all of us make decisions by using both the **thinking (T)** function and the feeling function, but our preferences of one over the other develop from childhood. People who have the preference of thinking become good organizers of facts and ideas, and they are analytical and want decisions and the resulting consequences to be fair. People with this preference strive to be objective and detached; even if they have strong feelings, they trust their logical thinking over their feelings.

As students, thinkers learn by challenge; they debate with teachers, authors, other students. They value professors who state the rules of the course clearly and provide a forum for discussion. Students with a preference for thinking can listen calmly to ideas to which they disagree because they do not generally attend to either their own feelings or those of the speaker. They enjoy manipulating and analyzing ideas and theories, whether or not they consider those ideas and theories to be true.

Feeling. People with a preference for **feeling (F)** in making decisions tend toward a personal, rather than an impersonal, approach to learning and to life. They are adept in human relationships and value harmony, and they usually intensely dislike conflict. They are the peacemakers. Compassionate, empathetic, subjective—all are adjectives used to describe people with this preference. As learners, they succeed best when they are supported and appreciated. They want to engage with the content material personally, and they value faculty members who establish rapport with the class. Such students struggle if both the content and the instructors are perceived as cold and distant.

By contrast, Jason has a strong preference for thinking. His choice of marketing as a career field reflects his comfort with work that is primarily competitive rather than collaborative. Jason is deliberate in his planning to maintain relationships with friends; he has formed his professional ethical rules early by modeling them after his father's behaviors. Jason is comfortable studying material that is logical and practical.

Case Study Question: What additional strategies can you recommend to Jason to help him more fully develop his *feeling* preference?

The two ways of acquiring information and the two ways of making decisions have a profound impact on how we prefer to learn and whether learning situations are easy or difficult for us. Understanding our own preferences across these dimensions helps us use our strengths and compensate for our weaknesses. Another dimension of our personalities outlined in Jungian psychology is whether we direct our attention primarily to the inner world of our thoughts and feelings or the outer world of people and events. That dimension is termed introversion/extraversion.

Focus of Attention and Energy

Introversion ⟵——————————————⟶ Extraversion

Jung used the terms *introversion* and *extraversion* to differentiate between two opposing aspects of how we generate our energy and focus our attention. As we begin to look at this dimension, we must note that he did *not* mean that people with a preference for extraversion have good social skills and those with a preference for introversion are shy. He created specific meanings for these two terms in order that we might understand our own behaviors.

Introversion. "According to Jung's ideas, introverts are more interested in their own inner world, their concepts and ideas and feelings, than in the outer world of people and things" (Myers & Myers, 1980, p. 7). People with a preference for **introversion (I)** are reflective, often preferring to think before they speak. Even more often, they prefer to think and then write. "Reflection, introspection, and solitude . . . produce energy, focus, and attention for the introvert" (Kroeger & Thuesen, 1988, p. 36). Introverts relish time alone and require solitude to replenish their energy and activity level. Although they may have good social skills, they usually have only a few good friends whom they know deeply.

As learners, introverts value reading and learn best by pausing to think. They need quiet to concentrate and prefer to study individually rather than in groups. Often they believe they are unskilled in public speaking or other forms of verbal expression (DiTiberio & Hammer, 1993, p. 6). They can dislike classes that focus on discussion and group work but can enjoy clear lectures.

Extraversion. By contrast, people with a preference for **extraversion (E)** tend to focus on people and events in the outer world. They are energized by other people and have multiple interests and multiple relationships. Usually sociable and gregarious, they often speak before they think. Rather than reflect, they prefer to talk about ideas or projects as the method for thinking. As students, they enjoy class discussions and group study and usually report feeling competent in verbal and interpersonal skills (DiTiberio & Hammer, 1993, p. 6). Quiet does not help their study concentration; in fact, they prefer background sounds. Because writing is a solitary activity, they usually do not enjoy it as much as group projects.

Jason's extraverted nature is easy for all to see. His sociable and gregarious manner has served him well throughout school, and it will certainly contribute to his future career in marketing. He makes friends easily, but recently he has made a deliberate decision to maintain his college friendships. (An extravert has to decide this action deliberately; an introvert automatically does it.) When he feels tired, he goes out with his friends and recharges his energy through activity.

Case Study Question: What additional strategies can you recommend to Jason to help him more fully develop his *introversion* preference?

Lifestyle Orientation

The fourth difference in preference is "which function—information gathering or decision making—you most naturally use as you relate to the outer world, verbally and behaviorally" (Kroeger & Thuesen, 1988, p. 40).

Judging. If we prefer our lives to be planned and controlled and if we prefer to be decisive and deliberate, then we are using our decision-making (judging) function more easily and more often than our information-gathering (perceiving) function. That characteristic is called **judging (J)**. Judgers like to make decisions quickly, rather than listen to new information, and they deplore indecisiveness. As students, judgers are organized. They plan in advance, usually work steadily toward a goal, and like to be in charge. They value faculty who are organized. Closure is emotionally satisfying to them.

Perceiving. If we value flexibility and spontaneity and are frequently uncomfortable with making and carrying out decisions, then we have a preference for **perceiving (P)** (information gathering). The great strength of perceivers is their continued willingness to be open to new information and circumstances. They are comfortable with spending the necessary time to learn everything they can learn. As students, perceivers work impulsively, and they like to solve problems spontaneously. They value faculty who are entertaining and inspiring.

No personality preference is more evident than whether we are judgers or perceivers. In families, the workplace, organizations, and so forth, judgers and perceivers can make each other crazy. Judgers feel compelled to always have an opinion, to plan, to schedule everything, whereas perceivers want to be spontaneous and easygoing. Conflicts are inevitable. However, each preference has its strengths, and we all have the capacity to improve our lives by deliberately exercising our nonpreference in this dimension, as in the other three. In other words, judgers can relinquish trying to control everything and learn to relax and play, and perceivers can push themselves to make appropriate and timely decisions.

Academic work is the outer world for students, and the preference for judging or perceiving can dominate how we handle the job of being a student. Both preferences have strengths and weaknesses, and it behooves us to pay close attention to how our particular preference helps us and hurts us in our academic pursuits. Jason is no exception.

Jason is clearly a perceiver, and it took him until his junior year in college to place his academic behaviors under control. Once he learned to set goals and monitor the management of his time, Jason began to make better grades. Jason is working hard to end his habit of procrastination of assignments through the use of self-regulation techniques. As he strives to develop his nonpreference for decisive academic behaviors (judging), he is also developing those habits that will serve him well in his career. Setting goals, managing time, making decisions—all are important professional behaviors.

Case Study Question: What additional strategies can you recommend to Jason to help him more fully develop his *judging* preference?

The MBTI® and other instruments help us determine our preferences, although they seem to be less reliable for older students. We frequently recommend that our older students use a questionnaire and an interview with a counselor to determine their preferences. *When all four preferences are determined,* the result is called a **type** or a **personality type**. See Figure 12.2 for descriptions of these types and preferences.

There are 16 types in the version of the Jungian system articulated by the MBTI® (see Figure 12.3).

We Recommend

If you have taken the MBTI®, we recommend a small booklet written especially for college students titled *Introduction to Type in College* by DiTiberio and Hammer (1993), published by Consulting Psychologists Press.

FIGURE 12.2   Personality Type and Learning Preferences

Acquiring Information	**Sensing (S)** *Detailed*	• Are observant, factual, concrete; notice detail. • Value practical knowledge. • Prefer to move from concrete material to the abstract in small steps. • Learn best with clear directions and assignments; like hands-on experiences.
	Intuition (N) *Big picture*	• See the big picture; focus on the relationship of information. • Learn best through independent thinking and use of imagination and creativity. • Occasionally careless about details as they like to focus on the overall concept. • Like to study theories.
Making Decisions	**Thinking (T)** *Logical*	• Are logical, objective, fair, impartial, detached. • Find that logic guides learning; learn best by critiquing and debating. • Want a logical rationale for projects and assignments. • Enjoy studying cause-and-effect relationships.
	Feeling (F) *Value oriented*	• Find that personal values dominate decision making. • Learn best by relating to the material personally. • Have a strong need to like the teacher. • Are motivated by teacher's encouragement.
Focus of Attention and Energy	**Introversion (I)** *Time to reflect*	• Focus on their own inner world of ideas. • Learn best by reflecting and thinking. • Are willing to share ideas with advance notice. • Need time to think before making a decision or participating in a discussion.
	Extraversion (E) *Excitement and enthusiasm*	• Focus on the outer world of people and external events. • Learn best by doing and discussing. • Prefer collaborative group work. • Like to connect facts, theories, and concepts to their own experience.
Relating to the Outside World	**Judging (J)** *Planned and organized*	• Are planned, scheduled, organized, goal oriented. • Learn best by planning and organizing material. • Like organized instructions and assignments. • Find that completing a task or an assignment is very reinforcing.
	Perceiving (P) *Spontaneous and flexible*	• Are adaptable, open to change, flexible. • Learn best by being spontaneous; want faculty to be inspiring. • Find that completing tasks and assignments on time is difficult. • Prefer less structured learning environments.

Source: Compiled from DiTiberio & Hammer, 1993; Lawrence, 1997; Myers & Myers, 1980.

As we work with individual students, the concept of type is the most powerful. There are numerous books and other resources that help students understand their own attitudes and behaviors through the lens of their type. We have listed many of those sources in the references at the end of the book.

If the types were distributed equally throughout the population, each type would comprise 6.25%, but interestingly they are not distributed evenly. Estimates vary because they are drawn from different sample groups that have been tested. In 1962, Myers made the following estimates (Myers & McCaulley, 1985, p. 45):

About 75% of the population in the United States prefer E.

About 75% of the population in the United States prefer S.

About 60% of males in the United States prefer T.

About 65% of females in the United States prefer F.

About 55% to 60% of the population in the United States prefers J.

Exercise 12.6

Matching Your Personality Type to Your Instructor's Type

Does your instructor's personality type influence your learning? This exercise will help you investigate that possibility.

1. Identify your personality type.

2. For each of your classes, try to determine the instructors' personality types (your best guesses) from the observations you have made thus far in each class.

3. Which instructors closely match your personality type? Do you have an easier time learning from these instructors?

4. How have you compensated for instructors with teaching styles very different from the way you prefer to learn?

TEMPERAMENTS

Another way of using personality type that is especially popular in business and education is the grouping of the 16 types into four temperaments. This method works well within groups, either familial or professional. Realizing the temperaments of the other people with whom we live or work helps us understand and accept their behavior and thus frequently reduce conflict. We can

FIGURE 12.3   Shared Personality Characteristics Among Four Temperaments

Temperament Percent of Population	Motto	Important Psychological Needs
Guardians (SJ) 38% ISFJ, ESFJ, ISTJ, ESTJ	*To serve is to be*	Membership/Belonging Responsibility/Duty
Artisans (SP) 38% ISFP, ESFP, ISTP, ESTP	*To do is to be*	Freedom/Action Excitation/Variation
Idealists (NF) 12% INFP, ENFP, INFJ, ENFJ	*To be is to do*	Identity/Self-actualization Meaning/Significance
Rationalists (NT) 12% INTP, ENTP, INTJ, ENTJ	*To know is to be*	Knowledge/Competence Willpower/Mastery

Source: Adaped from Fairhurst, A. M., & Fairhurst, L. L. (1995). *Effective Teaching, Effective Learning*. Palo Alto, CA: Davies-Black.

often deduce someone's temperament by observation, which is useful for college students because they spend hundreds of hours listening to and observing their professors. Understanding a professor's probable temperament can help a student determine how best to work with that professor.

Although there are several differing groupings, we focus here on the most widely used version articulated by David Keirsey (1998), an internationally renowned psychologist. He uses the term **temperament** to denote *the shared personality characteristics of four types of people.* Temperament theory is based in *constitutional psychology,* ancient systems from the Hindus, Greeks, and Middle Ages that categorized people based on their observable behaviors (Fairhurst & Fairhurst, 1995). The four temperaments and their corresponding Myers-Briggs preferences are Guardians (SJ), Artisans (SP), Idealists (NF), and Rationals (NT).

As evidenced in Figure 12.3, all four types of one temperament share two preferences. Guardians share the preferences of sensing and judging, whereas Artisans share sensing and perceiving. Rationals share intuition and thinking, whereas Idealists share intuition and feeling. It is interesting that the distribution of temperaments and types is not equal; there are far more Guardians and Artisans in the general population than there are Idealists and Rationals. In American colleges, however, there seem to be almost an equal number of all four temperaments among students (Porter, 1995).

Guardians

Guardians (SJ) comprise approximately 38 percent of the general population, 28 percent of college students, and 24 percent of college faculty (Porter, 1995).

Generally, Guardians stress order and responsibility, value routines and traditions, and plan carefully. This is the most stable of all the temperaments; they are loyal and do not like surprises. They prefer rules to be consistently enforced.

As teachers. Guardians want students to become good citizens. They establish consistent rules and routines, use meticulous lesson plans, and often lecture. They provide students with thorough, fair, and well-supported feedback.

As Students. Guardians tend to be serious and dutiful. They plan activities carefully and do not like to take risks. Often they do not like group work because they become angry at other students who are irresponsible (Fairhurst & Fairhurst, 1995).

Famous Guardians. Hillary Clinton, Bill Clinton, George H. W. Bush, George Washington, Queen Elizabeth II of England, John D. Rockefeller, Charles Dickens, Michael Jordan (Yoffe, 2008; Butt & Heiss, 2007).

Artisans

Artisans (SP) comprise approximately 38 percent of the general population, 21 percent of college students, and 5 percent of college faculty (Porter, 1995).

Artisans like freedom, spontaneity, and actions; in other words, they are flexible and sometimes impulsive. Good problem solvers and troubleshooters, they can focus on an immediate issue and take action. Many become athletic or artistic performers.

As teachers. Artisans create choices and opportunities for students and incorporate a wide variety of activities, some rapid and some tranquil. They prefer projects to tests and frequently overlook rules and constraints.

As students. Artisans are spontaneous and can distrust authority. They resist rules and other constraints because they want to feel free, not under someone's control. Often they procrastinate as a form of rebellion. However, their great strength as students comes when they get excited, even passionate, about a subject. Then their energy is contagious (Fairhurst & Fairhurst, 1995).

Famous Artisans. John McCain, George W. Bush, Lyndon B. Johnson, John F. Kennedy, Michael Jackson, Madonna, Lucille Ball, Tom Cruise, John Travolta (Yoffe, 2008; Butt & Heiss, 2007).

Idealists

Idealists (NF) comprise approximately 12 percent of the general population, 25 percent of college students, and 11 percent of college faculty (Porter, 1995).

Idealists are usually optimistic and romantic and try to bring out the best in others. They encourage harmony and dislike conflict. Idealists are diplomatic, cooperative, sensitive, and enthusiastic.

As teachers. Idealists value their own unique identity, and they encourage their students to express themselves as individuals. They use praise rather than criticism. They favor instructional techniques such as group discussion, creative writing, and peer tutoring, and they are skilled at individualization. Good listeners, they can elicit the best from their students. Sometimes they are charismatic and inspiring. However, they often procrastinate in the ordinary tasks of teaching such as grading or class preparation and then are forced to innovate.

As students. Idealists tend to be creative, flexible, unconventional. They are often either the best student in class or the worst, although usually they desire praise and thus work best in situations in which their work is complimented. These students treasure including everyone in activities, and they like to help others achieve. As Idealists, they often enjoy group work, and they act as catalysts for others' achievements. Usually they are good writers, with a gift for description by metaphor (Fairhurst & Fairhurst, 1995).

Famous Idealists. Barack Obama, Abraham Lincoln, Martin Luther King, Mohandas Gandhi, William Shakespeare, Oprah Winfrey, Bill Cosby, Robin Williams, Julia Roberts (Yoffe, 2008; Butt & Heiss, 2007).

Rationals

Rationals (NT) comprise approximately 12 percent of the general population, 28 percent of college students, and **60 percent of college faculty** *(Porter, 1995).*

People with this temperament value knowledge and mastery—that is, they like to understand and control. They want to be competent at whatever they do. If they do feel incompetent, then they are highly self-critical. They are skeptical, verbal, logical, and relentless.

As teachers. Rationals give challenging assignments and expect answers that use logic and reason. They especially want their students to develop their intellectual abilities. They enjoy being experts in a discipline because they are usually deeply interested in the subject and want their students to also become expert. They may lack interpersonal skills and sensitivity when interacting with students. Frankly, many college teachers who are Rationals care only about their subject and can be insensitive about the total workload of a student.

As students. Rationals want to be intellectually competent; they like Socratic questioning, independent projects, and competition. They live in the world of ideas, and they intend to change that world by understanding it. They focus on the *big picture,* the main idea, rather than the details, and they especially like unraveling complex systems. In groups, they tend to lead and they become impatient with members who learn or produce slowly. A primary characteristic is that Rationals will question everything, including professors! They tend to be quick learners and critical thinkers, but others often see them as arrogant (Fairhurst & Fairhurst, 1995).

Famous Rationals. Socrates, Albert Einstein, Sir Isaac Newton, Alexander the Great, Augustus Caesar, Whoopi Goldberg, Chevy Chase, Meryl Streep, C. S. Lewis (Yoffe, 2008; Butt & Heiss, 2007).

Temperaments provide a good method of understanding ourselves and our professors. We can use such insight wisely in our interactions in and out of the classroom. In the early weeks of a term, listen carefully to your professors and read the course syllabi. What are the values you discern? What temperament does each of your teachers exhibit in the classroom? All temperaments have advantages and disadvantages; however, understanding these concepts can help us communicate with others as well as understand ourselves.

Some of the most powerful uses of these concepts are in career counseling. Obviously, different preferences take us on different career paths. Your campus career center has numerous resources to help you explore the world of work through the concepts of temperament.

CONCLUSION

Talents and preferences—these two components of ourselves shape our educational experiences and accomplishments. Each of us makes myriad decisions about how we will use these components. Do we pursue only those goals that seem easy to us or are we determined to achieve even in areas in which we are not gifted? Are we confident in our abilities or afraid that we will fail? College is the testing ground for many people. It is in college that we can choose majors and move toward careers, not jobs. It is in college that our personal lives can take a new direction. Understanding ourselves is a key to thoughtful choices.

SUMMARY

- Individualism is one's self-concept, the image of oneself as an individual unit whose motivations and behaviors are aimed at individual goals.

- Individuality is the development of differences within the personality. We can differ physically, cognitively, and emotionally.

- Talents are those abilities that come as a result of the interaction of our genes, our environment, our experience, and our effort.

- We can differentiate human talents into eight categories of intelligence defined by Howard Gardner. These are logical–mathematical, linguistic, musical, spatial, bodily–kinesthetic, interpersonal, intrapersonal, and naturalist.

- These different multiple intelligences operate as a complement to each other. As individuals, we have a preference of one or more over others and tend to use those intelligences more often.

- Logical–mathematical intelligence is the ability to calculate, quantify, consider propositions and hypotheses, and carry out complex mathematical operations.

- Linguistic intelligence is the ability to think in words and to use language to express and appreciate complex meanings.

- Musical intelligence is the capacity to discern pitch, rhythm, timbre, and tone.

- Spatial intelligence is the ability to think in three dimensions.

- Bodily–kinesthetic intelligence is the capacity to manipulate objects and use a variety of physical skills.

- Interpersonal intelligence is the ability to understand and interact effectively with others.

- Intrapersonal intelligence is the capacity to understand oneself and one's thoughts and feelings and to use such knowledge in planning and directing one's life.

- Naturalistic intelligence is the ability to recognize, identify, and classify patterns in nature such as plants and animals.

- As individuals, we have cognitive and affective preferences. Based on Carl Jung's theory, we can define these preferences as personality type. We differentiate preferences based on the way we acquire information, the way we make decisions, our focus of attention and energy, and the way we relate to the outside world. The MBTI® is a means of assessing personality type.

- Sensing (S) or Intuition (N) is the way we prefer to acquire information.

- Thinking (T) or Feeling (F) is the way we prefer to make decisions.

- Introversion (I) or Extraversion (E) is the way we prefer to focus our attention and energy.

- Judging (J) or Perceiving (P) is our preference for how we relate to the outside world.

- Personality types can be grouped into four temperaments: Guardians, Artisans, Idealists, and Rationals.

KEY CONCEPTS

Affective

Cognitive

Individualism

Individuality

Intelligence

Learning styles

Multiple intelligences: logical–mathematical, linguistic, musical, spatial, bodily–kinesthetic, interpersonal, intrapersonal, naturalist

Myers-Briggs Type Indicator® (MBTI®)

Personality type

Preferences: sensing (S) and intuition (N), thinking (T) and feeling (F), introversion (I) and extraversion (E), judging (J) and perceiving (P)

Talents

Temperaments: Guardians, Artisans, Idealists, Rationals

GUIDED JOURNAL QUESTIONS

1. To understand more about yourself is the realization of your position on the individualism versus group-centeredness spectrum:

Individualism ⟷ Group centeredness

   Where would you place yourself on this spectrum and why?

   Have you been raised to choose and pursue your own individual goals or to do what is best for the group (family) to which you belong?

2. *Extraverts* are energized by being with other people; *Introverts* are energized by spending time alone. Which is most true of you and why?

3. *Sensors* value realism and common sense; *Intuitives* value imagination and innovation. Which is most true of you and why?

4. *Thinkers* value logic, justice, fairness, and one standard for all; *Feelers* value empathy and harmony and see the exception to the rule. Which is most true of you and why?

5. *Judgers* prefer knowing what they are getting into; *Perceivers* like adapting to new situations. Which is most true of you and why?

6. How are your multiple intelligences and personality type similar? How do they differ? Especially address learning approaches that are similar and different for each.

7. What are your strengths associated with your multiple intelligences and your personality type? What are your weaknesses associated with each?

8. Which of the multiple intelligences would you like to develop more fully? Explain several strategies that you can implement for yourself. Complete the same exercise for a personality preference that you would like to strengthen.

9. Based on your evaluation of your multiple intelligences and personality type, list at least three possible career choices for you to consider. Why are these careers good possibilities for you?

10. Look back over the descriptions of the four temperaments in this chapter. What temperament would you select for yourself and why?

The Last Word

Nothing has ever helped me understand myself and other people more than the concepts of talents and preferences.

—De Sellers

Appropriate Stress Reduction Techniques

13

*AAUUUGH *%^$# &!@ (I feel much better now.)*

CHAPTER HIGHLIGHTS

- Stress and Anxiety
- Stressors of College Life
- Stress Reaction Model
- Strategies for Managing Stress

Why *does everyone seem so tense and worried? I thought college was supposed to be fun.* You may have asked this same question after the first few weeks in the term. College is supposed to be exciting and fun as well as productive, but the first semester can leave you with feelings of exhilaration, terror, and a myriad of other emotions. You may feel tired, lonely, excited, homesick, apprehensive, or a combination of all these emotions and more.

If you are entering or reentering college, the first semester is a crucial passage time. Whether you live on campus or you are commuting, your life is undergoing enormous change. You are in a new environment that makes unfamiliar expectations and demands, and you are with new people who may or may not be like you. If you have moved away from your family home for the first time, you probably have a roommate, share a common bath, and eat in a dining hall. If you have left your job to return to school, you may be carrying a backpack instead of a briefcase. If your children are now in school, you may be packing your own school lunch as well as theirs. In all of these scenarios, there is tremendous change. Although change is wonderful and scary, times of intense change are stressful times. College students are particularly vulnerable to stress. "Indeed, students as a whole represent one of the most stress-prone groups in American society" (Rowh, 1989, p. 4). Almost one-third of college freshmen report feeling "frequently overwhelmed" about all they have to do. Twice as many women (40%) report feeling stressed as men (20%) (University of California, Los Angeles, Higher Education Research Institute, 1999). The focus of this chapter is the application of self-regulation strategies to manage stress and reduce anxiety. Strategies for specific academic anxieties regarding public speaking, math, test, and writing are in the Appendix.

Exercise 13.1

SELF-ASSESSMENT: Stress

Your thoughts and actions can either reduce or add stress to your life. As a college student, your ability to cope during stressful events is paramount to ensure your success. With 5 being "Almost Always" and 1 being "Almost Never," assess your coping skills. Rate each of the following statements honestly by circling the appropriate number. Completing this exercise will help you identify areas of concern you may have with your ability to cope with stress.

	Almost Always		Sometimes		Almost Never
1. I let go of negative thoughts and worries at the end of the day.	5	4	3	2	1
2. When I get angry I express it appropriately.	5	4	3	2	1
3. I have a high tolerance for frustration and discomfort.	5	4	3	2	1
4. I use positive self-talk during stressful situations.	5	4	3	2	1
5. I use my feelings of tension as an indicator that I need to do something to reduce or eliminate anxiety.	5	4	3	2	1
6. I experience a normal amount of anxiety during tests.	5	4	3	2	1
7. I take responsibility when I do something wrong or inappropriate.	5	4	3	2	1
8. I use relaxation techniques during stressful events.	5	4	3	2	1

9. I manage my time so as not   5   4   3   2   1
    to over schedule myself.

10. When I have a conflict with   5   4   3   2   1
    another person, I resolve it
    appropriately.

Add up the numbers you circled. Your total score will be between 10 and 50. The higher your score, the more likely you feel confident about your ability to cope with stressful events. For total scores below 30, write or reflect on items for which you have concerns and consider talking with a trusted friend, a family member, a teacher, a counselor, or an advisor.

STRESS AND ANXIETY

Stress is *the wear and tear that our bodies, minds, and feelings experience as we perceive and respond to everyday life.* It ranges from the negative extreme of actual physical danger to the exhilaration of falling in love or achieving some long-desired success. In between, day-to-day living confronts even a well-managed life with a continuous stream of potentially stressful experiences. Not all stress is bad. In fact, stress is not only desirable but also essential to life (Davis, Eshelman, & McKay, 2000).

Although stress and anxiety are often terms used interchangeably, we prefer to use them specifically. Think of stress as pressure, and pressure can be external or internal. **Anxiety** *is a feeling of worry, nervousness or unease, typically about an imminent event or something with an uncertain outcome* (Merriam-Webster, n.d.). In other words, anxiety is the emotional response to the pressure of stress. Anxiety can be acute and short-lived or it can be chronic and debilitating. Moderate levels of anxiety can improve our performance and enhance the quality of our lives. We feel energized and excited, our concentration improves, and we learn to set priorities and make wise choices. Thus, some anxiety keeps us alert and productive, but too much anxiety, especially over an extended period of time, can ruin our physical health, our ability to concentrate and create, and our relationships. Stress, both good and bad, is cumulative. For college students, that means that anxiety (the emotional response) resulting from family events, academic pressures, finances, relationships, and jobs combines to create physical, mental, and emotional effects within us. If the cumulative anxiety we feel is too great, quite negative effects occur. Figure 13.1 shows some of the probable negative effects of too much stress and anxiety.

FIGURE 13.1   Some Effects of Acute and Chronic Stress and Anxiety

	Acute (Short Term)	Chronic (Long Term)
Physical Symptoms	Cold, sweaty hands and feet, headaches, backaches, nausea, stomach knots, dizziness, rapid heart beat	Muscle strain, tension, stomach upset, gut or bowel problems, elevated heart rate and blood pressure
Psychological Symptoms	Worry, irritability, negative self-talk	Depression, specific fears or anxieties, anger

We develop our individual coping strategies to manage stress throughout our life span, and in this chapter, we look at the particular stressors of college life and the self-regulation strategies that work well for many students. Throughout your reading of the chapter, reflect about the stressors in your life and how well (or poorly) you manage them. If your anxiety seems overwhelming, please go to your campus counseling center. Issues such as Post-Traumatic Stress Disorder (PTSD), social phobia, and panic attacks are too intense and complicated for this text.

Exercise 13.2

Physical and Psychological Symptoms

Stress can affect your mind as well as your body. From the following list, check the physical and psychological symptoms you experience as a result of stress:

Physical

_____ Frequent sweating

_____ Frequent dizziness

_____ Inability to sleep

_____ Breathing difficulties

_____ Nausea

_____ Stomach knots

_____ High blood pressure

_____ Elevated heart rate

_____ Upset stomach

_____ Tension headaches

_____ Neck or back pain

_____ Skin problems

_____ Frequent illness such as colds

_____ Gut or bowel problems

_____ Ulcers

Psychological

_____ Constant worry

_____ Bad moods

_____ Negative self-talk

_____ Inability to focus attention

_____ Preoccupation with specific concerns

_____ Inability to concentrate

_____ Thoughts of inadequacy

_____ Irrational beliefs

_____ Depression

Consider talking with a trusted friend, a family member, a teacher, an advisor, a counselor, or a physician if you have concerns about your responses to this exercise.

STRESSORS OF COLLEGE LIFE

Most experiences of stress flow from the following sources: our personal circumstances, our thoughts, our bodies, and our environment (Davis et al., 2000). College students live within a complex structure of circumstances based on interpersonal relationships—boyfriends or girlfriends, family, friends, professors, roommates. Parents moving to another location or divorcing can be devastating to a student. Financial pressures; grade expectations from self, parents, or organizations; homesickness (a result of change); loss of a loved one; lack of personal connection to college teachers; loss of former identity; and peer group all contribute to college students' stress. For traditional-age students, the onslaught of personal responsibility for laundry, car, bills, food, and so forth is frequently overwhelming. Nontraditional-age students face their own unique stressors, from caring for family members of all ages to maintaining full- or part-time jobs to learning (or relearning) how to compete in an academic environment. Their families can either support or sabotage their return to college.

Our thoughts are both a powerful source of stress and an equally powerful antidote to it. Worry is the classic symptom that our thoughts are increasing our anxiety, rather than decreasing it. Our view of our own competence (self-esteem) and our self-talk creates an attitude toward the stressful events in our lives, as do our beliefs about success and failure. Classic examples of thoughts that can spin out of control and create extreme reactions such as anxieties about tests, math, speeches, or writing are described in the Appendix along with the appropriate self-regulation strategies.

How we manage our bodies greatly contributes to the stress we feel. If we deprive ourselves of sleep, eat large quantities of junk food, use alcohol or other drugs, or rarely exercise, then we are much more likely to suffer negative results of stress. Illness, injuries, and the time it takes to recover from these events are also stressful.

Our environment is the fourth source of stress. From the weather, geography, and pollens to the physical landscape of our campus, everyone has some challenges. We may have moved to another state or culture. Whether we live in apartments, dormitories, or houses, we may have changed our physical location, and adjustment can be difficult. Sharing small spaces with roommates can be challenging if we have had our own private space before. College classrooms are another specific environmental stressor. Immense lecture halls, small seminar rooms, and scholarly libraries can be intimidating. Too many strangers overwhelm many new students. Techno burnout is the 24/7 interaction with technology without downtime. "Eventually, the endless hours of unrelenting digital connectivity can create a unique type of brain strain" (Small & Vorgan, 2008, p. 19).

Exercise 13.3

Stressful Life Events

Past research has linked significant changes in a person's life to physical illness, especially when these changes occur in a short period of time (Holmes & Rahe, 1967). This adapted exercise will help you recognize possible causes of stress and anxiety.

Check those negative events that you have experienced during the past year:

_____   Death of a family member or close friend

_____   Divorce, separation, or breakup

_____   Arrest or sentencing to jail or prison

_____ Arrest or sentencing to jail or prison

_____ Personal injury or illness

_____ Trouble with an employer or fired from a job

_____ Unwanted pregnancy

_____ Sexual difficulties

_____ Life-threatening catastrophe (fire, earthquake, automobile accident, and so on)

_____ Other _____

_____ Other _____

Even positive events can cause stress and anxiety. Check those positive events that you have experienced during the past year:

_____ Graduation from high school or college

_____ Beginning college

_____ Transferring to a different college or university

_____ Beginning a new job

_____ Promotion at work

_____ Marriage

_____ Pregnancy

_____ Retirement

_____ Holidays

_____ Vacation

_____ Personal achievements

_____ Other _____

What conclusions do you draw from completing this exercise?

STRESS REACTION MODEL

Stress reactions vary dramatically across the population. What one person perceives as fearful and distressful, another may optimistically view as a challenge. Our perceptions of events are unique; they are based on our own life histories, our values, and our expectations. Our perceptions determine how we will initially react. Stress management techniques are those self-regulation strategies that can modify our reaction to a stressful event as well as decrease the negative effects. Because excessive stress is so prevalent in our culture and exacts such a high price on our health and happiness, hundreds of programs, books, and articles purport to give instant answers to stress reduction.

All of us have habits, physical and psychological, that affect how we will react to any event. Physical conditioning, self-talk, confidence, fear—all are examples of such habits. The event can be overt, an event observable by others, or covert, a psychological event within our minds. Each of us responds to an event in a unique way, and that perception, like the habits mentioned earlier, has a distinct effect on our reaction. We choose one of three reactions to an event we perceive as stressful: fight, flight, or manage. Obviously, we recommend the third reaction as preferable, and much of the rest of this chapter focuses on strategies to increase the likelihood that you will choose it in stressful circumstances. Note the **Stress Reaction Model** shown in Figure 13.2 that captures the flow of responses that an individual makes to his or her perceptions of an event.

FIGURE 13.2   Stress Reaction Model

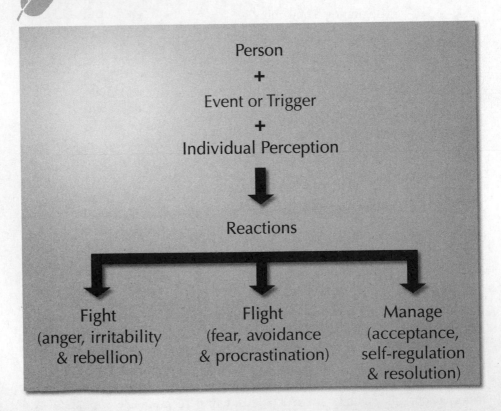

CASE STUDY

MARIA is a 25-year-old freshman who has just completed four years in the military. She is ambitious about making outstanding grades because she wishes to go to veterinary school. Maria was competitive in high school athletics and also in her work in the military. The lack of discipline she sees around her is confusing; her professors are not giving the explicit assignments that she had in the military; she feels alone in a sea of 18-year-olds. Although she has much experience in motivating herself, Maria is having headaches and muscle tension for the first time in her life. She also has nagging feelings of sadness and depression. She is feeling so discouraged that she has made an appointment to visit with a counselor on campus.

Case Study Questions: What will likely happen to Maria if she stays in school, but chooses to ignore or run away from her feelings? If she chooses to fight her feelings, what do you predict might happen? What are some actions she could take to manage her feelings?

Person

After visiting with her counselor and learning about the Stress Reaction Model, Maria now recognizes that the desired outcome is choosing to **manage**, that is, to *choose the appropriate manner to deal with the event with the least wear and tear on us.* To begin, each of us has a wide range of habits that contribute to how we will respond to stressful events. Some habits are clearly harmful, but there are also **defenders**, *habits that increase the likelihood that our reaction will be to manage, not to flee or to fight.* Maria has many defenders. She is self-disciplined in her habits and used to working hard. She has clear and explicit goals and a good academic plan. Although her family and high school friends are important to her, she has been apart from them for several years, so she is not homesick. Many of these self-regulated habits have already been presented in this text, including clear goals and planning, time management, timeliness, and ethical awareness. Others include regular exercise, healthy nutrition, assertiveness, and money management. A network of good and supportive friends and family is an important defender. The more we incorporate these strategies into our lives, the greater their effect will be.

Three areas of psychological research are especially relevant to this discussion of the individual differences within each person: Type A and Type B personalities, stress-hardy individuals, and gender differences.

FIGURE 13.3   Examples of Type A and Type B Personalities

Type A individuals tend to ...	Type B individuals tend to ...
Become irritated having to wait	Be patient
Like being in control	Follow others and not lead
Be more aggressive than passive	Be more passive than aggressive
Fidget	Be still
Be nervous and anxious	Be calm and collected
Be fast paced	Be slow paced

Type A versus Type B Personality

Just as we differ from each other in many ways, we differ in our abilities to manage stress. Psychologists and physicians have long divided people into Type A (driven) and Type B (laid back) personalities:

> A Type A person has a strong sense of time urgency, is highly competitive, and is easily angered when he [she] doesn't get his [her] way . . . Type B's don't suffer from chronic time urgency. They can play and relax without guilt and are not hostile or excessively competitive. (Davis et al., 2000, p. 9)

Many Type A's are perfectionists and workaholics; they push themselves to produce more in a shorter time, and they tend to suffer the physical effects of chronic stress. By contrast, Type B's tend to be team players; they are relaxed and forgiving, rather than critical or cynical (see Figure 13.3). Maria starts laughing when she reads these two definitions and claims that she and her older brother are the only type A's in her family. She has always driven herself to excel. Her friends even accuse her of scheduling her free time.

Recent research is revealing that a critical factor for Type A's seems to be the generalized hostility that many of them exhibit. The hostility is more harmful to the person than ambition or striving to achieve (Center for Social Epidemiology, 2004). After learning this, Maria becomes quietly reflective and then begins to talk about her brother. She says that he is angry all the time; everything is someone else's fault. She always wanted to be ambitious like him, but she just cannot get angry and blame other people. She cannot even tell most people how she feels. She just keeps everything inside.

Stress-Hardy Individuals

Another insight from research is that some individuals seem *stress hardy;* they have a natural tendency to resist or bounce back from the effects of stress. These people have specific psychological characteristics:

- **Stress-hardy people seek challenge rather than seek security.** "They view stressors as challenges and chances for new opportunities and personal growth rather than as threats" (Davis et al., 2000, p. 9).

- **Stress-hardy people feel capable rather than helpless.** "They feel in control of their life circumstances, and they perceive that they have the resources to make choices and influence events around them" (Davis et al., 2000, p. 9).

- **Stress-hardy people choose connection rather than alienation.** "They also have a sense of commitment to their homes, families, and work that makes it easier for them to be involved with other people and in other activities" (Davis et al., 2000, p. 9). They see their lives as worthwhile.

Maria gives herself high scores on the first two but admits that she is a real *loner* and rarely joins others in activities or organizations. She also states that she feels somewhat uncomfortable in school because she does not really know how to prepare for her college tests. Her discomfort causes her to feel less capable than when she was in high school.

Gender Differences

A provocative arena of research in the last decade is the deliberate investigation of gender differences in response to stress. Most of the early research on stress was conducted in predominantly male populations, so Taylor et al. (2000, 2002) began to study women and concluded that "females are more likely to mobilize social support, especially from other females, in times of stress. They seek it out more, they receive more support, and they are more satisfied with the support they receive" (p. 418). The initial and subsequent research by Taylor and other researchers has yielded the model of *tend and befriend,* a descriptive explanation of why and how women help other women cope with stressful experiences. Yet women often let go of friendships with other women when they get too busy with family and work (Apter & Josselson, 1998). Because women can be such a source of strength and nurture for each other, it is important to maintain those relationships in stressful times.

Case Study Question: What suggestions would you give Maria about connecting with other students on campus? With friends and family members?

What is the implication from this research for men? Many American males do not share with other men the most potentially stressful circumstances of their lives, such as failing relationships, work troubles, fear of unemployment, financial woes, sexual functioning, and addiction issues. Yet sharing with a trusted other person can relieve some of the stress and increase mental clarity. With a clearer mind, we can often find strategies to cope with the stressor. Some males find a trusted counselor or mentor; some choose a good female friend in whom to confide.

Exercise 13.4

Relaxation Response

One powerful habit or defender is the **Relaxation Response**, "the inborn capacity of the body to enter a special state characterized by lowered heart rate, decreased rate of breathing, lowered blood pressure, slower brain waves, and an overall reduction of the speed of metabolism" (Benson, 1984, pp. 4–5). The Relaxation Response is "a bodily reaction brought on by relaxational and meditative techniques that anyone can employ to strip away destructive inner stresses" (Benson, 1984, p. 24). Benson (1975, 1984) has explored the effects of the relaxation response through more than 20 years of meticulous medical research. Practiced regularly, the Relaxation Response is an extraordinarily powerful defender because it gives us the serenity and focus to avoid the fight-or-flight reactions and choose the *manage* reaction.

Are you stressed with no solution in sight? Find a quiet room to practice relaxing using this famous technique. Completing this exercise should help you lower your blood pressure and heart rate and alleviate stress. Here, in Benson's words, are the directions:

. . . . two essential steps to eliciting the relaxation response are:

1. Repetition of a word, sound, phrase, prayer, or muscular activity.

2. Passively disregarding everyday thoughts that inevitably come to mind and returning to your repetition.

This is the generic technique . . .

- Pick a focus word, short phrase, or prayer that is firmly rooted in your belief system.

- Sit quietly in a comfortable position.

- Close your eyes.

- Relax your muscles, progressing from your feet to your calves, thighs, abdomen, shoulders, head, and neck.

- Breathe slowly and naturally, and as you do, say your focus word, sound, phrase or prayer silently to yourself as you exhale.

- Assume a passive attitude. Don't worry about how well you're doing. When other thoughts come to mind, simply say to yourself, "oh well," and gently return to your repetition.

- Continue for ten to twenty minutes.

- Do not stand immediately. Continue sitting quietly for a minute or so, allowing other thoughts to return. Then open your eyes and sit for another minute before rising.

- Practice the technique once or twice daily. Good times to do so are before breakfast and before dinner. (Benson, 1975, pp. xxi–xxii)

Remember that *defenders* are habits that increase the likelihood that our reaction will be to manage, not to flee or to fight. Defenders are long-term strategies that yield powerful lifetime results. College students vary dramatically in how many of these strategies they have mastered and regularly use. What seems difficult for many students, of both traditional and nontraditional ages, is maintaining these good habits in the midst of the upheaval of entering collegiate life. As you have seen in this text, we strongly advocate the acquisition and maintenance of these behaviors as effective self-regulation methods.

The Event or Trigger

Events that trigger stress reactions can be external events such as a test, a confrontation with a friend, a visit home, or a financial setback. Remembering a painful or unpleasant experience is an example of an internal event, as are self-statements about expectations or beliefs. For example, a student may say to herself, *I feel like a real loser sitting at this table by myself; everyone else is surrounded by friends.* Another might say, *I know I'm going to mess up when I have to make my presentation in class on Friday.* An event is stressful only if you perceive it as stressful.

An important skill in managing stress is the accurate recognition of a truly stressful event. If you perceive that a particular event is genuinely threatening (e.g., a parent or grandparent is diagnosed with cancer, all three of your children come down with the flu simultaneously, your backpack with all your class notes is stolen), then you can marshal your forces. One key is to use self-talk helpfully as you plan to respond to the event: *As I support my family member, whom can I ask to support me? Who in my extended family can stay with the children while I'm in class? I'll call my teachers and ask for their help; maybe they can tell me the names of some good students who would let me copy their notes.* On the other hand, sometimes you perceive something as stressful that is only moderately taxing or disappointing. It is easy to exaggerate your feelings by using extreme, unhelpful self-talk: *I'll never pass that philosophy essay test because I just can't write! Everyone else has a date this Saturday night! I'm just too old to handle school; it's been too long.*

The stressful event in Maria's life is her first college semester. The challenge is new, and initially she did not understand that she would need support to handle so much change so fast. This experience is common for many first-semester students, regardless of age and prior experience. Older students often expect that they should be able to handle everything with little or no trouble, yet few do.

Individual Perception

Again and again in this chapter, we return to the realization that our perceptions are unique, grounded in our talents, preferences, and experiences. Whether or how we react to any event is determined by how we perceive it. Tests can be a challenge or a terror. Meeting new people can be exhilarating or painful. The adventure of doing something new can bring dread or delight. Much of stress management is understanding our own perceptions and, if necessary, changing them.

The Reaction: Fight, Flight, or Manage

Maria's reaction to the event of college is both psychological and physical. She has feelings of sadness and depression in spite of her desire to be in college and succeed there. Feeling uncomfortable and disturbingly incompetent fosters her depressive reaction. Her headaches and sore muscles, in spite of her excellent physical condition, are another sign of her body's reaction to her perception of this first semester.

We have looked at the first three parts of the Stress Reaction Model: Person, Event or Trigger, Individual Perception. Now we turn our attention to Reactions: Fight, Flight, or Manage. The fight-or-flight response has been studied for almost a hundred years, beginning with Walter Cannon, a physiologist at Harvard. The **fight-or-flight response** is "a series of biochemical changes that prepare you to deal with threat or danger" (Davis et al., 2000, p. 2). Although still useful in some physical circumstances, generally it is unhelpful in modern life. Our fight-or-flight responses are not always obvious. Sometimes we get irritable or angry (a fight response) as a reaction to a stressful event. Road rage is an extreme example. Far more likely is that we will be grumpy with or critical of our families or roommates and then feel guilty about our behavior. The flight response has less obvious outcomes. We may try to avoid situations in which we feel fear. Such avoidance can become a specific anxiety or phobia. A common example is social anxiety, in which people may avoid going to any type of gathering. Academic examples of flight responses are procrastination on assignments and a variety of anxieties regarding tests, math, speeches, and writing.

Maria wants to manage her collegiate experience in such a way that she meets her goals and is happy. One of her best strategies is simply to ask for help, to talk with another person about her feelings. She does not run away from her feelings and she does not blame herself or others. Instead, she thoughtfully analyzes the situation and her reactions and then is willing to try new strategies. She chooses to keep a journal of her feelings by recording her own internal dialog. Gradually her depressed feelings ebb as she begins to pass her tests through serious studying, and her body no longer hurts because she is resting more. Most important, she begins to make friends with whom she can share her feelings. Several visits home to her supportive family also bolster her spirits. By the end of the term, she is cheerful and confident.

Maria is successful in managing her stress because she has set clear goals, she monitors her actions, and she has the psychological strength or will to persist in helpful behaviors. She is willing to work diligently to solve this problem. One of the primary causes of self-regulation failure is underregulation, which "occurs because people lack stable, clear, consistent standards, because they fail to monitor their actions, or because they lack the strength to override the responses they wish to control" (Baumeister & Heatherton, 1996, p. 13).

STRATEGIES FOR MANAGING STRESS

As we said earlier, managing stress means that we use the strategies and the actions that will solve the issue and leave the least wear and tear on us. Let us use the four sources of stress—our personal circumstances, bodies, environment, and thoughts—as a method of organizing some useful strategies.

In terms of our personal circumstances, a basic goal is to keep our core relationships healthy. Who are the people who care about us and whom do we care about? Keeping connected through visits that encourage closeness (that ubiquitous term *quality time*) and by using telephone and electronic media helps maintain healthy relationships. Honesty, assertiveness, and compromise are assets in any relationship. As a college student, if you manage your time and your money so that you always have something extra for the unexpected demand, then that demand will not be so stressful and you can remain calm. Build a supportive system of people on campus; some possibilities include your roommate, hall director, adviser, mentor, counselor, and teacher. Join an organization and get to know the sponsor and the upperclassmen.

Strategies to protect our bodies are also important. Regular aerobic exercise, yoga, good nutrition, enough sleep, and vitamins all contribute to an increased self-awareness of our bodies and to becoming more stress hardy. Laughing helps all of us. The excessive use of alcohol, nicotine, and other drugs takes a toll on us. Counseling support groups help control these behaviors, as can Alcoholics Anonymous, Overeaters Anonymous, and Narcotics Anonymous.

We respond to our physical environment in subtle ways. Our first suggestion to students is to make where they live their home and their sanctuary, even if it is just half of a small room. Post pictures and mementos that bring good memories. Set up a quiet place to study (not your bed!) that has all the tools you need. Wear the right clothes, especially as the weather changes, and go to the doctor if you are ill. Regular physical checkups help too.

Our thoughts can be a source of stress, but they can also be a powerful tool for managing stressful reactions. Increasing our self-awareness of our beliefs and cognitive processes, changing our self-talk, meditating, participating in group or individual counseling, and using mental techniques to reduce phobic responses are examples of cognitive stress management strategies. The following sections explicate two cognitive stress management strategies: refuting irrational ideas and breaking the worry cycle.

CASE STUDY

ROY is a beginning freshman who has entered a college in a state 1,000 miles away from his home. He is excited to finally be in college, but within a few weeks, he reports that he is not sleeping well, has gained weight, and has trouble concentrating on his studies. What surprises him the most is that he is almost constantly worrying. He worries about the girl he left at home, he worries about his academic performance, and he worries that he will not fit in on campus even though he had a large circle of friends in high school.

Refuting Irrational Ideas

When Roy comes to talk with us, his self-talk pours out of him. Listening to our self-talk helps us realize what we are thinking and believing, so we ask him to write down all the things he is saying to himself. If what we are saying is irrational—*It is horrible when things are not the way I want them to be; I must be competent in everything I do; I need someone to decide for me; Everybody has to like me*—then we greatly increase the likelihood that our anxiety level will rise. Irrational beliefs not only lead to inappropriate stress; they can also lead to feelings of low self-esteem and depression. The easiest way to recognize irrational beliefs is to examine our self-talk for catastrophic and/or absolute words. Catastrophic words and ideas include *terrible, awful, all over, I'll get fired,* and *she'll leave me.* Absolute words include *should, must, never,* and *always.*

Roy's self-statements are classically catastrophic and absolute: *Why did I think I could succeed here? Everyone else is so much smarter than I am. Julie is going to find some other guy; she won't wait for me. She won't want to be with a failure.* We have the ability to change our self-talk (cognitive restructuring) to statements that are rational, such as *Things are the way they are, and I can handle that; I will try hard to do the best I can do, but I am not perfect; I am a competent person and can learn to make my own decisions.* If we are aware of what we say and strive to say and believe rational or logical statements, then our stress responses will be much lower.

Here is the five-step process Davis et al. (2000) recommend for changing unhelpful self-talk into helpful self-talk:

1. Describe the event that has triggered your stressed response.

2. Write down your self-talk and mark any irrational statements.

3. Write down your feelings during your response.

4. Challenge the irrational statements that you identified by replacing the catastrophic/absolute thinking with logical thinking.

5. Replace any irrational self-talk with rational self-talk.

Roy reluctantly agrees to try this exercise, so he chooses an event that had happened the night before. He had tried to call Julie, but he only got her voice mail. He immediately said to himself, *She saw my number and doesn't want to talk to me. I bet she's with someone else.* He felt low and dispirited and wanted to be home, not where he was at school.

Case Study Question: How do you think Roy would answer questions 2 through 5 above?

Exercise 13.5

Changing Negative Self-Talk

How frequently do you experience negative self-talk? Probably more often than you imagine. Completing this exercise will help you to become aware of your irrational statements.

1. Keep a log of your negative self-talk for one day. Write down both the trigger and your response.

2. Select one or two examples from your log and complete Davis et al.'s steps to change your unhelpful self-talk into helpful self-talk.

  • Describe the event that has triggered your stressed response.

  • Write down your self-talk and mark any irrational statements.

  • Write down your feelings during your response.

  • Challenge the irrational statements that you identified by replacing the catastrophic/absolute thinking with logical thinking.

  • Replace any irrational self-talk with rational self-talk.

Breaking the Worry Cycle

When we feel distressed, troubled, or uneasy, we are worrying. **Worry** is *a state of anxiety or uncertainty over actual or potential problems* (Merriam-Webster, n.d.). Worry can be healthy when it leads to problem solving such as: *I'm uneasy about that history test next week. I wonder if I can find a study group. I'd better make the time to go to the test review session.* When worry does not lead to productive solutions, it is unhealthy. You have a serious problem with worry if you

  • are chronically anxious about future dangers or threats,

  • consistently make negative predictions about the future,

  • often overestimate the probability or seriousness of bad things happening,

  • can't stop repeating the same worries over and over,

  • escape worry by distracting yourself or avoiding certain situations, and/or

  • find it difficult to use worry constructively to produce solutions to problems. (McKay, Davis, & Fanning, 1997, in Davis et al., 2000, p. 135)

Roy agrees that he has a serious problem with worry because almost all of the listed statements are true about him. Copeland (1998) recommends the following strategy to turn worry into problem solving:

  • Describe in detail one worrisome situation.

  • Make a list of possible solutions, that is, actions you can take to improve the situation.

- Choose the actions you can do right now (the others may be useful later).

- Make a contract with yourself to do up to three of those actions and set a date for completion.

- Evaluate your progress and set a new contract for other behaviors (Davis et al., 2000, pp. 137–138).

Roy chooses his concern about making a good life on campus as the focus of his exercise. The specific situation he chooses is that the past Friday night several guys who live on his floor went out to shoot pool and no one invited him. *Why didn't they include me? That hurts, especially since we usually eat dinner together in the dining hall.* As Roy describes this situation and his own internal dialog, he begins to speculate about what really happened. He admits that he was studying in his room with the door closed and his headphones on, and his roommate had gone out of town for the weekend.

Case Study Question: What would you recommend to Roy?

Exercise 13.6

Worry No More

If you are like most college students, you have probably worried about an exam or assignment. You may have worried about your performance or the consequences of doing poorly. You may have also experienced feelings of inadequacy. Think back to your most recent academic worrisome situation and follow Copeland's (1998) steps below. Completing this exercise will provide you a model to help you turn worry into problem solving.

- Describe in detail one recent worrisome situation.

- Make a list of possible solutions or actions you can take to improve the situation.

- Choose the actions you can do right now (the others may be useful later).

- Make a contract with yourself to do up to three of those actions and set a date for completion.

- Evaluate your progress and set a new contract for other behaviors.

CONCLUSION

In this and previous chapters, we have given you a powerful and complex set of self-regulation strategies that can help you structure and maintain not only your college life, but your professional and personal life beyond your college years. We hope that again and again you will return to these principles and adapt them to your current circumstances.

SUMMARY

- College students are particularly vulnerable to stress, for times of intense change are stressful times.

- Stress is the wear and tear that our bodies, minds, and feelings experience as we perceive and respond to the demands of everyday life.

- Anxiety is a feeling of worry, nervousness, or unease, typically about an imminent event or something with an uncertain outcome.

- Stress can be thought of as pressure (either external or internal), and anxiety is the emotional response to the pressure of stress.

- Moderate levels of anxiety can help energize and excite us, thereby improving our performance. However, too much anxiety over an extended period of time can ruin our physical and mental health.

- Anxiety can be acute and short-lived, or it can be chronic and debilitating.

- Most experiences of stress flow from the following sources: our personal circumstances, our thoughts, our bodies, and our environment.

- The Stress Reaction Model is a combination of the person, the event or trigger, and the individual perception that we have about ourselves. From these, we react to stress in one of three ways: fight, flight, or manage.

- Managing stress means choosing the appropriate manner to deal with the stressful event with the least wear and tear on us.

- Defenders are habits that increase the likelihood that our reaction will be to manage, not to flee or to fight.

- Three areas of psychological research relevant to individual differences are Type A and Type B personalities, stress-hardy individuals, and gender differences.

- The Relaxation Response is a physical reaction brought on by relaxational and meditative techniques.

- Two cognitive stress management strategies are refuting irrational ideas and breaking the worry cycle.

- Academic anxieties frequently occur in the areas of math, speech, writing, and testing.

KEY CONCEPTS

Academic anxieties regarding tests, math, writing, speeches

Anxiety

Breaking the worry cycle

Defenders

Effects of acute and chronic stress and anxiety

Fight-or-flight response

Gender differences

Manage

Refuting irrational ideas

Relaxation Response

Self-regulation strategies

Self-talk

Stress

Stress-hardy individuals

Stress Reaction Model: person, event or trigger, individual perception, reactions (fight, flight, or manage)

Stressors of college life

Type A and B personalities

Worry

GUIDED JOURNAL QUESTIONS

1. Within the last few months, how often have you become upset, really anxious, or stressed? What were the main causes? How did you react? Are you still experiencing these feelings? Explain.

2. What do you tend to worry about most often? Do you consider your worry to be unhealthy? What types of self-talk do you say to yourself when you worry? Explain.

3. What physical and psychological symptoms of stress and anxiety do you have? What is the primary cause (personal circumstances, your thoughts, your body, or your environment)? Explain.

4. Thinking specifically of your academic life and the courses you are currently taking, which ones are you most anxious or stressed about? Why? Do you suffer from any of the following anxieties: speech, test, math, or writing? If yes, explain.

5. What major changes have you experienced in the past year or two? Describe the stress and anxiety associated with those changes.

6. Are you primarily a Type A or Type B person in your academic endeavors? List several examples to support your choice. What do you think are the particular strengths and weaknesses of your characteristics? How content are you with this designation? Explain.

7. Do you tend to manage your stress or do you tend to fight or flee? Explain. When you do effectively manage your stress, what methods do you use? What methods might you consider now adopting (after having read the chapter) when you have the tendency to fight or flee from stress?

8. Describe an experience when anxiety actually improved your performance. Why do you think it helped you perform at a higher level?

The Last Word

I've always liked to live on the edge—not physically, but intellectually. The edge is lots of fun, but quite stressful, so I've learned to pull back from that edge a little, and life is sweeter.

—De Sellers

Appendix

Overcoming Specific Academic Anxieties

The fear response to a stressful event ranges on a continuum from a low level of anxiety (feeling mild physical symptoms and a desire to avoid the event) to a crippling level of phobic response in which a person cannot perform at all. People often think of airplanes, elevators, high places, snakes, and so on when they think of phobias. However, there are four common academic anxieties: speaker anxiety, test anxiety, math anxiety, and writing anxiety. Overcoming such an intense anxiety is serious business. What follows is a brief overview of the cognitive strategies used to subdue such a response. If you are mildly or moderately anxious in an academic situation, you can utilize these strategies; if you are intensely anxious in one or more of these situations, we recommend that you work with a counselor at your campus counseling center. Remember that you can learn how to *manage* rather than suffer the painful road of anxiety.

CASE STUDY

TODD is a senior who has avoided taking speech communication since entering college. He is a competent student but has always been terrified of public speaking. Now his department has mandated that he enroll in the freshman speech course, and he knows he must pass it to graduate. He has even had fantasies of leaving college, running away. When he had to take a short speech course in high school, he discovered that he felt nauseous, had trouble breathing, and usually forgot most of what he had planned to say. Todd is anxious, not just mildly nervous, but so anxious that he has extreme physical symptoms and cognitive interferences that inhibit his performance.

Four primary sources of academic anxiety are your academic reputation with others (what opinions other people will have if you perform poorly), your own opinion of your abilities and competence, your concerns about actualizing your goals, and your uneasiness about being unprepared (Divine & Kylen, 1982). What frequently happens to many students is happening to

Primary Sources of Academic Anxiety

- The opinions of others
- Your own opinions
- Your fear of not achieving your goals
- Your feelings of being unprepared

Todd. The memory of his poor prior performance increases his anxiety level, so there is an increasing spiral of intensity about his responses. In this state, his emotions cause his body to prepare for either fight or flight, which interferes with his ability to think clearly and rationally. His ability to attend and concentrate suffers; he feels intimidated and defensive. Thus, the cycle continues, and he wants to escape such negative emotions. He is even willing to fantasize about leaving college, just to achieve a sense of relief. "Brain-body misbehavior causes havoc" (Divine & Kylen, 1982, p. 74).

The purpose of anxiety reduction principles is to reduce or modify a fear response so as to be able to perform competently. Performance anxiety, sometimes called stage fright, is a learned response. That we learn to be anxious is actually good news because that means we can learn how to be calm. There are some common themes in the strategies to overcome these specific academic anxieties: appropriate content preparation, rehearsal, rational self-talk, physical self-care, and good use of time.

SPEAKER ANXIETY

Many students have similar feelings to Todd's. It is the *public* in public speaking that can intimidate so many people. Most of us have had little experience in public speaking through our high school years, yet it is a crucial professional skill. Increasingly, college instructors require public presentation of projects as required components of courses in differing majors. If you become nervous about making a formal presentation in class, the following strategies can help:

BEFORE THE EVENT:

- Keep your audience in mind when you develop your presentation. Adapt your vocabulary and examples accordingly.

- Complete research early so you know your topic, inside and out.

- Stand up and rehearse your performance several times. If you can't rehearse in the room where you will be speaking, at least try to imagine that room as you practice.

- Use rational and helpful self-talk.

- Focus on your message. Mentally review your opening lines, main ideas, and conclusion in the few minutes before you begin speaking.

DURING THE EVENT:

- Breathe slowly and deeply to counter the shallow breathing and rapid heart rate that accompany nervousness.

- Focus on your audience instead of thinking about your own nervousness. Search out and make eye contact with people who reinforce you positively with their nonverbal behavior.

- Use appropriate humor to get your audience laughing early and to help you relax.

- Make careful and deliberate use of your time.

- If you feel yourself becoming tense, refocus on the task using appropriate self-talk.

- Use rational and helpful self-talk throughout.

Additional Online Resources for Speaker Anxiety

Personal Report of Communication Apprehension
http://www.jamescmccroskey.com/measures/prca24.htm

Managing Nervousness During Presentations
http://www.lib.uoguelph.ca/assistance/learning_services/handouts/presentations.cfm

Reducing Speech Anxiety
http://www.muskingum.edu/~cal/database/content/speech2.html

OTHER SUGGESTIONS:

- Grab the audience's attention by using an audiovisual aid (distribute handouts at the end).

- Speak loudly enough for people in the back row to hear.

- Place a watch on the lectern to monitor your use of time.

- Deliver an effective, structured, and upbeat conclusion (a short summary of your main points will help the listener).

- Take advantage of opportunities to speak to increase your skill and confidence.

- Seek professional help from communication instructors, counselors, or other professionals trained in systematic desensitization and/or performance visualization. (Beebe, Beebe, & Ivy, 2009; Rowh, 1989)

Case Study Questions: Which strategies, both "before and during the event," do you think would most help Todd reduce his anxiety while preparing for and delivering his first speech? Why?

TEST ANXIETY

The most common academic anxiety is test anxiety. How many times have you lost points on a test when you knew the material? How many times have you raced through a test and turned it in without checking your answers because you just wanted to get it over with and escape? How many times have you worried more about a test than studied for it? A little anxiety can help motivate us and focus us on the task, but too much anxiety simply destroys performance.

Exercise

Test Anxiety Survey

Test anxiety is a frequent experience for college students. Look at the following checklist. How many of these characteristics describe you? Completing this exercise will provide an assessment of your test anxiety.

_____ You feel that tests are more of a threat than a challenge.

_____ You have a lot of worrisome or negative thoughts about what might happen if you do poorly.

_____ You have physical reactions (such as butterflies in the stomach, sweaty palms, altered heart or breathing rate) when you are about to take a test.

_____ You have trouble keeping your mind on the test items or remembering ideas you learned recently.

_____ You worry about other people scoring higher than you on the test.

_____ Your worries about tests have not decreased as you have matured (Divine & Kylen, 1982, pp. 60–61).

If you suffer from test anxiety, is your response generalized to all tests or is it specific to one course or subject? Your answer to that question is important. If it is specific anxiety about one course, then the strategies in this chapter can help you manage stress and increase performance. If you have been severely anxious in all testing situations for more than two years, then we strongly recommend that you work with a counselor on more powerful techniques such as progressive relaxation, cognitive desensitization, and thought stopping.

Many of the self-regulation techniques such as goal setting, timeliness, and key behaviors that we have described throughout this book can decrease test anxiety. Additional strategies stem from the following model to overcome test anxiety.

BEFORE THE TEST:

• Finish appropriate, timely, comprehensive content preparation, including all homework. In simple terms, read, study, and work with a study group. Go to any review sessions and be sure to go to class the week before the test.

- Use rational and helpful self-talk, such as *I have prepared sufficiently and I will answer the questions carefully.* Use the techniques for changing irrational self-talk and worry statements.

- Practice or rehearse your performance by answering practice questions.

- Get enough sleep, exercise, and good nutrition. Even if you study late the night before, get at least two to three hours of sleep.

THE DAY OF THE TEST:

- Grab the psychological edge by going to class on time with *all* the required materials.

- Be sure to take a watch so you can set specific time goals so you will have enough time at the end of the test to check your answers.

- Do not participate in the pretest fearful conversations that the other students are having.

- If you have a choice of where you sit during the test, sit away from friends and toward the sides or back of the room to minimize distractions when people finish early.

DURING THE TEST:

- Make careful and deliberate use of your time. Look over the test and allocate how much time you intend to spend on each section.

- If you feel yourself becoming tense or distracted, refocus on the question saying, *What is this question asking?* and breathe deeply.

- Use rational and helpful self-talk throughout. It is tempting to use *catastrophizing* and *awfulizing* statements; instead, deliberately use rational and calming statements.

Additional Online Resources for Test Anxiety

Test Anxiety
http://ub-counseling.buffalo.edu/
stresstestanxiety.shtml

Self-Help: Test Anxiety
http://www.utdallas.edu/counseling/selfhelp/
test-anxiety.html

Test Anxiety Sites
http://www.howtostudy.org/resources_skill.
php?id=16

MATH AND WRITING ANXIETY

Our abilities to solve math problems and to write college papers are procedural knowledge skills. Usually students who have math or writing anxiety have developed these responses over many years. An important initial step is to determine your level of competence in procedural knowledge skills. In other words, what is your competence when you are not anxious? Most campus learning centers have diagnostic tests to help you discern your skill level. If you are deficient in these skills, pursuing the appropriate remediation is imperative. You may need to learn these skills at the high school level before attempting a college-level class. Remedial courses or labs, computer tutorials, and individual tutoring are available through community colleges or local libraries. As you master each level, you will discover that your anxiety is lessening.

Many college students, however, have good procedural knowledge skills but freeze on the math test or in-class writing assignment. If that is your circumstance, review the following strategies.

BEFORE THE CLASS:

- Complete appropriate, timely, comprehensive content preparation, including all homework. Work with a tutor to clarify areas you find confusing and then attend study group and test reviews.

- Use rational and helpful self-talk. *I've practiced and gone to the test review. My tutor gave me some shortcuts that should really help.*

- Practice or rehearse your performance. For math, rework your homework problems and any additional problems available. Practice explaining to yourself how to do the problems. For in-class writing assignments, write possible questions and then outline your answer. Write thesis statements for each possible question.

- Get enough sleep, exercise, and good nutrition.

DURING THE EVENT:

- Make careful and deliberate use of your time. For math, immediately write the formulas down. Then plan how you will allocate your time on the various parts of the test. For the essay, quickly write down any key names, dates, and so forth to organize into an outline later.

- If you feel yourself becoming tense, refocus on the task using appropriate self-talk and breathe deeply. Refocus by saying, *Okay, what is this question asking and what do I know about it?*

- Use rational and helpful self-talk throughout. *These first few questions look just like the ones in the test review last night. I'm going to be fine.*

Additional Online Resources for Math Anxiety

Coping With Math Anxiety: A Workshop for Students
http://www.austincc.edu/math/documents/Coping_With_Math_Anxiety.pdf

Math Anxiety
http://www.counseling.txstate.edu/resources/shoverview/bro/math.html

Coping With Math Anxiety
http://www.mathacademy.com/pr/minitext/anxiety/index.asp

Additional Online Resources for Writing Anxiety

Writing Anxiety
http://web.princeton.edu/sites/writing/Writing_Center/handouts/html/Anxiety.htm

Writer's Block/Writer's Anxiety
http://owl.english.purdue.edu/owl/resource/567/01/

Writing Anxiety
http://www.unc.edu/depts/wcweb/handouts/writing_anxiety.html

Postscript

The Seven Characteristic Competencies of Becoming an Autonomous Learner

1. Autonomous learners have a realistic view of themselves and their academic abilities.
2. Autonomous learners are ethical.
3. Autonomous learners set realistic and appropriate goals for academic achievement.
4. Autonomous learners understand their own learning strengths and weaknesses.
5. Autonomous learners use effective learning strategies and adapt those strategies to new situations.
6. Autonomous learners manage their behaviors to reach their goals.
7. Autonomous learners use appropriate resources.

The transformation into a successful learner is neither easy nor ever completed. The seven principles of becoming an autonomous learner will serve you well in your academic, personal, and professional lives. You will, periodically, reexamine yourself through reflection and evaluate your academic abilities. Reflection and evaluation of your personal and, later, your professional lives will help you reap the benefits of a full life. But, remember, the realistic acceptance of what you discover allows you to face challenges confidently and helps you to move forward.

As you move forward, have the courage to move with integrity based on the ethics and fair-mindedness we hope you have come to see as an important part of your life. It is crucial to put into practice each day what you truly believe to be the right way to live. Whether it is in your academic, personal, social, or professional life, lead by example.

Always set realistic goals and expectations. When setting goals, try to achieve balance in all facets of your life. We live increasingly complex lives. To ensure that you live life to the fullest, set these goals based on an honest evaluation of your strengths and weaknesses. It is through an accurate self-assessment that you may choose the best path for you.

Knowing your strengths and weaknesses will help you to select the most appropriate strategies for learning and for life. As an autonomous learner, you will be able to adapt these strategies to fit an ever-changing environment, be it in the classroom or the boardroom. However, circumstances change and it is easy to let your actions hinder or even destroy your academic, personal, or professional achievements. You have the power to sustain your progress by maintaining behaviors that keep you on track and modifying those that slow your progress.

Finally, when you find you need help, always seek out the appropriate resources. If you break your leg, you do not want to be rushed to the dentist's office. If you are having difficulty with an essay for your English class, chances are a math tutor would not be your best alternative for help. As an autonomous learner, you know where to seek and whom to ask for assistance.

On this journey we have come full circle. All of the skills that we discussed throughout the text are adaptable to almost any facet of your life. We hope you will employ them not only in an academic setting, but in all the roles you will play in your life.

De Sellers
Carol Dochen
Russ Hodges

References

Adler, M. J. (1940). *How to read a book.* New York: Simon & Schuster.

Allen, D. (2001). *Getting things done: The art of stress-free productivity.* New York: Penguin Books.

Anderson, L. W., & Krathwohl, D. R. (Eds.). (2001). *A taxonomy for learning, teaching, and assessing.* New York: Longman.

Anxiety. (n.d.). In *Merriam-Webster's online dictionary.* Retrieved from http://www.merriam-webster.com

Apter, T., & Josselson, R. (1998). *Best friends: The pleasures and perils of girl's and women's friendships.* New York: Three Rivers Press.

Armbruster, B. B. (2000). Taking notes from lectures. In R. F. Flippo & D. C. Caverly (Eds.), *Handbook of college reading and study strategy research* (pp. 175–199). Mahwah, NJ: Lawrence Erlbaum.

Armbruster, B. B. (2009). Notetaking from lectures. In R. F. Flippo & D. C. Caverly (Eds.), *Handbook of college reading and study strategy research* (pp. 220–248). New York: Routledge.

Astin, A. W. (1993). *What matters in college?* San Francisco: Jossey-Bass.

Atkinson, J. W., & Feather, N. T. (1966). *A theory of achievement motivation.* New York: Wiley.

Augsburger, D. W. (1986). *Pastoral counseling across cultures.* Philadelphia: The Westminster Press.

Bandura, A. (1986). *Social foundations of thought and action: A social cognitive theory.* Englewood Cliffs, NJ: Prentice Hall.

Banks, J. A. (1993a). Multicultural education: Characteristics and goals. In J. Banks & C. M. Banks (Eds.), *Multicultural education: Issues and perspectives* (2nd ed., pp. 2–26). Boston: Allyn & Bacon.

Baumeister, R. F., & Heatherton, T. F. (1996). Self-regulation failure: An overview. *Psychological Inquiry, 7*(1), 1–15.

Baumeister, R. F., & Vohs, K. D. (Eds.). (2004). *Handbook of self-regulation.* New York: The Guilford Press.

Beebe, S. A., Beebe, S. J., & Ivy, D. K. (2010). *Communication: Principles for a lifetime.* Boston: Allyn & Bacon.

Benesh, B., Arbuckle, M., Robbins, P., & D'Arcangelo, M. (1998). *The brain and learning: Facilitator guide.* Alexandria, VA: Association of Supervision and Curriculum Development.

Benson, H. (1975). *The relaxation response.* New York: Quill.

Benson, H. (1984). *Beyond the relaxation response.* New York: Berkley Books.

Bloom, B. S. (1956). *Taxonomy of educational objectives.* New York: Longman.

Branden, N. (1994). *The six pillars of self-esteem.* New York: Bantam.

Bransford, J. D., Brown, A. L., & Cocking, R. R. (Eds.). (1999). *How people learn.* Washington, DC: National Academy Press.

Brewi, J., & Brennan, A. (1999). *Mid-life spirituality and Jungian archetypes.* York Beach, ME: Nicolas-Hays.

Burka, J. B., & Yuen, L. M. (2008). *Procrastination: Why you do it, what to do about it now.* Cambridge, MA: Da Capo Press.

Butt, J., & Heiss, M. M. (2007). *Typelogic.* Retrieved from http://www.typelogic.com.

Campbell, L., Campbell, B., & Dickinson, D. (1999). *Teaching and learning through multiple intelligences.* Boston: Allyn & Bacon.

Carter, C., Bishop, J., & Kravits, S. L. (2002). *Keys to college studying.* Upper Saddle River, NJ: Prentice Hall.

Caverly, D. C., & Peterson, C. L. (2000). Technology and college reading. In R. F. Flippo & D. C. Caverly (Eds.), *Handbook of college reading and study strategy research* (pp. 175–199). Mahwah, NJ: Lawrence Erlbaum.

Center for Social Epidemiology. (2004). *Job stress network: Type A behavior.* Retrieved from http://www.workhealth.org/risk/rfbtypea.html.

Chickering, A. (n.d.). *The seven vectors: An overview.* Retrieved from http://www.cabrini.edu/communications/ProfDev/cardevChickering.html.

Copeland, M. E. (1998). *The worry control workbook.* Oakland, CA: New Harbinger Publications.

Corey, G., & Corey, M. S. (1993). *I never knew I had a choice.* Pacific Grove, CA: Brooks/Cole.

Covey, S. R. (1989). *The 7 habits of highly effective people.* New York: Simon & Schuster.

Covey, S. R., Merrill, A. R., & Merrill, R. R. (1994). *First things first.* New York: Fireside.

Covington, M. V. (1984). The motive for self-worth. In R. Ames & C. Ames (Eds.), *Research on motivation in education: Vol. 1. Student motivation.* Orlando, FL: Academic Press.

Craik, F. I. M., & Lockhart, R. S. (1972). Levels of processing: A framework for memory research. *Journal of Verbal Learning and Verbal Behavior, 11,* 671–684.

Csikszentmihalyi, M. (1996). *Creativity: Flow and the psychology of discovery and invention.* New York: HarperCollins.

Csikszentmihalyi, M. (1999). If we are so rich, why aren't we happy? *American Psychologist 54*(10), 821–827.

Davis, A., & Clark, E. G. (1996). *Study skills: T-notes and others.* Metamora, IL: Davis and Clark Publishing.

Davis, M., Eshelman, E. R., & McKay, M. (2000). *The relaxation & stress reduction workbook.* Oakland, CA: New Harbinger Publications.

Deci, E. L. (1975). *Intrinsic motivation.* New York: Plenum Press.

DiTiberio, J. K., & Hammer, A. L. (1993). *Introduction to type in college.* Palo Alto, CA: Consulting Psychologists Press.

Divine, J. H., & Kylen, D. W. (1982). *How to beat test anxiety & score higher on the SAT & all other exams.* New York: Barron's Educational Series.

Dochen, C. W. (1993). *The effects of the targeted academic groupings learning community on retention and academic performance of university freshmen.* Unpublished doctoral dissertation, University of Texas, Austin.

Dunn, R., Dunn, K., & Price, G. E. (1984). *Learning style inventory.* Lawrence, KS: Price Systems.

Elder, L., & Paul, R. (1996). *Critical thinking development: A stage theory.* Retrieved from http://www.criticalthinking.org.

Ellis, A., & Harper, R. A. (1975). *A new guide to rational living.* Englewood Cliffs, NJ: Prentice Hall.

Entwistle, N. (1990). Teaching and the quality of learning in higher education. In N. Entwistle (Ed.), *Handbook of educational ideas and practices* (pp. 669–693). London: Routledge.

Erikson, E. (1963). *Childhood and society* (2nd ed.). New York: Norton.

Erikson, E. (1982). *The life cycle completed.* New York: Norton.

Fairhurst, A. M., & Fairhurst, L. L. (1995). *Effective teaching, effective learning.* Palo Alto, CA: Davies-Black.

Gagné, R. M. (1985). *The conditions of learning and theory of instruction* (4th ed.). New York: Holt, Rinehart & Winston.

Gardner, H. (1983). *Frames of mind: The theory of multiple intelligence.* New York: Basic Books.

Gardner, H. (1995). Reflections on multiple intelligences: Myths & messages. *Phi Delta Kappan, 77,* 200–210.

Gardner, H. (2000). *Intelligence reframed: Multiple intelligences for the 21st century.* New York: Basic Books.

Gardner, H. (2003, April). *Multiple intelligences after twenty years.* Paper presented at the American Educational Research Association, Chicago, IL. Retrieved from http://www.pz.harvard.edu/PIs/HG_MI_after_20_years.pdf.

Gardner, H., Csikszentmihalyi, M., & Damon, W. (2001). *Good work: When excellence and ethics meet.* New York: Basic Books.

Garrett, B. (2009). *Brain & behavior.* Los Angeles: Sage Publications.

Glasser, W. (1998). *Choice theory.* New York: HarperCollins.

Gollwitzer, P. M. (1995). The volitional benefits of planning. In P. M. Gollwitzer & J. A. Bargh (Eds.), *Psychology of action* (pp. 287–312). New York: Guilford Press.

Guralnik, D. B. (Ed.). (1986). *Webster's new world dictionary* (2nd ed.). New York: Prentice Hall.

Halpern, D. F. (1997). *Critical thinking across the curriculum.* Mahwah, NJ: Lawrence Erlbaum.

Halpern, D. F. (2000). *Thought and knowledge: An introduction to critical thinking.* Mahwah, NJ: Lawrence Erlbaum.

Holmes, T. H., & Rahe, R. H. (1967). The social readjustment rating scale. *Journal of Psychosomatic Research, 11*(2), 213–218.

Hosinski, T. E. (1992). Epistemology. In D. W. Musser & J. L. Price (Eds.), *A new handbook of Christian theology* (pp. 150–156). Nashville: Abingdon Press.

Hyerle, D. (2000). *A field guide to using visual tools.* Alexandria, VA: Association for Supervision and Curriculum Development.

Jonassen, D. H., & Grabowski, B. L. (1993). *Handbook of individual differences, learning, and instruction.* Hillsdale, NJ: Lawrence Erlbaum.

Jung, C. G. (1923). *Psychological types.* New York: Harcourt Brace.

Jung, C. G. (1971). *Psychological types. Bollingen Series XX. The Collected Works of C. G. Jung* (Vol. 6). Princeton, NJ: Princeton University Press.

Keirsey, D. (1998). *Please understand me II.* Del Mar, CA: Prometheus Nemesis Book Company.

Kolb, D. A. (1999). *Learning style inventory.* Boston: Hay/McBer Training Resources Group.

Kroeger, O., & Thuesen, J. M. (1988). *Type talk.* New York: Dell.

Kurtz, E., & Ketcham, K. (1992). *The spirituality of imperfection.* New York: Bantam Books.

Lakein, A. (1973). *How to get control of your time and your life.* New York: Signet.

Lawrence, G. D. (1993). *People types and tiger stripes* (3rd ed.). Gainesville, FL: Center for Applications of Psychological Type.

Lawrence, G. D. (1997). *Looking at type and learning styles.* Gainesville, FL: Center for Applications of Psychological Type.

Lee, W. (1978). *Formulating and reaching goals.* Champaign, IL: Research Press.

LeFrançois, G. R. (2000). *Theories of human learning.* Belmont, CA: Wadsworth/Thomson Learning.

Lipsky, S. (2004). *College study: The essential ingredients.* Upper Saddle River, NJ: Pearson/Prentice Hall.

McClelland, D. C. (1961). *The achieving society.* Princeton, NJ: Van Nostrand.

McKay, M., Davis, M., & Fanning, P. (1997). *Thoughts and feelings.* Oakland, CA: New Harbinger Publications.

McMillan, J. H., & Forsyth, D. H. (1991). What theories of motivation say about why learners learn. In R. J. Menges & M. D. Svinicki (Eds.), *College teaching: From theory to practice* (pp. 39–52). San Francisco: Jossey-Bass.

Merrill, A. R. (1987). *Connections: Quadrant II time management.* Salt Lake City, UT: Publishers Press.

Miller, G. A. (1956). The magical number seven, plus or minus two: Some limits on our capacity for processing information. *Psychological Review, 63,* 81–97.

Mischel, W. (1995). From good intentions to willpower. In P. M. Gollwitzer & J. A. Bargh (Eds.), *Psychology of action* (pp. 196–218). New York: Guilford Press.

Mulcahy-Ernt, P. I., & Caverly, D. C. (2009). Strategic study-reading. In R. F. Flippo & D. C. Caverly (Eds.), *Handbook of college reading and study strategy research* (pp. 177–198). New York: Routledge.

Myers, I. B., & McCaulley, M. H. (1985). *Manual: A guide to the development and use of the Myers-Briggs Type Indicator.* Palo Alto, CA: Consulting Psychologists Press.

Myers, I. B., & Myers, P. B. (1980). *Gifts differing.* Palo Alto, CA: Davies-Black Publishing.

Newman, B. M., & Newman, P. R. (1995). *Development through life: A psychosocial approach.* Pacific Grove, CA: Brooks/Cole.

Nist, S. L., & Holschuh, J. (2000). *Active learning.* Boston: Allyn & Bacon.

Olsson, F. M. (Ed.). (2008). *New developments in the psychology of motivation.* New York: Nova Biomedical Books.

Ormrod, J. E. (1999). *Human learning.* Upper Saddle River, NJ: Merrill/Prentice Hall.

Pauk, W. (1997). *How to study in college.* Boston: Houghton Mifflin.

Paul, R., & Elder, L. (2001). *Critical thinking: Tools for taking charge of your learning and your life.* Upper Saddle River, NJ: Prentice Hall.

Peck, M. S. (1978). *The road less traveled.* New York: Simon & Schuster.

Perry, W. G. (1970). *Forms of intellectual and ethical development in the college years.* New York: Holt, Rinehart and Winston.

Porter, D. B. (1995, October 26). *Total quality and educational enlightenment.* Lecture presented for the University Lecture Series, Southwest Texas State University, San Marcos.

Pressley, M., & Afflerbach, P. (1995). *Verbal protocols of reading: The nature of constructively responsive reading.* Hillsdale, NJ: Erlbaum.

Reavis, G. H. (n.d.). *The animal school.* Peterborough, NH: Crystal Springs Books. Retrieved from http://madalen.files. wordpress.com/2009/09/14037268-the-animal-school.pdf.

Rowh, M. (1989). *Coping with stress in college.* New York: The College Board.

Slavin, R. E. (2003). *Educational psychology: Theory and practice* (7th ed.). Boston: Allyn & Bacon.

Slavin, R. E. (2006). *Educational psychology: Theory and practice* (8th ed.). Boston: Pearson/Allyn & Bacon.

Small, G., & Vorgan, G. (2008). *iBrain.* New York: Collins Living.

Smart, L., & Wegner, D. M. (1996). Strength of will. *Psychology Inquiry, 7*(1), 79–83.

Smilkstein, R. (2003). *We're born to learn.* Thousand Oaks, CA: Corwin Press.

Taylor, S. E., Klein, L. C., Lewis, B. P., Gruenewald, T. L., Gurung, R. A. R., & Updegraff, J. A. (2000). Biobehavioral responses to stress in females: Tend-and-befriend, not fight-or-flight. *Psychological Review, 107*(3), 411–429.

Taylor, S. E., Lewis, B. P., Gruenewald, T. L., Gurung, R. A. R., Updegraff, J. A., & Klein, L. C. (2002). Sex differences in biobehavioral responses to threat: Reply to Geary and Flinn (2002). *Psychological Review, 109*(4), 751–753.

Tinto, V. (1987). *Leaving college.* Chicago: The University of Chicago Press.

University of California, Los Angeles, Higher Education Research Institute. (1999). *The American freshman: National norms for fall 1999—Record numbers of the nation's freshmen feel high degree of stress, UCLA study finds.* Retrieved from http://www.heri.ucla.edu/pr-display.php?prQry=21.

The University of Oklahoma Website. (2009). *Successful strategies for online education.* Retrieved from http://ou.edu/cls/online/success.htm.

VanderStoep, S. W., & Pintrich, P. R. (2003). *Learning to learn: The skill and will of college success.* Upper Saddle River, NJ: Prentice Hall.

Weiner, B. (1980). *Human motivation.* New York: Holt, Rinehart & Winston.

Weiner, B. (1986). *An attribution theory of motivation and emotion.* New York: Academic Press.

Weinstein, C. E. (1988, Fall). Executive control process in learning: Why knowing about how to learn is not enough. *National Association for Developmental Education, 12,* 1–3.

Winograd, K., & Moore, G. S. (2003). *You can learn online.* Boston: McGraw-Hill.

Woolfolk, A. E. (1998). *Educational psychology* (7th ed.). Boston: Allyn & Bacon.

Woolfolk, A. E. (2004). *Educational psychology* (9th ed.). Boston: Allyn & Bacon.

Woolfolk, A. E. (2007). *Educational psychology* (10th ed.). Boston: Pearson/Allyn & Bacon.

Worry. (n.d.). In *Merriam-Webster's online dictionary.* Retrieved from http://www.merriam-webster.com.

Yoffe, E. (2008, February 20). The supervisor, the champion, and the promoter. *Slate Magazine.* Retrieved from http://www.slate.com/id/2184696/.

Zimmerman, B. J. (1989). A social cognitive view of self-regulated academic learning. *Journal of Educational Psychology, 81,* 329–339.

Zimmerman, B. J. (2002). Becoming a self-regulated learner: An overview. *Theory into practice, 41*(2), 64–70.

Index